HORNS OF HEAVEN &EARTH:

THE POWER OF THE RESPONSE

*Revealed Mysteries of Spiritual
Communication Between God and Man*

SHARLENE SHANTALLE HYLTON

PROFESSIONAL PUBLISHING MEETS POWERFUL PROMOTION

A wholly owned subsidiary of TBN

Horns of Heaven and Earth: The Power of the Response

Trilogy Christian Publishers A Wholly Owned Subsidiary of Trinity Broadcasting Network

2442 Michelle Drive Tustin, CA 92780

Cover design by Scott Stubblefield

For information about special discounts for bulk purchases, please contact Trilogy Christian Publishing.

Manufactured in the United States of America

10 9 8 7 6 5 4 3 2 1

Library of Congress Cataloging-in-Publication Data is available.

ISBN: 979-8-88738-553-2

E-ISBN: 979-8-88738-554-9

DEDICATION

I dedicate this book to my first love, God Almighty. He inspired me to write this book to give His people an understanding of the power of the horn by revealing how it applies to our life and communication with God. Thank You, Jesus, for giving me life more abundantly through Your blood so I can be one with You. Thank You, Holy Spirit, for being my best friend and empowering me to write this book. I must say that I experienced some years of writer's block, but God helped me break through and gave me more than enough to write. I want to make my testimony known to all that He is faithful and always comes through.

I also want to dedicate this to my family, which has expanded from four to six since my last book. I want to thank God for gifting me with my two new additions, baby boy Ben-Ben, who loves me unconditionally, and my baby girl Liberty-Justice for being my heavenly surprise. I thank God for my older daughters, Harmony and Serenity, who have encouraged and prayed for me to begin writing again. Thank you, girls! You are my little angels. Most importantly, I thank God for my husband, Roger, for constantly building me up, walking by my side, encouraging me, praying with me, worshiping with me, caring for me, and listening to me. Thank you for sharing your excitement of the Word of God with me and for simply being a wonderful and supportive husband. Your support financially, emotionally, mentally, naturally, and spiritually has helped me to be the writer that I am today. Thank you for having faith in me to write. I love you.

I thank my mother, Margelee Hylton, for demonstrating strength; she serves as the founder of True Worshipers Global Worship Center, a ministry of which I am a proud member. I thank you for teaching me powerful revelations about the word of God. Your teachings have influenced me in so many ways. I thank my father, Tony Hylton, for demonstrating perseverance and wisdom. Thank you both for bringing me up in the Lord's way, pulling the best out of me, and never leaving my side.

Thank you also to my big brother, André Hylton, for always protecting me, building me up, and making it a duty to make me smile every day.

I also want to thank those who have brought guidance and support to my spiritual life. May God bless you for being a light of knowledge to the Body of Christ. I thank God for using you all to be of service to God.

I also dedicate this book to the enthusiastic follower of Jesus Christ, who yearns for the more profound things and the deeper revelations from God Himself. I pray that this book will help feed that hunger with the help of the Holy Spirit. Thank you for all your support!

TABLE OF CONTENTS

Chapter 9: We, the Royal Priesthood—Maintaining Spiritual Communication Through our Bodily Tabernacle 161

INTRODUCTION

A piercing sound from the great and mighty horn blasts from the highest mountain shaking everything around it! It releases a sound of awakening with the power of a mighty rushing wind. It is an ascending sound of the trumpet that ricochets across the four corners of the earth. It continues to sound with a thunderous blast heavily and repetitively across the land, rippling over waters to the nations! The sound it makes is powerful, resonant, penetrating, intensifying, full, and unbroken for all to hear! Some pause in shock, some are hit with fear, and some are alarmed. Some curiously look around, waiting for something to follow. Some run, some hide, some cover their ears, some shuffle back and forth in confusion, some gather their belongings with urgency, and some stop with expectancy. Some continue to do what they were doing before, completely ignoring the sound. Although different results occur from those that hear the sound, they all respond to it in some manner.

Have you ever heard a sound that caused you to react quickly or respond? Have you ever heard a sound that caused you to immediately be reminded of something? There is power behind sound. Sound is important to mankind and extremely significant to every living thing. We may not realize it, but sound triggers us to subconsciously connect to an object, a person, a memory, and/or emotion, just to name a few—which causes us to respond in some form due to this connection. That is because all sounds elicit a response. Sound causes us to harken to prepare us for the coming of something. Sound also impacts our concentration when performing tasks by pulling on the mind through the ears. There is a psychological explanation regarding our response to sound, but to simplify it down to a few words, we can see that our ears and our emotions are bonded together with a supernatural strength.

Although sound cannot be seen, it is very real. Sound is a wave that physically changes the formation of air molecules due to pressure. Pressure can only be created with something tangible…something real, which demonstrates the verifiable existence of sound. Pressure is known to be a physical force applied to an object.

In a biblical sense, we can see the importance of sound in various ways throughout the Bible. Beginning first with the book of Genesis, the very earth and everything in it was physically created by means of sound, which was by the voice of the Almighty God. Everything created was at the command of God's voice, which can be viewed as a supernatural instrument of sound. His voice is the physical force that was applied to the lifeless earth to bring creation into being. He spoke, and it was so.

We can also see in this day and time the astonishing power of God and the importance of sound through the development of babies. The first organ to form is the heart, and the sound of the heartbeat is what the doctors are trained to follow throughout the entirety of the pregnancy to make sure there is life and health. During our entrance into this world from mother's womb, we were stimulated in some manner to make a sound with our voice. That sound is required to clear our airways and lungs so that we could take our first breath. The stimulation was used to prepare the way for the entry of our voice into this world. How amazing it is to know that such actions are taken to make way for our sound to come forth as we are delivered into the earthly realm. It is by the will of God to make such preparation for our voice to come forth because our sound is who we are and what sets us apart from others.

Each human being has various means of identification to authenticate who we are, some of which include our fingerprints, our teeth, our DNA, known as our genetic blueprint, and our voice. Our voice carries a sound. For the purpose of this reading, we will be focusing on the sound that is released from our earthly vessel, which can include our voice, among many other things. Our voice is an instrument given to us, or gifted to us rather, as a solid means of communication. Our voice is the God-given instrument that was granted to us from birth. It is our instrument that requires the air we breathe to work and produce sound. God requires us to use this instrument as our first sign of entry into the earth realm. As a baby, we must cry out with the sound of our voice to show that we are alive and ready to begin the journey and tasks that lie ahead. We cry out in preparation to use our voice as the primary means of sound to communicate with others around us so they can understand us. That first cry from the time of birth releases our unique sound, a sound specifically assigned to us as an individual. Our first cry is our formal announcement of sound demonstrating our arrival to the world. To survive and function in this world, there is a requirement of having to communicate. Our voice is one of the main tools of communication.

The voice is a physical force that is unseen. Once we release our voice, the very atmosphere of the earth…meaning the air molecules around the sound of our voice, change formation. There are trillions of gas molecules found to be within the earth's atmosphere. With so many molecules existing within the earth, these same molecules have now come to know that a new force has made way into the earth. Meaning that when we speak, the formation of these molecules must change. This means we can cause the atmosphere to change with the sound of our voice. Just as God spoke and caused a change by creating things into being with the sound of His voice in Genesis chapter 1, we can do the same; because God gave us the power to make commands and change circumstances. What we release through the sound of our voice has power to change things. According to Proverbs 18:21 (NIV), "The tongue *[an instrument of sound]* has the power of life and death, and those who love it will eat its fruit." (Hereinafter, brackets added for clarity.)

It is through our life journey on earth that will help us to understand the authority that God has given us...but it comes through learning and coming in alignment with His plans. At the time of birth, we are given the opportunity to choose our path by the gift of free will. If we make the decision to choose the path of God during our journey, we come to know who He truly called us to be, in addition to understanding the authority He has given us to command change with our sound.

Our voice is a gift from God to use as a tool and weapon. Our voice is who we are and our identification on earth and in heaven. On earth, our voice is our unique sound, and in heaven, our sound is known to be our unique voiceprint. Our voiceprint is beyond the sound and voice that comes from our mouth; it is what comes from our heart and what communicates in the spiritual realm. It is our natural means and instrument of sound—it is our God-given trumpet embedded within from the time of birth. It is what we use to prepare the way for what is to come, to make declarations, to sound the alarm of warning, and it is what we use to cry out in times of need.

Now that we have taken a moment to understand what sound is about, may your mind and heart be prepared for the deeper things behind God's purpose of our voice and the sound that is produced from our voice. In this reading, you will get to understand the power behind the sound of our voice and how it relates to the power of the sound of God Almighty's voice. One thing you must know is that the sound of your voice is your horn. Since we are made in the image of Christ, we can know that the voice of the Lord and the sound that He produces can be viewed as the horn of all horns. You may wonder what I mean by this. However, by the end of this reading, as long as your heart is receptive, you will have no questions about the true power behind the horn. You will have knowledge that surpasses your own understanding. He who has an ear to hear, let him hear what the Spirit is saying. May the Spirit of the Living

God speak clearly to you, and may you receive this deeper gift He has to offer you.

In conclusion of this introduction, I would like to clearly tell you the purpose of this book. That purpose is to bring you to understand sound in general, what sound can be used for, the power of the sound of our voice, which is our horn, and what our horns are intended for. Our horns are our instruments of communication. You will come to find how our horn can change situations. You will get to know how to go beyond situations and furthermore cause a change to atmospheres. Not only can the sound of our voice cause atmospheric change, but it can also excel to the point of bringing forth a heavenly exchange. You will find out that the heavenly exchange is God's response to your sound. This heavenly exchange by means of sound only comes through communication between mankind and God, which is the main reason behind the sounds of the horn. Throughout this book, you will see that I will intermittently change between saying horn, saying voice, saying trumpet, saying shofar, and saying the sound of the voice or horn, but know that all of this boils down to the power of sound as it applies to being a tool of communication.

In addition to learning about sound, you will have a new sense of awe of the power of the heavenly horn, which is the voice of God and sound of God. You will have a better understanding of the power of His horn and be amazed at the vastness and might of His horn...how it can save, how it can heal, how it can set free, and how it can bring what was not in a man and make it come to be, as He communicates with us. You will come to understand how God was the initiator of communication and still is to this day. He began everything by making creation with His voice, and because He desired a relationship with creation, He made the first step to communicate with us through the power of His horn and patiently waits for our response. We are made in His likeness, so all that we learn about His horn, we are learning about ourselves. We will also conclude with how important our horn connects with God's horn all through the process of spiritual communication.

We will discuss in detail the process of spiritual communication and the protocols that must be followed to successfully get a response. God has a heavenly pattern of communication that He has given in the earth realm so we can connect with Him with divine understanding. We will come to know His pattern of successful communication through breaking down the Trinity, Father, Son, and Holy Spirit in likeness to the horn, understanding His protocol of communication through the tabernacle for the priests of the Old Testament, and how it connects to us utilizing our current day horn as current day priests and current day watchmen.

Now that you have a taste of what this book is about, prepare to be enlightened about the true meaning of the power behind the horn, which comes from your sound. We will begin by getting the background of how everything began.

CHAPTER 1

GOD, THE CREATOR, DESIRED RELATIONSHIP WITH MANKIND

(Spiritual Communication Established at the Garden of Eden)

God, in His sovereignty and awesomeness, sat in the heavens as the angels worshiped and adored Him. The angels were created for that very purpose. The divine duty for angels is to worship God. However, God wanted something more…something different. He desired a relationship with someone that is just like Him, someone in His own image that will worship and love Him, not because of it being their purpose and duty, but because of it being their desire and will to do so. With that in mind, God wanted to make creation in His own image and likeness. His desire caused Him to create mankind, which we can find in the book of Genesis.

"Then God said, 'Let us make mankind in our image, in our likeness, so that they may rule over the fish in the sea and the birds in the sky, over the livestock and all the wild animals, and over all the creatures that move along the ground'" (Genesis 1:26, NIV).

Man was created to have free will to love God, with the ability to make his own choices on his own terms. For man to be able to love Him and have a relationship with Him, it required a two-way flow. A flow that consisted of the following: God loves man…man loves God in return. How could this come to be? How could a man show love and relate to God? This could only come through communication and by keeping that flow of communication going.

The thing about it is that God is Holy, and He cannot look upon sin, which caused a soon-to-be conflict with the relationship between man and God. With the ability that man had to have free will, man was vulnerable to head in the wrong direction if he made bad choices. For God to honestly give man free will, He had to provide options for the creation of man. If God had not done so, He would have monopolized the heart of man. Meaning if man had no options to choose from, the heart of man would not have had the opportunity to truly be put to the test to show his real love for God. In God's omnipotence, omniscience, fairness, and truth, God was aware of this and placed an alternative within man's living space to really see where the heart of man would take him. Would it be towards God and loving God from the heart? Or would it be drawn away from God if man was provided the opportunity to go another route? God began to prepare by putting His desires of making creation with free will into action.

He began first by creating the heavens and the earth and all that was in it. Just as a pregnant mother lovingly prepares for her newborn child, so too did God prepare a place for His creation to live in so that God Himself could live among creation and stay in communion with creation.

This place that God prepared was the Garden of Eden. He then created the man, named him Adam, and gave him the authority and power to have dominion on the earth. God gave him a helpmate, a woman named Eve. He blessed them with the ability to be fruitful and multiply. Together Adam and Eve were able to walk with God and talk with God. God provided for them in every way. They knew no lack. Through this provision, they were able to eat from any tree except for one. This was the option that God placed within the middle of the Garden of Eden, which was the tree of the knowledge of good and evil. This was the only forbidden tree to eat from. It was placed alongside the tree of life. This caused them to have to be obedient to the commands of God. If at any point they made actions to eat of the forbidden fruit, that would be the day that they have made the decision to go against their Creator. This was the beginning of how free will began to test the connection that God so desired to have with us. The Garden of Eden is where communication between God and man was established. Communication between God and man was the main thing at stake and became imperfect due to one act of disobedience.

CHAPTER 2

God, the Voice of the Heavenly Horn—The Initiator of Spiritual Communication

The original plan of God was to be able to commune with mankind through a relationship. He wanted to be able to talk with man and walk with man. He wants us to have a relationship with Him, so He made the first step to communicate with us by directing us, guiding us, and providing His commandments. He also had a plan to live with us and give us eternal life by providing a way for us to commune with Him by sacrificing the life of His one and only-begotten Son.

Not only that, but He also sent His Spirit into the earth for us to bring comfort and to stand as a seal, a covenant, and a promise that He will one day come back for us. This goes to show that God is the Hornist in heaven, meaning He initiated the communication and played His chords first, which produced a sound that we, as humans (His creation), must grab a hold of and respond to it. Just as an instrumentalist that plays the horn controls the sound of the horn, makes the first step to initiate the horn's sound by placing his/her mouth upon the mouth of the horn to create the sound that he desires, so too does God do the same with His horn. He is the Instrumentalist and Hornist of heaven. He initiates communication with us by creating us and making it known to us through His word that He desires our love and a life of commitment to Him. He plays His horn. This, in turn, produces a sound, which is His voice. As God blows His heavenly horn, it produces a sound of His commands in hopes that we will fear Him, love Him, serve Him, and obey His commandments. God initiated conversation with mankind by stating all that He has blessed man with, followed by His command and call for them to obey.

"God blessed them and said to them, 'Be fruitful and increase in number; fill the earth and subdue it'" (Genesis 1:28, NIV).

This promise to Adam was the first covenant God made with mankind. He gave His commands to mankind and continued to speak with mankind directly in the Garden of Eden. There was no separation. God was and still is the initiator of communication with man due to His desire for a true relationship. To have a relationship, He would have to be able to relate to the man (His creation).

What exactly is a relationship? Relationship is a connection that bonds two parties together. It was clear that God had goals to make creation so He could have a relationship and true connection with them. As the definition says, he would have to have something that connected Him to the man. What more of a connection could be greater than creation being made in God's own image? Well, that is exactly what He did. This gave God more than enough reason to be able to relate with man. But as time went on, mankind began to fall away due to the sin that could not be thwarted because of the ability to have free will. Mankind began to draw away from God for the first time after the first sinful act, which was eating from the fruit of the tree of knowledge after God warned them not to partake from that tree. Even then, God initiated conversation by asking them a question, which caused mankind to respond. Here is a snippet of the conversation initiated by God in the Garden of Eden…

> *Then the man and his wife heard the sound of the LORD God as he was walking in the garden in the cool of the day, and they hid from the LORD God among the trees of the garden. But the LORD God called to the man, "Where are you?" He [Adam] answered, "I heard you in the garden, and I was afraid because I was naked; so I hid."*
>
> **Genesis 3:8–10 (NIV)**
> **(Hereinafter, emphasis added.)**

As one can see, God initiates a conversation with mankind by asking, "Where are you?" Then man responds. God continues this conversation by asking more questions, which led God to tell them what their punishment would be for their disobedience. Rewinding back to God speaking to mankind before the sinful act, it was mostly God initiating the conversation. God did most of the talking, which came by explaining to man all that He had given them, as well as giving warning ahead of time. His warning was to not eat from the tree of knowledge of good and evil—with this, they would surely die. Meaning God provided mankind with His expectations through the issuance of His commands. Commands only come from one who has power and authority. If someone has authority, that means they have the first say. Having the first say shows that that person is the first one to act, which leads us to discuss God as the commander.

God, the Commander
(The Spiritual Communicator)

In the introduction, the importance of sound was discussed. I mentioned earlier that all sounds elicit a response. Throughout the entirety of the Bible, we can see God, the Commander, at work. He makes a command, and something follows thereafter. For example, in the book of Genesis, we see God continuously saying, "Let there be…" and to follow, there was a creative response. Meaning the atmosphere heard the command, and creation came into being as a response to the command.

We can also see when God talked to Moses at Mount Sinai; He wrote His commands known as the Ten Commandments. This allowed humanity to be aware of right from wrong. If mankind were to go against these commandments, then that means they were sinning against God. God communicated through verbal and written communication. He spoke the commandment and then wrote it with His finger upon stone so that it would be recorded for the people to have direction in their life. God was operating as the commander over His people as He created these commands.

We can see God as the commander in the book of Exodus, as He communicated to Moses and through Moses to Pharoah and to the Israelites. He commanded that His people be let go, and the Pharoah couldn't help but to comply. In Leviticus, God provided instruction through His commands for the building of His tabernacle. In Deuteronomy, He provided the blessings that would come from obedience and the curses that would follow for disobedience…all of these were commands issued from the Commander Himself. We can also see God commanding during the times of Joshua and King David when providing instruction for battle. These are only a few samples of the Commander at work because the list can go on and on.

Let's discuss God as the Commander a little more from a different stance. We previously discussed Genesis 3:8 based on God initiating conversation, but let's view this scripture from another angle. Naturally, we can see that commanders have authority in the military. They issue a command to those that they are responsible for. Those who are under the commander are obedient to his/her command. Think a little bit deeper about what happens when a commander first enters the room or area where a group of soldiers that they head up are located. The soldiers will stop what they are doing and take position, even though the commander hasn't yet opened his mouth to audibly say something. The response of the soldiers taking position based on the commander's entry happens because authority has made its way into the room—they must stand at attention. The soldiers are trained to respect the authority of the commander just by his or her very presence. The commander carries this type of authority for soldiers to shape up, get orderly, get in position, and stand at attention even before the commander makes his command. The mere presence of the commander communicates to the soldiers because it elicits a response to get into position. It is in their training.

As we revisit Genesis 3:8, we can see the same scenario mentioned above playing out in this scripture.

> *Then the man and his wife heard the sound of the Lord God as he was walking in the garden in the cool of the day, and they hid from the Lord God among the trees of the garden.* But the Lord God called to the man, "Where are you?" He answered, *"I heard you in the garden, and I was afraid because I was naked; so I hid."*

Genesis 3:8–10 (NIV)

Here we see the authority of God, the Commander, by simply being present. In the italics text above, within the scripture, we can see that Adam and Eve heard God walking. In other words, they knew that God was present. The very sound of His presence caused a physical and emotional response from mankind. The physical response was that they acted by hiding from the Lord within the trees of the garden. The emotional response was that they were afraid. We can see that they were afraid due to the sinful act they committed, and that fear caused them to physically take action to hide from the commanding authority, which is God. Also, keep in mind that fear comes naturally when mankind encounters God in their midst. This response is due to the awesomeness and bigness of God.

With this knowledge, we can see clearly that communication comes from more than the voice alone. It is the authority that one carries that can also cause a response. God is the Commander, and the authority He carries as a commander always results in a response from those who experience His presence. Now that we understand His role as the Commander, we're going to go into another exciting part—the voice of God and the response of the audience that hears His voice.

God's —The Thunder of Heaven

In this chapter, we are going to focus on the voice of God, which is powerful beyond what we can ever fathom. His voice is also His sound. In the word of God, we can see that God's voice and the sound of the Lord are interchangeable because they are one in the same. One may ask, "Where is the proof, and how can this be?" We can find this based on the study of His word through various translations that are available. Now let's take a look at the same scripture we have been reviewing in the previous section. We are going to dissect this verse a little bit more from the perspective of God's voice. In italics, we can see the sound of the Lord and the voice of God being represented in the same scripture.

> Then the man and his wife *heard the sound of the LORD God* as he was walking in the garden in the cool of the day, and they hid from the LORD God among the trees of the garden. But the LORD God called to the man, "Where are you?"

Genesis 3:8–9 (NIV)

28

Let's look at another translation…

> And they *heard the voice of the* LORD *God* walking
> in the garden in the cool of the day: and Adam and
> his wife hid themselves from the presence of the
> LORD God amongst the trees of the garden. And the
> Lord called unto Adam, and said unto him, Where
> art thou?

Genesis 3:8–9 (KJV)

As we can see, the sound of the Lord and the voice of the Lord are both represented in the same scripture based on the translation. When studying the word of God, it is important to review different translations. This should help to get better knowledge, clearer understanding, and a broader perspective. By merely utilizing both translations, we can clearly see that God's voice and God's sound are one and the same. Which goes back to what was mentioned in the introduction of this book…that our voice is our sound. Our voice is what identifies us. Since we are made in the image of God, then we can automatically understand that God's voice is what also identifies Him.

The King James Version of this scripture is boggling to the mind because, based on our earthly understanding of a voice, it is hard to comprehend how a voice can be heard walking. But this only goes to show how powerful, how astonishing, and how magnificent our God is. Everything about God is beyond our understanding, and we can see it demonstrated in this scripture. Now we all know that for something to walk, it must have life. That means if the voice of the Lord God was heard walking, then His voice is alive. His voice, the identifier of God Himself, is life. The scriptures support this fact because we see that what God spoke into existence with His sound and by the directives of His voice was created and given life. Whatever God commanded to be created with His voice replicated the voice of God by being created. Meaning the things that

God used His voice to speak into creation turned into life too! This is the mind-boggling power of God's voice.

The voice of the Lord is powerful and is made known throughout various scriptures in the Bible. There is reference to His voice as rumbling thunder. As one may know, rumbling thunder here on earth comes with a sound that causes things on earth to physically shake. That is because sound is equal to vibrations that travel in waves. When sound passes through air, gas, water, and/or anything solid, it causes that very thing to vibrate as well. Have you ever been inside your home or any building when thunder rumbles? Sometimes the walls shake, especially when the sound is first released. I am sure that my home is not the only home that it happens to at the time of the sound. That means the whole area shakes for many to feel it at one time. If this is what happens with the natural sound of thunder…imagine the power of the sound of the voice of the One who created the thunder, which is the sound of the voice of God!

God's Voice Is Thunder in a Vision

I can attest to God's voice sounding like thunder as well. I had a dream of God speaking from the heavens. He was formed within the galaxy of the stars. He began to search the earth, picking up individuals one by one and speaking with them. The time came for Him to speak to someone who was next to me. With a loud and thunderous voice, He said, "You!" His voice in the dream was unforgettable, so much so that it caused me to be in awe the next morning I awoke from the dream. It was so real, and the feeling that I felt when God spoke in the dream was still there when I woke up. It was hard to shake. His voice indeed sounded like thunder and caused me to fear. It brought on a feeling that caused me to look quickly within myself by doing a life check. You know how people usually say, "My life flashed before my very own eyes"?

In this dream, my life flashed before my eyes by me checking to see if I did everything that I could possibly do for God in terms of serving Him here on earth. His voice caused me to search myself deep within.

The Formula of God's Voice as Thunder

In Psalm 29:3–9 (NIV), it discusses the voice of the Lord and demonstrates its power:

> *The voice of the* LORD *is over the waters; the God of glory thunders, the* LORD *thunders over the mighty waters. The voice of the* LORD *is powerful; the voice of the* LORD *is majestic. The voice of the* LORD *breaks the cedars; the* LORD *breaks in pieces the cedars of Lebanon. He makes Lebanon leap like a calf, Sirion like a young wild ox. The voice of the* LORD *strikes with flashes of lightning. The voice of the* LORD *shakes the desert; the* LORD *shakes the Desert of Kadesh. The voice of the* LORD *twists the oaks and strips the forests bare. And in his temple all cry, "Glory!"*

These verses say so much about the voice of God that it doesn't need to be broken down into anything more than what it says. What the word says is exactly what God's voice is and what His voice does. His voice is over the waters; His voice is powerful and majestic; it thunders; it can break things, shake things, twist things, and strip things. For now, let's focus on the verses that discuss His voice being thunder. Notice how I said His voice being thunder instead of being "like" thunder. There is a difference. In verse 3, it says, "The voice of the LORD is over the waters; the God of glory thunders, the LORD thunders over the mighty waters." It later says, "...the voice of the LORD strikes with flashes of lightning." Think of it, when we see flashes of lightning naturally, it is most likely that we hear the sound of thunder with it. Based on this verse, we can see that God's voice and thunder are somehow connected. It is almost like a math equation showing that two objects are the same, such as A = B. We can apply that same concept to the scripture in the following manner as it relates to God's voice being equal to, or the same as, God's thunder:

"The voice of the LORD *is* over the waters." (The voice of the Lord equals "V.")

"V" is over the waters.

"The God of glory thunders." ("T" equals the God of Glory thunders, aka the Lord thunders.)

"The Lord thunders over the mighty waters."

"T" is over the mighty waters.

Since "V" is over the waters and "T" is over the waters, we can hypothesize that "V" equals "T." In conclusion, our Psalm 29:3 formula is V = T. This can also be written as the voice of the Lord equals the God of Glory thunders.

As we can see, the voice of the Lord is thunderous, which can be supported by the following scriptures: Job 37:4–5, Job 40:9, Psalm 18:13, Psalm 77:18, Psalm 104:7, and John 12:28–29. Not only is the voice of the Lord thunderous, but it can also come with lightning. Psalm 29:7 (NIV) says, "The voice of the LORD strikes with flashes of lightning." Let's explore how lightning ties in with God's voice and thunder.

God's Voice as Thunder at the Throne of Heaven

As we just read, the *voice of the Lord* strikes with flashes of lightning in Psalm 29; based on our formula, this can also be viewed as the *"God of Glory thunders"* and strikes with flashes of lightning. We can see this demonstrated in Revelation 4:5. This chapter describes the throne of heaven, but in this verse, John saw these very things coming from the throne of God, which confirms what we were just discussing that the voice of the Lord is equal to the thundering of the God of Glory. It reads, "From the throne came *flashes of lightning*, rumblings and peals of *thunder*" (Revelation 4:5a, NIV). Since we know this throne is the throne of God, we know that everything described coming from this throne was in reference to what was coming from God Himself as He sat on His throne. God, the Father, is the subject of this verse. Notice how this scripture gives reference to "flashes of lightning" and peals of "thunder." These are the same words that came as a result when we converted the "voice of the Lord" to the "God of Glory thunders" in Psalm 29:7. That means the thunder in Revelation 4:5 belongs to God since He is the subject of this verse in Revelation 4:5. With this understanding, we can conclude this is the thundering of the God of Glory, this, in other words, is the voice of the Lord. So, if we apply Psalm 29's formula to Revelation 4:5, we can also understand the "flashes of lightning, rumblings and peals of thunder" to be the voice of the Lord. In the Psalm 29 formula, God is appearing as the God of Glory. We can see from this scripture that when God appears as the God of Glory, His voice can also come with thunder. Thunder is a powerful sound and terrifying sound, which means the voice of God is powerful and can also be terrifying.

God's Voice as Thunder at Mount Sinai

Let's backtrack to Exodus chapter 19 because it also provides a deeper understanding of the voice of the Lord and how it relates to thunder. This was the time when God was going to give the Ten Commandments to Moses by communicating to Him from the cloud on the mountain. He wanted the people to witness Him talking to Moses so that they could trust Moses as their leader. God said that He would appear in a dense cloud, and the people would hear Him speaking with Moses. However, God had to have

Moses prepare the people for His coming by having them be consecrated, wash their clothes, and refrain from intercourse for three days. When the time came for God to appear, it says that flashes of lightning and thunder came, and a thick cloud was present over Mount Sinai.

In Exodus 19:16 (NIV), it says, *"On the morning of the third day there was thunder and lightning, with a thick cloud over the mountain and a very loud trumpet blast..."*

In verse 19, it says, *"As the sound of the trumpet grew louder and louder, Moses spoke and the voice of God answered him"*; in other translations, it says, *"God thundered His reply"* (Exodus 19:19, NLT).

This verse shows God answering with thunder. We must also take into consideration that when God answers with thunder, it brings about fear.

In this chapter, we can see the mountain began to tremble, Moses was in fear. Hebrews 12:21 (NIV) says, *"The sight was so terrifying that Moses said, 'I am trembling with fear.'"* Additionally, in Exodus 20:19, it says the people who heard the voice of the Lord speaking to Moses were also trembling with fear so much that they begged to not hear His voice anymore because they believed they would die.

The very atmosphere that was created on Mount Sinai to accompany the voice of the Lord was memorably associated with terror. The word says the whole mountain was covered in smoke while violently trembling. In other translations, it says the mountain quaked at the presence of the Lord. Think about it, we know how high and how vast mountains are. To behold a mountain in its fullness, you must hold your head up so much so that the back of your neck must recognize something is happening because the neck muscles begin to ache. The neck muscles must compensate for supporting the adjustment of the head at such an angle. If that happens to us at the sight of viewing a mountain from a distance, just imagine viewing a mountain being covered with the presence of the Lord. The voice, the smoke, the fire, the lightning, the quaking, the loud blast of the trumpet, the dense cloud, the darkness, and of course…the thunder. Just choosing one of the items previously listed is enough for itself, but all the above at once is what the people experienced, which resulted in their fear. It was too much for the people to bear at Mount Sinai. This all goes to show the power of God and what comes with His voice that can come as thunder.

God's Voice Is Not Limited to Thunder Only

We can also see that God's voice can appear in various ways throughout the word of God. Remember, He is the I Am that I Am. In Hebrew, that means "Ehyeh Asher Ehyeh." Depending on the situation and scenario, the revelation of who God is at that moment can vary, and the way He communicates can also vary. He comes as who He needs to be for the purpose of why He is needed. But at the same time, He always is the I Am because He is the same, yesterday, today, and forever; He changes not, according to His word. So, I must reiterate that God is not limited to but instead limitless in all things. He uses many ways to communicate with us. However, for the sake of the study of God's voice being thunder, we were previously reviewing the scripture from this perspective. We must also realize that the voice of God can come as a still, small voice. He can speak to our hearts. He can use the voice of a donkey. He can speak through a burning bush. He can speak through the voice of an angel; He can speak through dreams and visions and so much more. I wouldn't be able to catch everything because He is too big and too vast. There are many ways His voice can speak because that is how awesome He is. He appears as how He chooses to appear as He sees fit. As mentioned before, thunder is one of the many marvelous ways the voice of the Lord can be heard. This study simply capitalizes and highlights His voice as thunder, so we can understand Him and the power of His voice in that matter in reference to communication.

Speaking of power, let's move on to the power part of the Trinity...the Holy Spirit. He is the breath of God, the Ruach, and the one who helps us to maintain communication with the Father through Jesus. In the next chapter, we will discuss a quick vision the Lord gave me that will help bring clarity to the role of the Holy Spirit in our spiritual communication.

CHAPTER 3

HOLY SPIRIT, THE BREATH OF THE HEAVENLY HORN— THE TRANSLATOR AND MAINTAINER OF SPIRITUAL COMMUNICATION

The Heavenly Vision of Horns and Communication

In the year 2015, the Lord gave me a dream. I was taken into the heavens to sit before the choir of heaven to witness worship. There were beautiful beings in white robes with covers on their heads. They stood in a group joined in unison, releasing songs from heaven, worshiping God. They had faces with eyes and noses, but there was a major distinguishing item on their face that was not like that of a man. Their mouth. It was bewildering for me to see that the mouth was made of a horn. The dream then ended. When I awoke from the dream, I had to ask myself, "Why would their mouths be actual horns? I know dreams are symbolic and have meaning, but what are You trying to tell me, God?" The Lord gave me an answer years later, but He required that I do my part by studying and seeking to find out more about horns.

Since the Lord showed me a horn in the place of where the mouth should be, I took the first step by thinking about what a mouth represents. We can see that the mouth is what we use as an instrument for communication. It is used to bring forth a message as a sender to the recipient and used to be a responder of a message from a sender. God knows me and how I think. Once I come across certain words, I begin to ponder and break things down in my mind for easier understanding. Additionally, with a background in communication, I get excited when I come across anything that has to do with communication.

What does communication have to do with heavenly worship? That's a great question. Before I was able to find out the connection to worship, the Lord had me look first into the basics of communication. First and foremost, communication is an exchange. It is not one way only. It is a message that includes both a sender and a hearer. One party transmits information, hopefully in a clear and understandable manner, so that the one who receives the message hears it, interprets it, and may even respond to it, depending on the scenario. As we communicate, we are sharing or imparting a message with a recipient. Communication is "a process by which information is exchanged between individuals through a common system of symbols, signs, or behavior, or an exchange of information."[1] This exchange of information within communication can be verbal, nonverbal, written, or visual. Let's quickly break this down into four parts:

- **Verbal**—can include communicating in person, by phone, and through media platforms.
- **Nonverbal**—can include body language, personal appearance, eye contact or lack thereof, smell, facial expressions, etc.
- **Written**—can include letters, emails, books, magazines, websites, newspapers, written information through media platforms, etc.

- **Visual**—can include creativity by hand, such as art, drawings, and carvings; creative expressions, such as playing instruments, dancing, etc.

This demonstrates that communication comes in various forms that go beyond the limitations of what can be heard audibly. When we are delivering our message during the communication process, we can speak as a form of communication, we can use our body language as a method of communication, and we can write as a method of communication. When we are the recipient of communication, we can listen to the message, interpret the message, and possibly respond to the message.

The Seven Concept Model of Communication

The Shannon-Weaver Model of Communication, which was developed in 1948, states that there are seven key concepts in communication: sender, encoder, channel, noise, decoder, receiver, and feedback.[2] Let's break this down to get a closer look at the specifics of each concept:

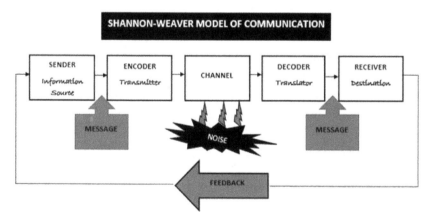

1. *Sender*—the source that provides the message and sends it.

2. *Encoder (transmitter)*:

    a. The device that changes the message into signals for it to be sent to the recipient. *(For example, phone.)*

    b. The person that transmits the idea of the message in various forms (verbally, nonverbally, written, or visual) to the recipients.

3. *Channel*—how the information from the sender is transmitted. For example, internet, electrical wires and cables used for a landline phone, frequencies, and bands (network) used for cell phones.

4. *Noise*—the interruption that may take place with the message while it is being sent to the recipient.

    a. Internal noise—when a sender makes a mistake encoding the message or a receiver makes a mistake decoding the message. (For example, not speaking clearly through verbal communication; typos or incorrect spelling through written communication.)

    b. External noise—when an outside source disturbs the message from being encoded or decoded correctly. (For example, background noise that can distract or make it hard to hear over the phone.)

5. Decoder:

    a. The device that changes the signals back into a format that can be understood by the recipient.

    b. The means by which the person interprets the message that is being received.

6. Receiver (destination)—this is the final point of the message, where the recipient receives the remainder of the message after it has encountered noise.

7. Feedback—the recipient can respond to the sender of the message to complete the communication loop. Keep in mind that feedback does not always happen.

If we connect this back to spiritual communication, a great deal of understanding can be pulled from the seven concepts of communication. As we can see, there are seven steps in communication. Seven represents "completion" spiritually, which means our communication with God should be something established and made complete in our spiritual walk. If you notice, the last step to completing the communication loop is feedback. Feedback can also be referred to as a *response*. This demonstrates communication reaches the stage of completion when the recipient does something with the message received. Complete communication has more than one party doing the communication. There should be a communication loop.

What is a communication loop? It is basically something that is continuous. The sender sends the message to the recipient, the recipient receives the message and responds. The recipient then becomes the sender during the response, and the one who was originally the sender becomes the recipient and then receives the message and responds...and the communication loop continues on. This is what we call healthy communication, and this is what God desires for us to have with Him. To have a healthy relationship with someone, healthy and clear communication is required. Meaning that both parties in that healthy relationship are maintaining the communication loop by staying in constant communication. God wants us to be able to completely communicate with Him, with the hopes of it going beyond the one-way message by getting to the final step. The final step is the response, and as previously noted in the seven concepts of communication model, this step does not always happen. It should be our goal to make sure that the seventh step does happen. We should get to the point of communication where it reached the advanced stage of having a conversation.

The question is...how can we ensure that we make it to the seventh step? In other words, how can we make sure that we reach the step of response in our relationship with God? How can we maintain or complete the communication loop? Well, as you move further into the reading of this book, you will get the answers. But before moving on, take some time to think about how this can be done personally and then apply it to the reading. Now that we have the gist of what communication entails, let's go a little bit further into some communication history. We will start first by discussing what God challenged me to do.

My God Challenge Assignment

After looking into what communication was about, God gave me an assignment. He did this by directing me to find out what the first phone looked like. At first, I was wondering where God was going with this because, at the time, it seemed a bit odd to me. But a few seconds later, I got an "aha" moment. I understood why God said to look up a phone because a phone is a common device we use daily to communicate. With that in mind, I eagerly followed His command. After pulling up various results, I saw that the first workable phone looked like an actual horn! The phone was invented by Alexander Graham Bell in 1876 while he was researching on the subject matter of *hearing and speech.* It is exhilarating to know that the details that God had me research have a great deal to do with communication. Everything was so tied together. I was amazed to see how God was only trying to emphasize the fact that the horn represents communication.

Being the researcher that I am, I took additional steps to find out what the name Alexander means. The biblical meaning behind the name Alexander is "defender of men."[3] The meaning of the name Alexander is very applicable to this reading. Why? That is because God is our defense. God is the ultimate defender of men (mankind). We will learn more about God as our defense when we study the Horn of Salvation and the meaning behind the exalted horn later in this book. Keep in mind, to be the defender of another, one must understand the story and the needs of the person who is in need of defense. Understanding someone requires hearing and knowing their story, which involves communication. The Word of God can bring some clarification to this point.

> In you, LORD, I have taken refuge; let me never be put to shame; deliver me in your righteousness. *Turn your ear to me,* come quickly to my rescue; be my rock of refuge, a strong fortress to save me.

Psalm 31:1–2 (NIV)

Take a closer look at the italicized part of the scripture…which is when the psalmist says, "Turn your ear to me." This is another way of saying, "*Listen* to me; I have something to say." Listening is a major part of communication. The sender (David) in this scripture is preparing the recipient (God) to take the time to listen to his message. David's message would be concept two (encoding) in the communication process because it was released from the sender and transmitted. The channel used in this matter is prayer, which is concept three. We understand that concept four includes noise, in other words, anything that interrupts the message. In this case, we can assume that it could be his fear, anxiety, weakness, or any means of flesh that he could have been experiencing. The listening part would happen in concept five (decoding). This is where the receiver, which in this scenario is God, interprets the message being sent. Interpretation requires active listening if it is a verbal message, and observation is required from the recipient's side if it is a behavior…this further leads to the recipient to come to some form of an understanding of the message being sent. After this stage, the message is received by God, which is concept six.

In this scripture, we can see that David prayed with an urgency. He was in desperate need to be delivered and rescued. In this Psalm, David goes on to further explain why he needed God's help. His very bones were getting weak, and his strength was failing him due to all that was coming against him. His problems included having so many enemies that those close to him were fleeing from him. He went on to say that there are people even plotting to take his life. So, this was a life-and-death situation that required God's urgent attention. David was hoping to get a response from God after his message was sent. The question is, would the communication loop be activated, meaning would this message get to concept seven? The answer is yes because David received his feedback when God responded. God rescued David and came to his defense. Although David had many enemies, not one of them prevailed against him. God remained faithful and kept David strong, kept him in a place of safety, and gave David a long life.

Now going back to the heavenly vision of the choir that had horns for mouths, you may wonder how communication ties in with this vision. Based on my research about horns, we see the first workable phone (a tool for communication) was in the likeness of a horn. Due to this, we can determine that if the choir was using their horns to bring forth worship through song, that means their horns of worship are a tool of communication in the heavens. If communication is involved, that means there is an exchange of information, there is a sender, and there is a recipient. In this case, the choir was the sender, their song was their message, and the recipient of their message was God.

In summary, the horns for mouths of the heavenly choir released a sound and a song of worship, communicating a message of worship to God. Their mouths were horns, and their horns were horns of worship. If horns represent communication in the heavenlies and their horns were horns of worship in the heavenlies, that leads us to make a final determination. Horns signify communication and produce sounds of worship in the heavenlies, showing us that the sound of the horn is worship in the heavenlies. Worship is the sound of communication in the heavenlies. Worship is the sound of the horn, and the horn is the tool of communication in the heavenlies! To simply put it, worship is communication.

Spiritual Communication, Worship, and the Breath of God: Holy Spirit

As God revealed to me the revelation about worship being communication, He began to expound on that note by revealing to me that the choir represents giving worship to God through song. The very sound they made during worship was by that of a horn. Remember, a wind instrument requires breath to produce a sound. In the heavenlies, it takes the breath of the choir to produce the sound of worship. The Lord then began to emphasize the word "breath." He reiterated who the breath of God is. The breath of God is His Spirit...the Holy Spirit. He also began to reveal that the wind instruments invoke the Spirit of God. Why? Because the Holy Spirit is the wind part of the Trinity. The Holy Spirit is the Ruach and the breath of the Almighty. The Holy Spirit is the breath that comes from God's nostrils and the breath the comes from God's mouth. He is the wind, the essence of God, the one who maintains and sustains life. The Holy Spirit is the Spirit of God. The Holy Spirit is the wind within the instrument of heaven; He is the breath behind communication in heaven and the wind within the horn of God!

To break things down a bit further, we can see that wind instruments are important when it comes to worship. There is a special and unique sound that comes from the horn—a sound that brings life to worship. The Holy Spirit continues to be the one who helps us to communicate to God. He is the translator of our communication from earth to heaven. He is the life that is breathed upon our message that is being sent out. He is also the life that is breathed upon the word of God to bring it to life, meaning He brings the understanding of the Word of God to us if we invite Him to do so.

As we know, in the beginning of Genesis, during the time of creation, it says in verse 2 that the Spirit of God "*hovered over the* *waters."* This shows that the Holy Spirit was present during the time of creation. In Genesis 2:7 (NKJV), it says, *"And the LORD God formed man of* the dust of the ground and breathed into his nostrils the breath of life; and man became a living being."* This demonstrates that creation requires breath to function, and the Holy Spirit was the breath of God that breathed and gave life to Adam for him to become a living being.

God places an importance on the Holy Spirit when it comes to worship and when it comes to the sound. The breath of God, His Spirit, is required to produce sound and, in turn, produces His response. With that in mind, God had me review the four types of communication, as well as the seven concepts of communication. He then propelled me to apply this knowledge to the vision. In response, I followed His command with great enthusiasm, which I will now share with you.

I was first able to identify the communication type involved. As previously noted, there are four types of communication, verbal, nonverbal, written, and visual. Based on my perspective, I was able to determine that the type of communication represented in this vision was nonverbal communication. That is because the choir with horns for mouths produced a sound, not by words, but by the sound of their horn. Their sound produced music. Music is an expression of art that starts from the inward part of a being that can be from emotions and expressed outwardly, communicating to the hearers of the sound tugging on their emotions by way of their ears. Now, if by chance they were singing audible words to a song, I could consider it to be verbal, but I only heard sounds of a horn. But keep in mind the determination I made is based on my earthly perspective, so this is by no means the final and correct answer. Additionally, my observations could completely differ from the thoughts of God. It is also important to note that music can be communicated verbally, through singing words, nonverbally, through the playing of instruments, and written, through the written sheets of music and written lyrics. Music is a form of communication that goes past the barriers and limitations of language, serving as a form of communication understood by all. The heavenly choir vision shows that there were no limits that were successfully communicated and understood by God.

Seven Concepts of Communication Identified in the Heavenly Vision and Spiritual Communication

I then moved on to the seven concepts of communication found in the Shannon-Weaver Model of Communication and applied it to the heavenly vision. We already know the sender of the vision is the choir, and the receiver is the Lord. But what about the concepts of communication that exist in between? Let me break down the answers in bullet format and by a flow chart so we don't miss any details.

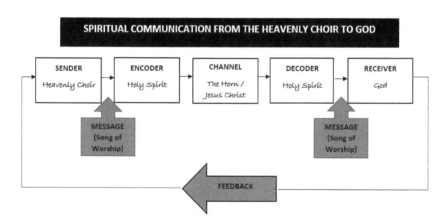

1. *The sender—the heavenly choir*—is the originator of the message.

2. *Encoder (transmitter)—the Holy Spirit* is the transmitter of the message. The Holy Spirit searches the heart of the heavenly choir and interprets it. He then breathes life

upon the heart of their message so it can be expressed into a form that can be communicated to the hearer. In this instance, He turned the message of their hearts into a sound of worship by breathing life into it so it could be transmitted and heard. He was the breath of their horn, giving life to the sound of their heart so it could be heard.

    a. *Spiritually.* The sound of worship comes from the heart. It is the Holy Spirit who searches the heart, interprets the message of the heart, and then moves upon the heart of the sender to give God ultimate worship. The Holy Spirit moves through us, worships through us, and prays through us. He understands us more than we understand ourselves. It is Holy Spirit who helps us to do such things because we can't do it on our own. He helps us to release what is in our hearts, which goes beyond the flesh and into the inward parts of our being so that it can be expressed through communication to God.

In the same way, the Spirit helps us in our weakness. We do not know what we ought to pray for, but the Spirit himself intercedes for us through wordless groans. And he who searches our hearts knows the mind of the Spirit, because the Spirit intercedes for God's people in accordance with the will of God.

Romans 8:26–27 (NIV)

3. Channel. The horn and Jesus Christ are the channel of the message. The channel is the mouth made of a horn of each being within the heavenly choir because this is what the sound of worship (their message) came through, but the access to God from their horn comes through the main channel, which is always through Jesus—no one and nothing can come to the Father except through Him.

    a. *Spiritually.* The sound of worship (which is our message) comes from our heart, but our worship cannot ascend to God without going through the Door, who is the access and gateway to God Himself. Jesus and the blood He shed for us gave us access to communicate our message of worship. Through Him, we are no longer disconnected from God. Jesus says, "I am the way, the truth, and the life. No one comes to the Father except through me" (John 14:6, NIV).

4. *Noise.* The noise is a disruption in the flow of communication. It is any interruption that prevents the message from being sent clearly to the recipient, which can be internal or external. In this vision, there was nothing found to be interruptive to the heavenly choir's message of worship that would be considered as noise.

   a. Spiritually. We would consider noise to be anything that stops, muffles, distracts, or tries to buffet the message of our heart of worship from flowing to our recipient (God) in its entirety. This can happen in two ways: internally and externally.

      • Internal noise. This is when there is an inward distraction preventing our heart from sending a message to God. Meaning we have a hindrance within our person that stops us from communicating with clarity to God. In this case, it can be the mind, the flesh, and the sin that comes with it because the mind and flesh are always at war with the Spirit. These noises are controllable if we allow the Spirit of God to help us.

         • According to Galatians 5:17 (NIV), it says, "For the flesh desires what is contrary to the Spirit, and the Spirit what is contrary to the flesh. They are in conflict with each other, so that you are not to do whatever you want."

         • First Corinthians 2:14 (NIV) says, "The person without the Spirit does not accept the things that come from the Spirit of God but considers them foolishness and cannot understand them because they are discerned only through the Spirit."

- According to 1 Corinthians 7:35 (NKJV), "And this I say for your own profit, not that I may put a leash on you, but for what is proper, and that you may serve the Lord without distraction."

- *External noise.* This is when there is an outward distraction preventing our heart from sending a message to God. Meaning we have an outside hindrance that can distract us from communicating with clarity to God. External noises are not caused from within our person but instead, from the prince of the air (Satan), who controls the spiritual environment within the earth. These distractions can include temptations, arguments, destruction, intimidation, attacks, accusations, confusion, condemnation, conflicts, division, lies, opposition, and all other fiery darts sent from the enemy.

  - John 10:10a (NIV) says, "The thief comes only to kill, steal, and destroy…"

These are interruptions that we cannot control, but we can stand and fight against them with the authority and power God has given us for spiritual warfare:

Finally, be strong in the Lord and in his mighty power. Put on the full armor of God, so that you can take your stand against the devil's schemes. For our struggle is not against flesh and blood, but against the rulers, against the authorities, against the powers of this dark world and against the spiritual forces of evil in the heavenly realms. Therefore, put on the full armor of God, so that when the day of evil comes, you may be able to stand your ground, and after you have done everything, to stand. Stand firm then, with the belt of truth buckled around your waist, with the breastplate of righteousness in place, and with your feet fitted with the readiness that comes from the gospel of peace. In addition to all this, take up the shield of faith, with which you can extinguish all the flaming arrows of the evil one. Take the helmet of salvation and the sword of the Spirit, which is the word of God. And pray in the Spirit on all occasions with all kinds of prayers and requests. With this in mind, be alert and always keep on praying for all the Lord's people.

Ephesians 6:10–18 (NIV)

1. *Decoder (translator). The Holy Spirit* is the translator of the message—the sound that the Holy Spirit created through the heavenly choir's horn by breathing life upon the message of their heart so it could be heard is a translation of their heart that can be understood by the heart of God. He translated the message of their heart into a sound and song of worship that communicates to God.

   a. Spiritually. The Holy Spirit translates the sound of our thoughts, heart, tears, mouth, and actions into the language of heaven, by which God can understand...and that is only by the Spirit because God is Spirit. God does not communicate with the flesh and does not see the outward but instead the heart. The heart is where the truth of a person resides and where their worship truly comes from, and it is the Holy Spirit that translates this message so it can be understood by God.

Yet a time is coming and has now come when the true worshipers will worship the Father in the Spirit and in truth, for they are the kind of worshipers the Father seeks. God is spirit, and his worshipers must worship in the Spirit and in truth.

John 4:23–24 (NIV)

1. *Receiver. God* is the recipient of the message—He is the final destination of the message sent from the heart of the heavenly choir. God is the one who receives their message of worship.

   a. Spiritually. Our message that has been transmitted and translated from our heart by the Spirit through Jesus becomes our worship, which has a sound and communicates to God as our worship. Our worship is our message to God; He is the one from who we intend to receive this message.

2. *Feedback.* This is the response of God that is communicated back to the heavenly choir. In this case, it was His very presence being among them.

   a. Spiritually. If the communication is clear, that means our worship is true. Upon this matter, it ensures the message of worship we are sending to God from our heart is true and, therefore, received by the Father. Our worship will cause Him to respond in various ways, which includes His presence among us.

Now that all bullet points of communication have been identified in the vision, we can have a better understanding of spiritual communication. Take a closer look, though; do you realize how much the Holy Spirit is involved in spiritual communication? We can see that the Holy Spirit is involved in concept two and concept five, meaning He is the transmitter (encoder) and translator (decoder) in the process of communication. The Holy Spirit is the Breath of God, and anything that belongs to God comes with life, which, therefore, comes to life. He hears what we, as fleshly beings, are saying and transmits it to God by translating our message into a spiritual message so God can understand us. Remember, flesh is death...but the Holy Spirit is life. He breaks through the barrier and the limits of our flesh by adding the life to our message so that it can ascend into the heavens through Jesus. Did you just catch it? Do you see what is happening during this process? Just in case you did not catch it, here it goes:

We can see that *complete* spiritual communication requires the participation of the Trinity, meaning the Father, Son, and Holy Spirit are actively working together as one for the communication to process. God, in all His power, never ceases to amaze. He always has an order to everything He does. It is for us to tap into His order. He wants us to realize that communication requires unity in the realm of the Spirit to be fulfilled.

Since we have taken the time to know about spiritual communication through the means of the heavenly vision and through the prayer of David, let's dissect it even more, to be more general, so it can apply to all aspects within our spiritual walk. As we do so, take a mental note of this and meditate on it daily so you can soon apply it to your lifestyle by the help of the Holy Spirit. Let us begin…

In general, spiritual communication requires the following if the message begins with us as humans (also subject to change based on the scenario):

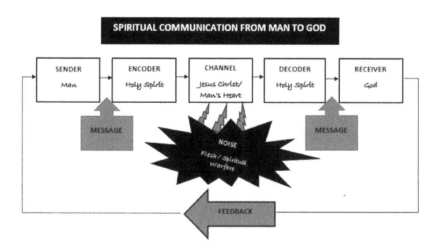

1. Sender—man,

2. Encoder—Holy Spirit,

3. Channel—our heart and Jesus,

4. Noise—flesh/spiritual warfare,

5. Decoder—Holy Spirit,

6. Receiver—God,

7. Feedback—God's response.

God's message to us is likened to the following (also subject to change based on the scenario):

SPIRITUAL COMMUNICATION FROM GOD TO MAN

1. Sender—God,

2. Encoder—Holy Spirit or God's angels/messengers,

3. Channel—God's heart and Jesus,

4. Noise—flesh/spiritual warfare,

5. Decoder—Holy Spirit/God's angels/messengers,

6. Receiver—man,

7. Feedback—man's response.

Jacob's Ladder—Heaven's Diagram of Spiritual Communication

In the book of Genesis 28:10–22, we can see spiritual communication being demonstrated in the life of Jacob when he makes a vow in Bethel after he gets a message from God in a dream. In Genesis 28:10–12, Jacob begins to dream about the angels of God ascending and descending on a ladder.

> *Then he dreamed, and behold, a ladder was set up on the earth, and its top reached to heaven; and there the angels of God were ascending and descending on it. And behold, the Lord stood above it and said: "I am the Lord God of Abraham your father and the God of Isaac; the land on which you lie I will give to you and your descendants..."*
>
> **Genesis 28:12–13 (NKJV)**

This was a manifestation of the spiritual communication process all wrapped up in a dream. The ladder is a representation of the connection between God and man. That connection comes through the maintenance of clear communication. The angels ascending were the angels that were taking the earthly message/prayers/commands from man to the heavens. The angels descending are the angels on an assignment to bring forth God's will or carrying out God's commands/instructions/answers from heaven to man on earth.

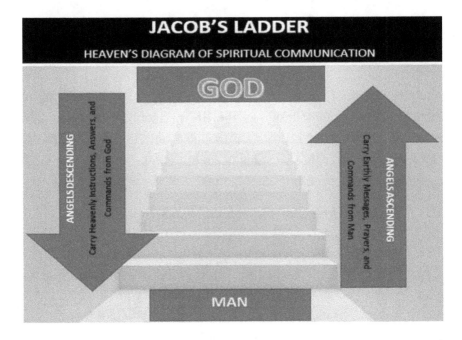

The fact that the Lord stood above the ladder shows that God is the ultimate source of communication in the heavens. His angels are only messengers of the message that He sends. He is the sender, and He can also be the recipient if we respond to Him and maintain communication. Jacob's ladder, or may I even say the heavenly ladder of spiritual communication, is an evident demonstration of transactions taking place between heaven and earth and between God and man. Now keep in mind, even though angels are mentioned in this passage, this also applies to the work of the Holy Spirit.

We can also see Jacob's ladder and the seven concepts of spiritual communication being played out in the book of Daniel chapter 10 when Daniel prayed for an answer, but there was a war in the heavenlies that delayed the answer from coming sooner. Daniel was the sender during his prayer for God to have mercy, found in Daniel 9:17–19 (NIV):

> *Now, our God, hear the prayers and petitions of your*
> *servant. For your sake, Lord, look with favor on*

your desolate sanctuary. Give ear, our God, and hear; open your eyes and see the desolation of the city that bears your Name. We do not make requests of you because we are righteous, but because of your great mercy. Lord, listen! Lord, forgive! Lord, hear and act! For your sake, my God, do not delay, because your city and your people bear your Name.

Then God became the sender when He sent forth an answer through an angel…in this case, the angelic messenger was the encoder and decoder. The noise, in this case, was from the hindrance that came through the prince of the kingdom of Persia, who caused a spiritual war in the heavenlies creating a twenty-one-day delay. The angel said Daniel's words were heard, and he came because of Daniel's words. Let's emphasize the word "heard." Hearing is an active part of communication, and this can be found in Daniel 10:12–14 (NIV):

Then he continued, "Do not be afraid, Daniel. Since the first day that you set your mind to gain understanding and to humble yourself before your God, your words were heard, and I have come in response to them. But the prince of the Persian kingdom resisted me twenty-one days. Then Michael, one of the chief princes, came to help me, because I was detained there with the king of Persia. Now I have come to explain to you what will happen to your people in the future, for the vision concerns a time yet to come."

Let's take a closer look at this scripture at verse 12. The angel said to Daniel, "…your words were heard, and I have come in response to them." Hearing takes place within the sixth concept of communication, which is basically when the recipient receives the message from the sender. The next phrase, "I have come because of your words," reveals that there was a response to Daniel's request. This demonstrates that his communication made it to the final concept of communication, which is the recipient's response. The communication loop began because the Lord became the sender of the message, the angel was the channel, and Daniel became the recipient. Actions were made to answer Daniel's prayer, but the noise from the prince of Persia caused the delay during this phase of communication.

First Phase of Communication: Daniel is the sender. God is the recipient.

I am a visual person, so I love to put things into perspective based on visualizing how everything plays out. If we focus back on Jacob's ladder, we can apply Daniel's experience to the ladder. When we think of the angels descending and ascending on the ladder, we can see that Daniel clearly made it through with the ascension of prayer. Meaning the angels ascending on the ladder were those who were able to take the message from man and give it to the Lord...who was waiting at the top of the ladder. In Daniel's case, this was a success because the angel said his words were heard from the first day. No noise was present because Daniel humbled himself before God and had a heart prepared to understand. This caused clear passage for the message to ascend to God...his prayer in this phase of communication was complete, and it reached the final concept because the response came. This marks the beginning of the communication loop due to the response.

Second Phase of Communication (Loop 1): God is the sender. Daniel is the recipient.

The descension of answered prayer took place, meaning the angel was able to descend to earth with the message from God. Unfortunately, there was a high level of noise that came during the process of communication through the prince of Persia, which caused a twenty-one-day delay before the response got back to

Daniel. Even so, the angel was still able to bring God's message back to Daniel, which can be found in Daniel 10:10–14. The communication process completed here as well because Daniel responded.

Third Phase of Communication (Loop 2): Daniel is the sender. The angel is the recipient. This can be found in Daniel 10:15 (NIV): *"While he was saying this to me, I bowed with my face toward the ground and was speechless."*

In this part of the scripture, Daniel responds through nonverbal communication. He first looked down towards the ground because he was at a loss for words. This was nonverbal, showing that he understood, but his body language was doing the talking. The angel responded, completing this phase and continuing the loop of communication.

Fourth Phase of Communication (Loop 3): The angel is the sender. Daniel is the recipient. This can be found in Daniel 10:16a (NIV): *"Then one who looked like a man touched my lips..."*

This demonstrates nonverbal communication because the angel touched the lips of Daniel in response to Daniel's actions... continuing the loop of communication.

Fifth Phase of Communication (Loop 4): Daniel is the sender. The angel is the recipient. This can be found in Daniel 10:16b–17 (NIV): *"...and I opened my mouth and began to speak. I said to the one standing before me, 'I am overcome with anguish because of the vision, my lord, and I feel very weak. How can I, your servant, talk with you, my lord? My strength is gone, and I can hardly breathe.'"*

In this scripture, we see that Daniel responded to the angel who touched his lips in a manner that was nonverbal and verbal. His nonverbal response was Daniel making the action to open his mouth in preparation to speak. His verbal response was his message back to the angel as he spoke about his anguish and weakness and then questioned the angel on how he could talk to him in such conditions. As Daniel responded, he became the sender of the message...continuing the loop of communication.

Sixth Phase of Communication (Loop 5): The angel is the sender. Daniel is the recipient. This can be found in Daniel 10:18–19a (NIV): "Again, the one who looked like a man touched me and gave me strength. 'Do not be afraid, you who are highly esteemed,' he said. 'Peace! Be strong now; be strong.'"

As one can see, this scripture demonstrates that the angel communicated both nonverbally and verbally. When the angel touched Daniel again, this was a nonverbal response to Daniel's question. The angel then proceeded to speak to Daniel by encouraging him with actual words, which was a verbal response.

We can break this scripture down further to analyze communication, but since the point is clearly made, we can stop right there for now. We can conclude that Jacob's ladder helps to bring things into perspective regarding the process of communication between heaven and earth. This also helps us get a better grasp of the communication process that was taking place in this reading between God, the angel, and Daniel. Keep in mind, this process is not limited to this chapter in the book of Daniel, but it can also be applied to all chapters of the Bible. This was only a simple breakdown as teaching ground for us to better understand how to use these same concepts for the studying of the word of God. Spiritual communication can be found throughout the word of God, and the Holy Spirit helps us to maintain the communication. If our communication is not clear, He helps us to realize this so we can maintain our connection with God. It is for us to take heed to His nudge to do something about it and not quench Him.

Also, as mentioned earlier, spiritual communication can be found in every area of the Bible. Please take note that in the Old

Testament, the Holy Spirit came upon people to communicate spiritually; the Holy Spirit was not yet moving within people. Reason being is that Jesus had not yet come to earth to release the Holy Spirit to move from within the hearts of people. He had to sacrifice Himself first through the shedding of His blood; the veil had to be ripped to show that the barrier of having access to God is no longer necessary since we can now get to God through Him, and He had to ascend to the heavens so that the Comforter, the Holy Spirit, could come and live within us. We can see the Holy Spirit moving within people in the New Testament after the death and resurrection of Jesus. Jesus made it possible through the sacrifice of His life and shedding of His blood. Jesus gave humanity the direction and explanation that He must go so that the Holy Spirit could come. Not only can we find the Holy Spirit moving within the hearts of people in the New Testament, but it still stands to this very day and applies to us right now. It is ordained for God and man to be able to communicate clearly and freely between one another. With that in mind, it is imperative that we understand the flow of communication by the help of the Holy Spirit—the breath of God...the One who maintains our closeness and communication with God through Jesus.

The Earthly Functionality of Horns and the Breath of Man

Since the Lord placed such an emphasis on wind instruments by having us focus on the horn, I thought it would be best to take a closer look at what wind instruments are all about. After my research, I discovered information that I never knew about wind instruments, which ties into what I previously shared with you about horns and the breath of God. Let us start off with the basics.

The first subject matter to acknowledge about wind instruments is that they come in various sizes and shapes. They all make unique sounds, from the tuba to the trumpet, to the saxophone, to the flute, to the harmonica, to even that of a whistle. The sounds that come from wind instruments help assist a certain mood. These moods can include sounds that are calming, soothing, dramatic, romantic, alerting, joyful, suspenseful, etc. As we know, wind instruments produce sound only if a person blows air into the mouthpiece of the instrument. In other words, it takes the breath of an individual for the wind instrument to work. It has also been found that playing a wind instrument can bring numerous health benefits. That's right, health benefits.

A benefit that comes from playing a wind instrument is improved health for respiratory functions.[4] Meaning, the player of the instrument becomes more disciplined with inhaling and exhaling in such a way that the lungs begin to open more, increasing the capacity of the lungs, thus, strengthening the health of the lungs. To keep it simple, playing such instruments help the individual to breathe better. On top of that, it strengthens the abdominal muscles due to the pressure placed on these muscles. This pressure occurs in the muscles every time a breath is taken to make a sound. It also helps bring relaxation to the mind and relieves stress. Another exciting fact is that the playing of wind instruments helps coordinate distinct parts of the body, which includes the eyes, hands, breath, and mind. These parts and functions are required to be in unison to produce the sound of music. As previously mentioned, the mind is already relaxed while playing a wind instrument, so if the body coordinates with the mind, the body then becomes relaxed as well, which is another example of a great benefit. Amazingly, people that have asthma are still able to play wind instruments. So, if an asthmatic individual decides to play a wind instrument, it can be a method of therapy for that person. According to studies, asthmatic wind instrumentalists are found to have less constriction to breathing functions, have fewer panic/fear responses, and are more energetic in comparison to asthmatic non-wind players.[5] Playing wind instruments helps with energy, mood, and our panic-fear response. With this knowledge, we can see that there are many advantages to not only listening to the sounds that come from a wind instrument but also many advantages that come through the actual act of playing a wind instrument.

Now you may ask, "What does this have to do with the Holy Spirit?" Just as it takes breath of an individual to make a wind instrument work, so too does it take the breath of God for us to communicate. He is the wind and the breath within our horn, causing it to sound and communicate, which comes with health benefits in spiritual communications.

The Holy Spirit's presence is necessary during worship because He helps us to worship God the way God deserves and desires to be worshiped. The Holy Spirit knows exactly what sound is needed for certain times and certain situations. He knows what is necessary to get the attention of God. He also knows what we need to express our love and our giving of worth to the Father. The Holy Spirit connects us to the Almighty because it is His duty to help us stay in communion with the Father bringing health to our spirit and health to the spiritual communication we have with God. When it is time to worship, we must always ask for the help of the Holy Spirit so we can go beyond ourselves into that place of honoring the Lord. As we go beyond ourselves by the help of His Spirit, healthy communication begins to activate by causing a breakthrough. We break through the boundaries of flesh, and everything within us begins to align with the Holy Spirit...our mind, all parts of our body (eyes, hands, feet, etc.), and breath/spirit begin to coordinate with one another because they are now being steered by the Holy Spirit as He takes us to a spiritual place of communication with God. Fear and panic take a back seat because we are now operating through His Spirit. As He communes with the Father through us, we operate in His likeness by the evidence of His fruit taking a front seat in our spiritual communication, which consists of "love, joy, peace, patience, kindness, goodness, faithfulness, gentleness, and self-control" (Galatians 5:22b–23a, NLT). The more we allow the Holy Spirit to help us worship by breathing life into our communication, the more our spirit man becomes strengthened, and our spiritual lungs that help us to bring our message of worship begin to strengthen. The stresses of this world are nonexistent when we allow the Holy Spirit to help us communicate because He takes us to a place beyond the earthly realm of limitations connecting us to God in the heavenly realm with no limitations.

When that connection takes place, the Lord can respond freely with no hindrances. Whenever true worship takes place, there is an exchange, an exchange that comes with correction, direction, and empowerment for the sake of His glory, which proves the Holy Spirit brings health to our spiritual communication with God. The Holy Spirit is life. If He is life, then He maintains our health spiritually as we allow Him to operate through us daily. When He comes, He breathes life into us (meaning our spirit), thus, making us more effective in worship. We go beyond worshiping through the means of the power of ourselves into a place of spiritual power that gives us access to an intimate place with God Almighty. The Holy Spirit activates what was once dead and brings it to life. That is, the Holy Spirit brings life to our worship and, in turn, life to our spirit. He takes us beyond our sinful flesh and brings us to being alive in the spirit. The word of God tells us that the flesh and the Spirit are always at war. When the flesh is at work, "But if Christ is in you, then even though your body is subject to death because of sin, the Spirit gives life because of righteousness," according to Romans 8:10 (NIV). When we give way to the Spirit, we give way to life in our worship. When our spirit man is at work, we can clearly connect with God because God communicates only through the Spirit.

We must remember that God does not look at the outer, meaning the flesh, and does not communicate with the outer; according to 1 Samuel 16:7, He looks at the heart. The heart and the spirit are one. It is important to note that God is Spirit; according to John 4:24 (NKJV), "...those who worship Him *must* worship in spirit and truth." This scripture alone tells us that we cannot worship in our own might but only by His Spirit. In other words, God's Spirit is necessary and is required to truly worship Him. This brings me back to the necessity of having the Spirit of God present when we worship. Genesis 1:2 (NIV) relays this message well; it says, "Now the earth was formless and empty, darkness was over the surface of the deep, and the Spirit of God was hovering over the waters." Notice, this scripture explains the earth was lifeless, in other words dead, but the Spirit of God was present. Meaning "life" was hovering over the waters but had to be invoked. How? By the activation of the Commander's voice. The Holy Spirit was there doing His part from the beginning of creation, but for all things to be created with completion, it took the unity of the Trinity. God's spoken word came from His breath, His breath is His Spirit, and His spoken word is Jesus; Jesus is the Living Word. We discussed God the Father being the Commander and initiator of communication; we just concluded the Holy Spirit as the breath and life of communication; we will now go into Jesus as the way of communication.

CHAPTER 4

JESUS, THE HEAVENLY HORN, THE HORN OF SALVATION—THE WAY OF COMMUNICATION

Communication between heaven and earth is possible, but only by the means of the access giver. The access giver is Jesus. Remember, we are focusing on the horn. As we have previously discussed, the horn represents communication; it represents sound. If we take time to literally examine an actual horn and revisit what we previously discussed, we can see that the horn can only make a sound when someone uses their mouth to play it. Spiritually, the person initiating the sound would be God, the Commander. To hear the sound, it requires the breath to create the sound, which is the Holy Spirit. Now, we are moving on to what we have not yet discussed, which is the actual instrument, the vessel that the sound is coming through, that is, Jesus, the Horn of Salvation. Horn of Salvation, meaning He is the instrument that heaven uses to bridge the gap of communication between God and man and between heaven and earth. He is the tunnel that the life and communication go through. He is the trumpet. He is the one who sits at the right hand of God; He has authority and direct access to hear from God, the Father, and perform what God desires in heaven and on earth. All things must go through Him. "I am the way and the truth and the life. No one comes to the Father except through me" (John 14:6, NIV).

As we study Jesus, the Horn of Salvation, we may wonder why He is "the Horn of Salvation." Why is it so specific to Salvation? Why couldn't it be Jesus, the Horn of Love? Or Jesus, the Horn of Righteousness? Or Jesus…the Horn of (fill in the blank)? Well, there is a reason. There is always a reason why God does what He does and why heaven is set up the way it is. All names have a significant meaning. This means Jesus, as the Horn of Salvation, comes with a specific and inevitable purpose. Let's look deeper into this name.

Horn of Salvation.

A horn is an instrument; its sole purpose is to produce sound naturally. A horn is an apparatus, something that is tangible, something that can be seen, held, and utilized by the one who plays it. A horn is a tool. A horn is something created to express what the instrumentalist of the horn wants to release to the hearers through sound. A horn is simply a reflection of the one who plays it. The horn is completely dependent upon the instrumentalist of the horn. The horn simply does what the instrumentalist of the horn desires it to do. It makes a sound only when guided to do so by the directives of the one who holds and plays it.

We will now look into the "of Salvation" part. Firstly, the word "of" means association, belonging to, relation to something. Secondly, the word "Salvation" means to be saved and delivered from the penalty and consequences of sin, which includes death, ruin, harm and/or loss. Salvation comes from a source that preserves, protects, and keeps one safe from something. In other words, salvation brings help and aid to those who need it.

When we put everything together, we can see that Jesus fits the description perfectly. When we talk about the horn being a tool, instrument, apparatus, and vessel that could be seen…He did just that. He came down here on earth in the form of flesh. He walked on this earth as man; people were able to walk with Him, talk with Him, eat with Him, touch Him, and see Him in a tangible form. He came as an instrument of God, one that could be used by God so that God's will could be done on earth as it is in heaven. He did not come in His own strength but by the strength of the God. He was and still is the word.

According to John 1:1 (NIV), "In the beginning was the Word, and the Word was with God, and the Word was God."

Jesus is the Word. Since Jesus is the Word, we can interchange "the Word" with "Jesus," so it now reads, "In the beginning was *Jesus*, and *Jesus* was with God, and *Jesus* was God." This goes to show that Jesus was not only with God, but He is God. He is the Son of God, God in the flesh, the tangible form of the Almighty God. He reflects God, the Father in heaven. He is a chosen vessel that gave of Himself to act upon the commands and directions of the One who sent Him. Remember, when Jesus prayed in Gethsemane, He realized the great task that was ahead of Him, a task that no human could bear.

But as Jesus prayed, He said in Luke 22:42 (NIV), "Father, if you are willing, take this cup from me, yet not my will, but yours be done."

This scripture demonstrates that Jesus did only what God desired for Him to do. He was a willing instrument, completely committed and sold out to what the instrumentalist (God, the Father) desired to come from the vessel of His Son, Jesus. It was through Jesus that God the Father could bring a solution to this lost and dying world. Jesus is the Horn, the tangible form of God, the Word made into flesh…the Living Word.

As we go into Jesus being the Horn "of Salvation," we can see that He has many names. Remember, the "of" means belonging to something; in this case, it is salvation. As mentioned before, salvation is being saved and delivered from the consequences of sin. Jesus came and gave His life as the ultimate sacrifice paying for our sin once and for all so we can have life and so we can be saved from the power of death. He brought us aid even though we were undeserving of it. The blood of an animal sacrifice could not even compare or come close to the wages of sin, so He brought us salvation through giving up His very own life. No one on this earth could ever do what Jesus did for us. That is why it was important that He came as a vessel, a horn, who could save us from our sins and bring us salvation. Which demonstrates why He is the Horn of Salvation.

The purpose of this Horn had to be none other than "of Salvation" because salvation was crucially necessary for humanity. We had to be saved for everything else that comes from Him to follow. So, it is important that we understand and recognize His sacrifice and the power behind why He is our Horn of Salvation. We have life once we accept Him, honor Him, reverence Him, and recognize His sacrifice as being that pliable vessel of God, one who was a willing instrument sent by God to act upon God's command to bring us life through His death and set us free by giving us victory. He now has power over sin, death, and the power of the grave.

"Where, O death, is your victory? Where, O death is your sting?" (1 Corinthians 15:55, NIV)

Jesus holds the authority over the power of sin and death because of His selfless sacrifice.

Since Jesus is the Horn of Salvation, that means He is the One who holds all power, authority, dominion, and strength to save mankind. He is our strength; He will deliver us and save us from our enemies. According to Zechariah's song in Luke 1:68–75 (NIV):

Praise be to the Lord, the God of Israel, because he

has come to his people and redeemed them. He has raised up a "horn of salvation" for us in the house of his servant David (as he said through his holy prophets of long ago), salvation from our enemies and from the hand of all who hate us—to show mercy to our ancestors and to remember his holy covenant, the oath he swore to our father Abraham: to rescue us from the hand of our enemies, and to enable us to serve him without fear in holiness and righteousness before him all our days.

The above scripture is explaining that Jesus has brought forth redemption to us; He is the One who came as the Horn of Salvation from the line of David, which was promised long ago. We can run to Him and be safe from our enemies. We can find protection from those who hate us and want to harm us. This scripture serves as a reminder that God provided a promise to Abraham that we shall be delivered from the hands of hostility if we serve Him. When He makes a promise, it cannot return to Him void, for He is a man who cannot lie. This is His oath and covenant, which serves forevermore.

Jesus came to our rescue by giving us salvation. He has saved us and preserved us from harm, loss, or ruin. Through Him, there is deliverance and liberation from sin. That is why in the days of old, if a person was to be harmed due to a crime that they may have committed, that person could grab on to the horns of the altar to claim sanctuary for safety and mercy. By doing so, the person who committed the crime has placed themselves under the saving grace of God, washing away sin and obliterating deserved punishment. The blood that was found on the horns of the altar was symbolic of God's grace and salvation for a sinner. However, it must be noted that the saving grace, safety, and mercy that came from the "horns of the altar" did not apply to those who committed acts that were premeditated.

"But if anyone schemes and kills someone deliberately, that person is to be taken from my altar and put to death" (Exodus 21:14, NIV).

The horns of the altar were symbolic of Jesus and what He was called to do, even before He walked the earth. Although He had not yet walked the earth in the Old Testament, He was still very much present. I am reminded of what I mentioned in the earlier part of this book about God being our defense during my God challenge assignment. God is our defense as He operates through God, the Son, who is the Horn of Salvation.

Through the blood of Jesus, we, who serve Christ and believe in Him, are saved and redeemed from death. He is our salvation and strength. We are preserved from harm and protected by His saving grace. His blood provides atonement and cleansing. The very name of Jesus means God is our salvation. His name has given us the power to be set free. But we must remember not to take advantage of this promise by deliberately sinning. Deliberate sin (which can be viewed as intentional sin, willful sin, and lawlessness against God) is iniquity. God shared His thoughts about the matter of the lawlessness of a man when He said, "I never knew you. Away from me, you evildoers!" (Matthew 7:23, NIV)

With this in mind, we are to embrace the access God has given us to be delivered and redeemed. We are to follow Him by submitting to His will and not our own. As we follow Jesus, we can know that He has saved us from harm; we can always hold on to Him and be fully confident that His protection is certain. He is our refuge, and His strength surpasses the strength of our enemies and everything set to try to destroy us. He is the Horn of Salvation that we can hold on to, our promised protection; there is no need to fear.

A good example of Jesus as the Horn of Salvation was during the time Abraham was about to sacrifice his son Isaac to show his love for God. At the nick of time, God put the sacrifice to a stop and provided a saving substitute, which was the ram in the thicket caught by its horns. The ram substituting the sacrifice of Isaac represented Jesus Christ Himself as being the ultimate sacrifice, taking our place to save us from our sins. This brought salvation to us, even though we did not deserve it. This was symbolic of Jesus, being the Horn of Salvation.

As we reflect on Jesus being the Horn of Salvation, we can now understand that He is the trumpet of heaven. God is the instrumentalist, the hornist, and the trumpeter, the Holy Spirit is God's breath within the Horn, and Jesus is the Heavenly Horn, that trumpet that we see throughout the word of God.

We are a people that are in dire need of Jesus as the Horn of Salvation to be saved. We also need to maintain a life of holiness, righteousness, and purity by submitting to the call of God. To be in communication with God, we have to accept and acknowledge the sacrifice made by Jesus and recognize that all communication must go through Jesus.

Jesus plays a significant role of spiritual communication. In order to get to the Father, we must go through the Son. Jesus saved us so we could have the opportunity to connect with God. His sacrifice brought us salvation, which is why He is our Horn of Salvation.

"The LORD is my rock, my fortress and my deliverer; my God is my rock, in whom I take refuge, my shield and the horn of my salvation, my stronghold" (Psalm 18:2, NIV).

CHAPTER 5

TRINITY COMMUNICATION— THE ENSURED SUCCESS OF SPIRITUAL COMMUNICATION

In the previous chapters, we discussed spiritual communication in three ways by specifically focusing on God, Jesus, and the Holy Spirit operating in their own avenue. But even though they operate differently, they are still operating as one. God, Jesus, and the Holy Spirit moving together as one is what we know to be the Trinity. In this chapter, we are going to discuss the Trinity.

Before going into the depths of the Trinity, I believe it is important to view how we, as human beings, are made up as an individual, which will help us to see the Trinity through our makeup. We, as individuals, are made up of three parts: the mind, soul, and body. Our mind helps us to think and where our actions start from. Our soul is our essence; it is who we are in spirit. It is the life within that activates that which is outside. Then we have our body, which is our flesh, which is what houses the mind and soul. It is what people can see and touch. Even though we, as individuals, are made up of these three different parts doesn't mean we are three different people.

We can also see this theory from psychological teachings. According to the teachings of Sigmund Freud, the human personality is complex and is made of three different components: the id, ego, and superego. According to Freud's psychoanalytic theory, "*The id is the primitive and instinctual part of the mind that contains sexual and aggressive drives and hidden memories, the super-ego operates as a moral conscience, and the ego is the realistic part that mediates between the desires of the id and the super-ego.*"[6]

To simplify Freud's theory, the id represents our body and fleshly desires. The ego represents the soul, which is our inner and serves as a mediator within us. The superego is our mind. Our thoughts within our mind help us to decipher right from wrong. With this teaching, we can still see three at work within us as an individual. If we were to compare the three components of the human personality with what is within the Trinity, we could see that the id represents the body. The ego represents the Spirit. The superego represents the mind.

The three parts within us make us one whole as an individual. Just as we have the mind, body, and soul, in the Trinity, you have the same. Just as we have the id, ego, and superego, in the Trinity, you have the same. We are made in His image, so if we see ourselves first, we can understand the makeup of the Trinity easier. God, the Father, represents the mind and superego of God; He is the mastermind behind all things. Jesus represents the body and id because He came on earth as flesh and walked among us. The Holy Spirit represents the soul and ego; He is the Spirit of God and the very essence of God. Just because they are three different parts doesn't mean that they are not one. Together, the Trinity is God in His complete form. They are three different parts of One Perfect God in His wholeness.

Each part of the Trinity has a specific purpose and performs differently yet remain One. God, the Father, is the Godhead. He heads everything up and makes the commands for things to get done. God, the Son, is the Doer. He hears the commands and takes the actions to do them. God, the Holy Spirit, is the Power behind everything. He activates and brings to life whatever it is that needs to get done. We now have a general understanding of how the Trinity is made up of three parts, and each part functions differently, but they remain one. We also see that our makeup as humans is the same as the Trinity because we are made in the image of God. With this foundational knowledge, we can better understand how the Trinity functions differently but move together in unity, which always results in success.

In this chapter, we are going to view the Trinity with a different spin. To prepare your mind and heart, it will be from the perspective of business to effectively explain how they successfully operate together through unity. I will refer to the covenant that God has with us from the viewpoint of a business plan. When I say business plan, I also mean God's covenant. The business plans that we will discuss will be summarized in my own words but will be based on the scripture. Before going into this, let's briefly review what we just learned in the previous three chapters about all three within the Trinity.

God, the Father, and the Creator is the initiator of communication. God, the Son, is the way of communication. God, the Holy Spirit, is the maintainer of communication. Spiritual communication is not complete without having them all move together as one; that is why they always operate as one. God wants us to realize and take note of the power of unity. He demonstrated it in the beginning of the Bible, throughout the entirety of the Bible, and concludes the Bible with the unity of the Trinity. Unity and continual communication create healthy communication, and the Trinity in operation is the ultimate example of healthy communication.

Think about it...a business operation cannot function with only one department. There are always several departments within a business moving in their own function to complete a specific task to make the business run. These departments are part of a whole; as they operate individually, they are completing one goal collectively, which is the success of the business operation. This is also applicable to the Trinity. Each part of the Trinity has a job to perform, and together, they perform their job to complete one mission. They operate differently in three parts, but the separate parts are bound together as one whole. I found a perfect explanation of this in an article titled "Understanding the Trinity" by Kelli Mahoney (2018), which explains the "Trinity" as "Tri-Unity":

> *Many people have stopped using the term "Trinity" and started using the term "Tri-Unity" to explain the three parts of God and how they form the whole.*
>
> *Some use math to explain the Trinity. We cannot think of the Holy Trinity as a sum of three parts (1 + 1 + 1 = 3), but instead, show how each part multiplies the others to form a wonderful whole (1 x 1 x 1 = 1). Using the multiplication model, we show that the three form a union, thus why people have moved to calling it the Tri-Unity.[7]*

I found this to be interesting because God, Jesus, and the Holy Spirit operate in unity, as I previously mentioned. They move three different ways but move together as one, which equals one. As they move together, they magnify one another, which results in one perfect result. "Tri," meaning three. "Unity," meaning one. Together it forms the word—"tri-unity." They are three but one.

The Development of the Trinity Business Plan

What exactly is the purpose of the Trinity in operation? What are their goal and mission? To answer that, let's revisit why God created man in the first place. God desired worship from creation in a different way than what had been before. God was already getting worshiped by the angels because they were created and designed to worship Him. It is the duty and purpose of angels to worship God. The angels were not given a choice to do so because there was no need for choice. Reason being is that angels were designed for that very purpose, which is to worship God. It is not that God lacked being worshiped because the angels were already doing that. But God desired worship in a different way, a heartfelt way, a sincere way, a way of choice. So, He created and designed man to worship Him slightly similar to the angels, but the difference is that God gave mankind a choice to do so. Because of this, a plan was created by the Trinity to make creation worship God from the heart and own free will. To do this, there had to be a plan. It wasn't that simple, though; the creation had to be designed in a certain way that was different from His previous creation. Creating a plan required a time to review, devise, weigh options, develop, analyze, etc. As we know, for such strategies to come about, it required a meeting for plan development.

We can find the development of this plan in Genesis 1:26, which is when God began to have a discussion among Himself during the time of creation. This happened on the sixth day. I use the word "discussion" because He makes a statement using the words, "Let us…" To have a discussion takes more than one person. That means there is someone else present in addition to who is speaking. When the word "us" is used, that means the one who is speaking is referring to themselves and one or more other people as they are speaking. This shows there is a conversation involving others outside of the person who is sending the message. Who is the speaker in this case? God, the Father. Who else is He speaking to? God, the Son, and God, the Holy Spirit. This was the first example of a conversation and clear communication within the word of God. This is also the first meeting and first conference made known in the Bible.

Before moving forward, let's look into why meetings and conferences are held in the world of business. Conferences and meetings are found to be a gathering of a set, a group, members, or committees for the purpose of a discussion. These meetings and conferences can be held to develop, resolve, plan, and make decisions. This can be applied to the Trinity in operation. Since we are going to apply it in this manner, for easier understanding, let's refer to this operation as the Trinity operation.

So, what exactly is the purpose, goal, and mission of this operation, and how was it developed? To keep things simple, let's briefly break it down into bullet format:

- *Purpose*: For God to be worshiped from the heart and own free will of His creation.
- *Goal*: Make creation. God and creation shall be one.
- *Mission*: To give creation dominion, like God. Because of this, this creation will be made in the image of God. They are to be fruitful and multiply. They are to love Him, obey Him, and follow Him. Upon the compliance of this condition, creation will live with Him and have everlasting life.

We were originally viewing the Trinity from a business standpoint because it helps us understand how the Trinity operates together as one. Even though we are seeing it from this perspective, it is not fiction; God is the first businessman. The Trinity is God in three persons. We must remember that God chose to send His Son through the race of the Jews. With that in mind, let's review business by focusing on God's chosen people...the Jews.

The Trinity's Union, the Torah, and Business Success

Jews are known to be amazingly blessed and gifted to do business. This gift helps Jews to be wealthy and successful due to the blessing from God. In an article "Why Are Jews So Successful?" written by Michael Sebastian in 2016, it states,

> *Jews comprise a tiny percentage of the world population, about 0.2%, yet they hold enormous wealth and power. 10 of the 50 billionaires are Jews-which is a highly disproportionate representation.*[8]

This goes to show that not all Jews are wealthy and successful, but in comparison to their small percentage within the world's population, they are significantly prevalent among the successful. Another article released in 2008 titled "Why Jews Are Disproportionally Successful?" by Rabbi Levi Brackman states,

> *The fact that Jews are disproportionally successful in many fields of endeavor is undeniable. The statistics simply speak for themselves. Jews make up less than half of one percent of the world's population, but they consistently have made up more than twenty percent of the Forbes 400 list of the world richest people.*[9]

The Jews are small in number, but the proportion of the wealthy Jews among the wealthy of other races is extremely high. They are simply reflecting the ultimate One by whom we are all made in the image of, which is God Almighty, the Great Businessman. Everything He does is astonishing and clearly indicates His power. He does great things with small numbers.

Think about the story of Gideon, when God said, *"You have too many men. I cannot deliver Midian into their hands, or Israel would boast against me, 'My own strength has saved me'"* (Judges 7:2, NIV). Because God was God, and wanted His power and might to be recognized, He decreased the army from 32,000 to 300. With this small number, God gave Gideon and His army the victory. This goes to show it was by none other but God Himself that brought deliverance. God does not need a large population to bring success and accomplishment. He prefers just a few so we can see His power at work. The number 300 is a sign of God's perfection of "3 x 100." The number three goes back to the beginning of creation where the Trinity—"Tri," meaning three, was at work. God is making a powerful statement through that number. It only took three through the Trinity to make creation. It only took 300 to gain victory for Gideon's army. It doesn't take large numbers for God to bring success.

Going back to the Jews and their small percentage in population, they are the least in population, yet their presence is largely represented among the wealthy and successful because God's hands of blessing are on them. The Jewish race is simply a reflection of God. They are blessed and gifted with business because God, the Businessman of all businessmen, had already prepared the way through His example and by giving them the wisdom through the Torah. In the article I previously mentioned by Rabbi Levi, he explains the book he wrote titled *Jewish Wisdom for Business Success*, which is about how business success of the Jews is inspired by the Torah and how the Torah is known to be "the divine blueprint for success."[9] Rabbi Levi concludes the article by stating,

> *...areas such as negotiations, positive thinking, will power, the approach to failure and reactions to fear—the Torah has wisdom for all of it. It is therefore little wonder that Jews who have studied the greatest book of wisdom ever written—the Torah—are disproportionally successful in every arena of endeavor. And even those who do not actively study the Torah still benefit from its wisdom in the form of attitudes and*

teachings that Jewish parents and communities teach and pass down, albeit mostly without being aware that they originate from the Torah. If this divine blueprint for success exists and it has helped us as Jews become successful it is about time we both recognize where the wisdom comes from and share it with others.[9]

Based on these quotes, we can see the Torah serves as a foundation of business success for the Jews. The Torah is also known as the Five Books of Moses (Genesis, Exodus, Leviticus, Numbers, and Deuteronomy). These books contain the laws, instructions, and teachings given to Moses by God to give to His people for righteous living. Moses wrote the God-given instructions within these books, which were birthed from his experience with God at Mount Sinai in addition to what God revealed to him about the requirements necessary for the tabernacle. Let's not forget the tablets that contained the Ten Commandments written by the hand of God Himself, who serves as the Author and Finisher of our faith. All of which caused the establishment of what we know to be the Torah. The Torah is about the covenant between God and man, and it also is believed to be the actual blueprint for God's creation. The word "blueprint" is described as "an original plan or prototype that influences subsequent design or practice; it is a detailed plan of action, a detailed outline, a model; a prototype."[10]

God had to have a blueprint developed for creation to serve as a blueprint for mankind. It took strategy, togetherness, analyzation, a thought process, and much more for the blueprint to serve as an outline and an original plan for creation. It had to be just right to put it into effect, production, and have it executed. That is why God had to hold the meeting among Himself to successfully come up with a solution, that is, upon the unanimous agreement amongst the Father, Son, and Holy Spirit. All had to be present to come up with a result. Agreement was required from all for the result to be reached. All had to make a commitment to make sure the agreement could be executed. With that being said, let's look deeper into God's example by reviewing the business plan of the Trinity operation.

Trinity Communication During the Creation of Adam (the Beginning of Mankind)

God, the Father, had a meeting with His counterparts (the Son and the Holy Spirit) to develop a plan for creation. As mentioned before, all had to be present, and all were present. This can be found in the first three verses of Genesis chapter 1.

In Genesis 1:1 (NIV), it says, "In the beginning *God* created the heavens and the earth." This shows that God the Creator, who is the Father, was present.

In verse 2 (NIV), it says, "Now the earth was formless and empty, darkness was over the surface of the deep, and the *Spirit of God* was hovering over the waters." This shows that the Holy Spirit was present.

In verses 3 to 4 (NIV), "And *God said, 'Let there be light,'* and there was light. God saw that the light was good, and he separated the light from the darkness." This shows that Jesus, the Son, was present because He is the light of the world and the Word of God.

The three discussed what needed to be done to accomplish having creation worship Him by factoring in free will. They realized this could be done, but they had to work together to get it done. God, the Father, was the mastermind behind it all. He had to do His part by envisioning and creating it by speaking it. Jesus, the Son, knew that once the Father speaks it, He had to do it by putting action to it; it had to go through Him first for creation to be made. Once this was accomplished, the Spirit of God had to breathe into what was spoken to give it life. This is the power of unity. To accomplish anything, there must be clear communication, there must be agreement, and there must be oneness. They worked together then, and they are still working together even now. This is the first example of the sound of the *Heavenly Horn*, the wind instrument of heaven, who is Jesus, being played by the Hornist, who is God, and being sounded by the wind, who is the Holy Spirit.

As I mentioned earlier in this book, when playing a wind instrument, it causes the mind, body, and spirit to be in unison. When creation was being formed, we could see the unison of the mind, body, and spirit through God (the mind), Jesus (the body, but not yet formed), and Spirit (the breath).

God thought first—that was His mind at work. God is the mastermind behind creation. God came in agreement with the Spirit by speaking out His thoughts with the sound of His voice. The power part of the Trinity, which is the Holy Spirit, began to do His work by breathing life into the thought. The breath is what helped produce the sound of God's voice, which is the Word that was released through the mouth of God. Whatever God says becomes the Word of God. When God speaks, it is His Word that causes things to be created.

The Word of God is God, and the Word of God is Jesus. He existed in the beginning, although not flesh as yet, He always was there. Through Him, all things were created. That means creation could not come into being without the presence of the Son, Jesus Christ. John 1:1, 3–5 (NIV) backs this up significantly; it says:

> *In the beginning was the Word, and the Word was with God, and the Word was God. Through him all things were made; without him nothing was made that has been made. In him was life, and that life was the light of all mankind. The light shines in the darkness, and the darkness has not overcome it.*

That Word became flesh according to John, and Jesus says it Himself in John 8:12 (NIV), "I am the light of the world. Whoever follows me will never walk in darkness, but will have the light of life."

Jesus was with God in the beginning. All things came through Him, and there was not one thing that was created without His participation. When God said, "Let there be light," that Word released (which is the sound released from the voice of God) was Jesus Himself. This shows that Jesus was at work during the time of creation as well. As we can see, there is a united effort that takes place by way of the Trinity, the Father, the Son, and the Holy Spirit to make things happen...all by way of sound.

This demonstrates the presence of all three; it also demonstrates the power of unity. All of them worked together in different capacities to accomplish one great task that lay ahead of them. God, the Father, initiated the desire for creation, so He made it known by speaking it. Remember, He is the Initiator and the Voice of the Horn. He placed His lips upon the Trumpet, who is the Horn of Salvation, and by way of the Horn, God's thoughts became reality. His thoughts were formed by way of the Word of God. Every time we see the words "God said," we can also view it as God's Word. God's Word is the Word of God. The Word of God is Jesus. We also know that in order for a voice to be released, it takes breath. As God voiced His words through the horn, it had to be done by His breath. His breath is His Spirit, the Holy Spirit. His breath brought the creation to life by the sound of His Trumpet. This is unity at its very best; one could not do without the other, which took the necessity of clear communication.

The Trinity had to agree to accomplish all things they desired to accomplish. All duties of each were required to succeed and accomplish the final goal. To have agreement, there must be communication, and the communication must be consistent. The Trinity at work is the epitome of what healthy communication is all about. Every successful business derives from healthy communication and the power of agreement. As far as the Trinity operation is concerned, there was an original business plan, and inadvertently, there had to be an amended business plan. The sin of man (through disobedience to God) caused the business plan to be amended by God, which we will look into shortly.

The purpose of the Trinity was to make mankind in their image and likeness to rule within the earth, and mankind was created to walk with God, talk with God, and have a relationship with God out of free will. Since we were made in the image of God, that means that we operate like Him.

In Genesis 2:15 (NIV), it says, "The LORD God took the man and put him in the Garden of Eden to work and take care of it." Keep in mind that this is only a reflection of what God does. Genesis 2:2 gives reference to God just finishing His work of creating. Meaning we are to work; therefore, we produce, and in so doing, we are taking care of what we were given. Working is a characteristic of God, and He does this daily by taking care of us.

In Genesis 2:18 (NIV), God said, "It is not good for man to be alone. I will make a helper suitable for him."

If God said we are not to be alone, and we were created in His image, that means that God desired the same for Himself. That is why He created a helper suitable for Himself, which is mankind, aka humanity. In other words, the church is the betrothed Bride of Christ. We were created to love Him, worship Him, and be at one with Him. We are bone of His bone and flesh of His flesh. But it is a choice. It is for us to stay in communion with Him through a life of repentance and by the blood of Jesus. We are to be faithful to Him as a wife should be to her husband. When the Garden of Eden was created and mankind was placed within it, the ultimate purpose was for us to always be with Him. Of course, through the sin of Adam, we were disconnected from the original purpose, but we had to be reconnected to Him. That is how the Trinity put the business operation into a new purpose by developing a new mission, which was to bring the Bride back to Him.

With that in mind, let's view the three propositions that I can imagine having been discussed by the Trinity, which includes the original plan, conditional plan, and the final plan. Below you will find the imaginary minutes taken from the Trinity operation's business meeting. All plans developed required the communication of the Trinity.

Business name: Trinity operation.

Business owner(s): God, the Father. God, the Son. God, the Spirit.

Attendees: God, the Father. God, the Son. God, the Spirit.

Original Business Plan

- *Goal*: Let's create humanity. Humanity is to be like us. We will give them authority, dominion, and power over the earth. They will be one with Us through continuous relationship and worship. They will have the ability to love Us by their own will, which differs from My created angels.

-

- *Mission*: In order to create humanity, they must have a living space to abide in. We will create the heavens and the earth. Within the earth, We will prepare a place called the Garden of Eden, a place of fruitfulness and multiplication. Humanity will live there, have dominion, be fruitful, and multiply. As they live in this space, I will live with them and care for them. If they remain faithful to Us, they will have everlasting life with Us forevermore. This will be My covenant.

Unfortunately, man sinned after being swayed by the serpent Satan, lost dominion over the earth, got kicked out of the Garden of Eden, and, therefore, kicked out of God's presence. The dominion and authority of mankind were lawfully handed over to Satan due to their disobedience. This caused the original business plan (original covenant) to be broken, and mankind was separated from

God and destined to die. But God is merciful. He still desired the connection with man. Out of His love, mercy, and compassion for us, He had to develop a new plan to reach the ultimate goal again, which was for man and God to be connected. But since man disobeyed God, the connection, which was the main goal, could not happen immediately. It wasn't going to be as easy as before because now a new issue had to be dealt with. That issue to deal with was sin. Sin and God cannot cohabitate. God had to develop a new plan to deal with the sin so that God and man could be one again. This could only happen by having man be reconciliated back to God through sacrifice and worship.

Plans had to be rearranged. God could not look upon sin because He is Holy. With this, He designed a way for man to be reconnected by way of the tabernacle. To do this, it had to take the sacrifice of something pure and free from sin to take on the sins of man, which would come from bulls, goats, oxen, etc. The blood from this sacrifice would serve as atonement to reconnect man back to God. With this, God would dwell within the tabernacle. Through their acceptable sacrifices, they would receive forgiveness, mercy, and avoid the judgment of death. This would serve as a conditional/temporary plan until the final plan came into play. With that in mind, God developed and released this plan at Mount Sinai. Even here, we will see that the Trinity was present and communicated through unity.

Trinity Communication at Mount Sinai

God released the conditional business plan to Moses at Mount Sinai in Exodus chapter 19. As this conditional business plan was brought forth to Moses, we can see that all parties were present. Remember, for a plan to be successful, it takes communication, agreement, attendance, complete participation of the responsible parties, and commitment for it to be executed effectively.

In Exodus 19:16 (NIV), it says, "On the morning of the third day there was thunder and lightning, with a *thick cloud* over the mountain and a very loud trumpet blast." In verse 19 (NIV), it says, "As the *sound of the trumpet* grew louder and louder, Moses spoke, and the *voice of God* answered him."

We can see that the Father, Son, and Holy Spirit were present. God, the Father, was present because He was the Voice speaking to Moses on the mountain. He was the One who provided the instruction to Moses so that it may be written.

God, the Son, Jesus Christ, was also present. He was the Word being released from the mouth of God that became the laws and teachings of God for the Israelites, and Jesus was the Word written upon the two tablets of stone, which served as the Ten Commandments. Jesus was also the loud trumpet being heard, preparing the way for what was about to come, which was the release and creation of the covenant of law (conditional business plan). Remember, He is the way, the truth, and the life.

We can also see the Spirit of God was present. He was the thick cloud that was over the mountain. Just as the Holy Spirit hovered over the waters in Genesis 2:2, the Holy Spirit hovered over the mountain during the time the covenant of law (conditional business plan) was being released. As we can see, all parties of the Trinity were present supporting one another for the goal to be accomplished. They were all working together to achieve one goal and one purpose. Let's take a look at the conditional business plan below...

Amended Business Plan (Conditional)

- *Goal*: Let's restore the connection between man and God that was broken due to the sin of man. I will make a proposal with conditions. They are to love Me and stay in relationship with Me. This is Our courtship, and they will be betrothed to Me if they accept My proposal and remain faithful. It will be My responsibility to care for them, provide for them, and protect them. Upon complete faithfulness, they will be My people, and I will be their God forevermore.

- *Mission*: Due to the sinful nature of man, this is My proposal: We will create instructions for holy ways of living. This will help mankind to know right from wrong and be accountable for their actions. This will guide them in Our ways and help them to be connected to Me. I will be their God, and they will be My people. I will instruct them to make a dwelling place for Me on earth that is in likeness to My dwelling place in heaven. So that what is done in heaven can also be done on earth. That way, they can understand My ways from their perspective, which is an earthbound perspective. It will be set apart for Me, and I will live among them within this place. This place will be My tabernacle.

- Upon following My instructions through the tabernacle, they will receive mercy and avoid the judgment of death. Although I live among them, they cannot come to Me directly. They will have indirect access to Me through My chosen vessels, who have been set apart to do My work only. I will have chosen vessels that will come from the tribe of Levi, and I will make them priests for My daily service. The Levites will have Me as their inheritance and serve in My earthly dwelling place, the tabernacle.

- The tabernacle will be a place of sacrifice and a place of mercy. The people will be required to make continual sacrifices and offerings that are found to be acceptable so that they may receive my forgiveness and be in communion with Me. The tabernacle will be set apart for Me and where man can connect with Me through the priests. But they can only have direct access to My holy presence and receive atonement for their sins once a year through one man who is worthy enough to enter in. This man will be

My chosen high priest.

- The ark of the covenant within the tabernacle is where My presence on earth will be housed and upon it will be the mercy seat. A place by which My mercy will be shown. I will show them evidence of My presence in various ways. Cloud by day, fire by night. They will also see My presence through various signs.

- But there are conditions: they must follow My commands, which is the law, I will give them. There will be blessings for obedience and curses for disobedience. This will be My covenant.

With this conditional business plan, mankind could not come to Him directly where He dwelled. There had to be men set apart to stand in proxy for them to be of service within the tabernacle, which is the priests. There could only be one particular man that was set apart within the priesthood to offer the sacrifice on behalf of the people for atonement for their sins within the most holy place, which was the high priest. There was a veil that separated God's presence from man. No man had direct access but the high priest. Even then, the high priest could be among God's presence only once a year. They had to follow His laws and continuously make sacrifices. This would have to be a continuous act to remain connected to God. This was a hard task, and they had to rely on their own strength to maintain a life dedicated to God.

The Trinity Identifies a Recurring Problem, Creates the Ultimate Solution

God saw that the task was too hard for man in their own strength to follow the law of the covenant through the tabernacle. There were also limitations with this conditional business plan. It wasn't enough. All the continuous sacrifices and offerings just to get close to Him once a year were far from the original goal that God intended for the relationship to continue between Him and mankind. It didn't quite meet the expectation of what God really desired from us and didn't even take away sins. The scriptures say, "It is impossible for the blood of bulls and goats to take away sins" (Hebrews 10:4, NIV).

It also says, "...'Sacrifices and offerings, burnt offerings and sin offerings you did not desire, nor were you pleased with them'— though they were offered in accordance with the law" (Hebrews 10:8, NIV). God truly desired to have a relationship with man without all these restrictions required by law. The sin of Adam really set things back and threw everything off course.

God saw that there was a recurring problem with mankind. This had to be communicated among the Trinity so that a new plan could be developed. Here was the problem.

- *Problem*: Mankind is weak and easily falls into temptation, even with tabernacle in place. They still do wickedness and worship idols created by their own hands while also making sacrifices unto Me at My tabernacle. They go through the actions of making the sacrifices and offerings at My tabernacle, but their hearts are far from Me. This defeats the purpose of what the tabernacle was originally intended for, which is to serve Me, stay in communion with Me, and live holy.

After identifying the problem, the Trinity had to come up with a solution. All businesses experience failures, even the successful ones. The Trinity operation experienced a failure. The business plans from before were good for the moment, but then something happened to stop it from succeeding. There was a recurring problem, which was that man kept falling away from Him through disobedience and unfaithfulness. The Trinity operation observed that mankind keeps being deterred by the enemy, which caused God's anger and a disconnection between God and man. It also caused a temporary allowance of the enemy to oppress them (mankind). To overcome this recurring problem, there had to be a solid solution, a solution that would stand the test of time and give mankind a promised future with God that was not temporary but permanent. The covenant law was found to be a temporary solution that became watered down. A permanent solution was now necessary. So, the Trinity operation had to find what plans of action were necessary to tackle this recurring problem. Here is the solution.

- *Solution*: We will do away with the requirements of the law of bringing continual sacrifices of lambs, goats, oxen, etc., to take on the sins of man because this is not enough. It is hard for man to follow My ways in their own strength. Instead, we will have one sacrifice that is pure and holy to take on the sins of man once and for all. This sacrifice will break the disconnection between God and humanity.

Since man sinned and brought death to mankind, it had to take a man that was free from sin to bring forgiveness, cleansing, and life to mankind. God had to create a new business plan that didn't require the continual sacrifices and offering that the law spoke about. He had to do something once and for all.

"For by one sacrifice he has made perfect forever those who are being made holy" (Hebrews 10:14, NIV).

He had to send a man of flesh and blood (the second Adam) to fix what a man of flesh and blood (the first Adam) broke. So again, the Trinity communicated with one another and devised a finalized plan that would bring mankind back to God. This would serve as the final solution forevermore, which required clear communication, their presence, and unity.

Trinity Communication During the Creation of Jesus, the Second Adam

God released this plan of sending Himself down to earth in the form of flesh in the New Testament during the creation of the second Adam, Jesus Christ. This plan is beyond imaginable. In our own human thoughts, it is hard to fathom how God, in all of His awesomeness, and all of His deity, could recreate Himself in the form of a small little seed implanted within the womb of a human being. As we also know…nothing is impossible or too hard for God. He did just that—He came to earth as the incarnate Son of God.

We know that the Trinity is constantly at work as One within the word of God. The creation of Jesus was well thought out and began from the Old Testament, which is too detailed for us to go into right now. It begins from Abraham, Isaac, Jacob, Judah, David, and everyone else, after which can be found within Matthew 1:1–16. Each person I previously listed, plus many more, has a story found in the Old Testament, by which God had to come and direct them, keep them, instruct them, discipline them, and protect them. God had to guide them, which included promises and covenants. Some of the covenants were unconditional, but other covenants required their obedience and telling the generations thereafter. The generations that came before Jesus had their own share of trials, but God delivered them out of everyone. The genealogy of Jesus included forty-two ancestors in total, before Jesus came into the earth…forty-two that came in segments of three, fourteen for each segment. The generations from before were all a part of God's bigger plan to bring the Savior into the world. Matthew 1:17 (NIV) says, "Thus there were fourteen generations in all from Abraham to David, fourteen from David to the exile, and fourteen from the exile to the Messiah."

1. Fourteen from Abraham to King David.
2. Fourteen from King David to Josiah.
3. Fourteen from Josiah to Joseph.

The number "fourteen" is extremely significant in the word of God. It means double completion. "Seven" means completion. (7 x 2 = 14.) Let's view both of Jesus' completions. Firstly, He was completing His ministry and purpose as Jesus, the incarnate Son of God, manifested on earth as flesh. Secondly, He also completed and thus ended the need for the sacrifice of animals by making Himself the ultimate sacrifice. His sacrifice fulfilled the law once and for all.

We will first discuss the conception of Jesus within the Virgin Mary. It all begins with God turning the Word into flesh. Count it not strange the explanation of God the Word coming in flesh is found in verse 14 of John chapter 1.

"The Word became flesh and made his dwelling among us. We have seen his glory, the glory of the one and only Son, who came from the Father, full of grace and truth" (John 1:14, NIV).

Now that we see the Word became flesh and dwelled among us…let's jump to the book of Luke. This is where we can see the details of how the Word becoming flesh came into being through the Virgin Mary. Doing so had to first come from a plan. As we previously discussed, it takes clear communication, the unity, and presence, all three within the Trinity, for any plan to be complete and to be successful. We will see how this applied to the birth of Jesus through the life of Mary in the scriptures below:

> In the sixth month of Elizabeth's pregnancy, God sent the angel Gabriel to Nazareth, a town in Galilee, to a virgin pledged to be married to a man named Joseph, a descendant of David. The virgin's name was Mary. The angel went to her and said, "Greetings, you who are highly favored! The Lord is with you."
>
> Mary was greatly troubled at his words and wondered what kind of greeting this might be. But the angel said to her, "Do not be afraid, Mary; you have found favor with God. You will conceive and give birth to a son, and you are to call him Jesus. He will be great

*and will be called the Son of the Most High. The Lord
God will give him the throne of his father David, and
he will reign over Jacob's descendants forever; his
kingdom will never end."*

*"How will this be," Mary asked the angel, "since I
am a virgin?"*

*The angel answered, "The Holy Spirit will come on
you, and the power of the Most High will overshadow
you. So the holy one to be born will be called[b] the
Son of God. Even Elizabeth your relative is going to
have a child in her old age, and she who was said to
be unable to conceive is in her sixth month. For no
word from God will ever fail."*

*"I am the Lord's servant," Mary answered. "May
your word to me be fulfilled." Then the angel left her.*

Luke 1:26–38 (NIV)

In this passage, we can see the presence of the Trinity during
the conception of Jesus. Although the scripture does not say that
God was literally among them, He was there. It reminds me of
what happened during the creation of mankind, although Jesus,
God the Son, was not there in the flesh...He was there as the Word.
That's why Jesus said, "...before Abraham was, I am" (John 8:58b,
ESV). He was the light and the very Word of God in the beginning.
Which is like what happened during the second creation. Now that
Jesus was present in the flesh, we don't see the words "God said"
during this conversation with Mary, as we saw during the creation
of mankind and as we saw during the times of Moses at Mount
Sinai. Instead, God used the angel Gabriel to deliver His message.
Even though we don't see the words "God said," God still "said"
because God was present in a different form. It was just in a way
that was different from before. His message through Gabriel indicates God was there.

As we previously learned, God is the Voice of the heavenly horn and the Initiator of communication. He was the initiator of this conversation by sending His message through the angel Gabriel. In Luke 1:26 (NIV), the word says, "God sent the angel..." Gabriel was a representative of God, and the message that Gabriel delivered was directly from God, which represents God's presence through His messenger. So, in essence, God was there. God started this conversation and was communicating with Mary through His angel Gabriel. In addition to that, the angel said, "the Lord is with you," which indicates that God was with her. If the Lord was "with her," that means God was present with her. God is omnipresent, meaning He is everywhere at the same time. We can also see healthy communication between God and Mary because God was the sender of the message, and Mary responded to God's message through a third party (Gabriel) by saying, "...May your word to me be fulfilled..." (Luke 1:38, NIV) This shows that they reached concept seven in the communication process.

We can also see the presence of the Holy Spirit during the creation of God, the Son, in the form of flesh. I was intrigued to see that the Holy Spirit presented Himself in similar ways during creation, Mount Sinai, and now the creation of the incarnate Son of God. In all three scenarios, the Holy Spirit was hovering over something. In the creation of mankind, the Holy Spirit "hovered *over* the waters" (Genesis 1:2, NIV), and during the time God revealed Himself at Mount Sinai, the Holy Spirit was the "thick cloud *over* the mountain" (Exodus 19:16, NIV). Now, during the time of the conception of Jesus, the Holy Spirit came upon Mary and "*over*shadowed" her (Luke 1:35, NIV). Once Mary agreed by saying, "May your word to me be fulfilled in me," the Holy Spirit was given permission to come with power, hover over her, and bring life to the Word within her. And it became so; she was impregnated with Deity. Creation of the Son of God, the Word of God in flesh, was now a reality. This directly shows that the Holy Spirit did His part to allow the plans of God to come to pass. This clearly shows the Holy Spirit was present.

Lastly, in this case, we can see that God, the Son, was present. The Word, who is God, was within the womb of Mary. As it states in the passage above from Luke chapter 1, Gabriel, directed by God, told Mary that she would give birth to the Son of the Most High, whose name shall be called Jesus, whose kingdom will never end. He came to the earth in flesh and blood, was born unto us to save us and take away the sins of the world. Jesus, God in the flesh, was conceived, born, grew, began ministry, died for us, and rose again, fulfilling His purpose on earth. He was present during this time, and because of it, history was changed forever, and prophecy was fulfilled.

This was a plan that could only come by the complete dedication of all three of the Trinity. It required healthy communication to accomplish this task. They had to discuss the matter, plan it out, come in agreement, be present, stay committed, and do their part for this plan to come to pass. Remember, we are looking at this through the eyes of business. The Trinity operation is the perfect example of the perfect business. They serve as a heavenly example of what a successful business looks like, what it takes to accomplish success in a business, the importance of healthy communication, and, most of all, the power of unity. Now that we see all three were present again, let's envision how the Trinity operation handled the meeting. Since we are looking at the Trinity as a business for the purpose of this chapter, let's imagine how this plan was developed and discussed and what the meeting would have been like for the creation of the Word of God in flesh to come to pass. Remember, God, the Father, is the Mastermind behind everything, the Initiator, and the Voice of communication. With that in mind, let's view what His plans may have looked like as He communicated them with Jesus and the Holy Spirit.

Final Business Plan

- *Goal*: Let's restore the broken connection between God and man and remove the judgment of death due to the sins of mankind. We will cancel out the law, and this will be done by purchasing them through a blood sacrifice that will be provided by us, which will be the Lamb of God, who is pure, holy, and acceptable. I will send My Son as a man and as the Lamb of God to die for them to take away the sins of the world once and for all. He will restore the authority, dominion, and power back to mankind. He will go through the more perfect tabernacle that is not made by mankind, and His blood will serve as eternal redemption for the sins of mankind. He will be a deliverer to those who are faithful to Me and remain in covenant with Me. Whoever believes in the Lamb of God will be born of Me and will not perish but have everlasting life. They will receive victory and overcome the world. I will be their Bridegroom, and they will be My bride. We will be one forevermore.

- *Mission*: We first must learn the ways of mankind and understand their ways. We will come upon the earth in the form of flesh from within the womb of a woman and walk the earth from birth to manhood. To do this, My Word will become flesh and will be conceived within My chosen vessel, Mary. To accomplish this, My Spirit will overshadow My chosen vessel Mary so that she may conceive a child. He will be named Jesus, meaning "The Lord Saves," because I plan to save mankind from their sins. This child will be My Son, and He will save My people from their sins. We will learn what it is to be tempted and experience everything that mankind faces daily. As we learn their ways, we will show by example how to overcome these things. We will teach them our ways as we walk with them so that it may go into their heart.

- My Son will come as the Horn of Salvation to fulfill the law by giving His life for the sins of My people once and for all. This will break the curse of sin, break the barrier that is between God and man, and it will defeat the enemy. My Son will die, but He will rise again by the Spirit and be seated at the right hand of God, conquering death and gaining the victory over death. He will be raised to the heavens. Mankind will not be alone during this time. I will send My Comforter, My Holy Spirit, who will help them follow Me. They will no longer need to depend on the law by bringing the same sacrifices because the law brings death and only reminds them of their sins. Instead, I will make a new covenant, and by the Spirit, I will put My laws in their hearts and minds. I will send My Spirit to guide them in My ways, and they will rely on Spirit in all things.

- They are to teach My ways to others by spreading the Gospel of Christ and increase My Kingdom by being fruitful and multiplying by making other disciples. They are to have authority, dominion, and power through My name. My Spirit will dwell within mankind until I return. My Spirit will also be my provided evidence that I am coming back for them. When I come back, I will defeat the enemy once and for all, overcome the world, and the enemy will have no power over them; they will have victory and live with Me. I will build a new heaven and earth; they will have access to Me always in My most holy place and live with Me, worship Me, and be one with Me. They will be My wife, and I will be her husband. We will be one. This will be My new covenant.

This final business plan was accomplished. Because all three of the Trinity communicated effectively with one another, were committed, and did their individual part to make each purpose and each planned goal be a success. The original business plan, conditional plan, and finalized plan all went into effect after clear communication and commitment of the Trinity. The Father, the Son, and the Holy Spirit all needed each other to get the job done because they are one.

God, the Father, planned everything out because He had an

ultimate desire to be worshiped by His creation, which had the gift of free will. This came into effect and is still to this day in effect, but only by means of planning with His counterparts, the Son and the Holy Spirit. God had to communicate His ideas with them; they had to understand, come in agreement, and do what was necessary to make it come into fruition.

They experienced challenges and bumps in the road along the way, but through clear communication, they developed solutions to overcome the challenges, which brought results of success. Why do I say success? Because God received the victory—the book of Revelation tells us so. Although man slipped away through disobedience, another man, Jesus, God in the flesh, fulfilled everything necessary through careful planning and communication of the Trinity to redeem the lost connection between man and God.

The Trinity stands as the perfect and primary example of a successful business that is still in operation today and forevermore. Every successful business, for the most part, withstands the test of time, even through hardships, and we see that the Trinity operation has done just that. The Trinity operation is the ultimate example of business success. Now we have a clear understanding of the Trinity through the eyes of business. The Trinity, may I also say Tri-Unity, are separate but one, moving individually in their function but moving collectively as one. They continue to do so through clear communication, attendance, unity, and commitment. God has given a tool to us as well through His word; it serves as a living manual for success. If we follow Him, follow His precepts, stay in communion with Him, and stay committed to Him, we will succeed in life and in anything we put our minds to—He has already shown us the way.

CHAPTER 6

SPIRITUAL COMMUNICATION DISCONNECTED AT THE GARDEN OF EDEN

We just discussed how the Trinity communicates. We discussed how the Trinity had to plan things out to fulfill the ultimate goal of God, which was to create humanity, be worshiped by humanity, and be one with humanity. The Trinity had to revise the original plan due to the sin of man caused by disobedience, as we previously discussed. Now that we have a general understanding of what God had to do to provide a resolution to be one with mankind, let's go into the detailed background of mankind to break down why God had to find resolution in the first place.

Let's begin first by this statement…man falls short of God's glory through sin. "Man," meaning us, meaning you and me, which is humanity, fall short of God's glory because we are sinners. When we sin without asking for forgiveness and refrain from repenting, we begin to draw away from God. It is impossible to avoid it because sin is innate within us from birth.

Even when a baby does something that they know they are not supposed to do, sometimes they run away from the authoritative figure, such as the mom or father, and find someplace to hide. At other times, they may put their heads down in shame and barely want to say anything. Sometimes they will even cry before they are disciplined because they know what lies ahead. The action of the baby doing wrong, even when he or she knows the right thing to do, is not learned. Sin is inborn within humanity. They haven't lived long enough on earth to know how to sin and hide in shame. However, we see that even though they are babies, they sometimes do wrong when they know the right thing to do. In short, they know better but didn't do better. Paul expressed it very well when he said, "For I do not do the good I want to do, but the evil I do not want to do—this I keep on doing. Now if I do what I do not want to do, it is no longer I who do it, but it is sin living in me that does it" (Romans 7:19–20, NIV). No matter how hard we try to be sin-free, we continue to sin because our flesh and mind are vulnerable to disobedience.

It all began from the Garden of Eden when Adam and Eve went against the ruling of God by falling for temptation by eating from the tree of knowledge of good and evil. This action introduced sin among humanity. Sin brought on the penalty of death. Sin divides us from God. We, as humans, deal with temptation daily. In the book of Genesis, we can see the original plan that God had for humanity, which was to live among humans, walk with them, and be in constant communion.

It says in the word of God that God walked in the cool of night with man. The air that man breathed was the very presence of God. He was our oxygen; the survival of man depended on His presence.

God created man in His image and gave man the ability to have free will. He wanted us to be able to love Him from our hearts, out of freedom of choice. We were given the access to have a close relationship with God, with no need for any barriers. There was no separation between God and man. We were able to talk with Him, walk with Him, and have everlasting life. However, temptation grew strong when the serpent presented an idea to Eve to apparently "justify" why it should be okay to eat from the forbidden fruit. She fell for the temptation and brought Adam into going against the ruling of God, which caused them both to lose the access and close relationship they once had with God. They realized their nakedness and began to hide from God, which is one of the first signs of sin. Due to their sin, God expelled them from the Garden of Eden:

The Expulsion from Paradise

> *The LORD God made garments of skin for Adam and his wife and clothed them. And the LORD God said, "The man has now become like one of us, knowing good and evil. He must not be allowed to reach out his hand and take also from the tree of life and eat, and live forever." So the LORD God banished him from the Garden of Eden to work the ground from which he had been taken. After he drove the man out, he placed on the east side of the Garden of Eden cherubim and a flaming sword flashing back and forth to guard the way to the tree of life.*
>
> **Genesis 3:21–24 (NIV)**

Sin is what separates us from God. We see here that sin was introduced to the relationship between God and man. The sin of mankind started the division between God and man and furthermore, a division between heaven and earth. A veil was created to separate us from God, and the cherubim guarded the east gate. The east gate represents the glory of God and the way to His presence. Moreover, the cherubim were placed on post to guard the presence of God with a sword of flame. Free access to God was no more. Not only was the communication between God and man severed, causing man to be kicked out of the Garden of Eden, but man was also cursed with death. Sin equals death, which was now a part of creation. This is humanity.

We, as humans, are prone to sin from the time of birth. Humanity sins, and because of this, we fall short of being pure, holy, and righteous. These three characteristics are necessary to enter the presence of God and necessary to have access to God. Additionally, we must be repentant. This means we must ask for forgiveness for our sins with the intention of not doing that sin again. That is why God used the prophet Samuel to say that obedience is better than sacrifice (1 Samuel 15:22).

We can see a sample of a servant of God who also fell short of being pure, holy, and righteous when he lusted after Bathsheba within his heart, which led to additional sins. In Psalm 51:16–17 (NIV), King David began to repent for his sin with Bathsheba, "You do not delight in sacrifice, or I would bring it…My sacrifice, O God, is a broken spirit; a broken and contrite heart you, God, will not despise." King David was aware that God looks at the heart; if we love God, we will obey Him. What good is it to give the sacrifice of a burnt offering as a payment for his sin and for his heart to be far from God? Such sacrifices are despised by God… only a ritual that holds no power. David was aware of this, and he wanted to make things right from within his heart. He was repenting from the depths of his very being. He was aware of his sin, sorry for it, ashamed of it, and wanted to turn from it completely, no matter the cost. He was desperate to be in right standing with God again. This was true repentance.

King David was known to be a man after God's own heart, but even he was faced with temptation and bit from the apple of sin. He disobeyed the commandments of the Lord—even though he loved God with all his heart. Why? It is because of the limitation that is placed on humanity. We are disobedient. We are sinners. We need the grace and mercy from God that comes only through the blood of Jesus. King David is just one of the many followers of Christ that demonstrated a man that fell short and sinned. Sampson, known for his supernatural God-given strength, was "dedicated to God from the womb" (Judges 13:5, NIV). His prophesied birth was a miracle; his barren mother was visited by the angel of God to announce that she would have a son. She was given specific instructions to follow since he would be a Nazirite. She was chosen to be a mother of a baby boy that would deliver Israel from the Philistines. Despite her son being dedicated to God and having such a powerful calling on his life, he, too, was disobedient. He fell for temptation through the likes of Delilah and lost his strength. How could someone like him, that was used so mightily by the hand of God, fall for temptation and turn from God's instructions? Again, the answer is he was human. Humanity sins. Humanity disobeys. As we move along to review others within the Bible, we can see the sins of humanity. Moses struck the rock when God did not give him instruction to do so. Saul became the first king of Israel and was chosen by God. However, he became consumed with jealousy and disobedient to God. He was directed by God to destroy the Amalekites with nothing left to spare. Saul took it upon himself to spare the king and some livestock. The sins of Saul only snowballed after this; he then committed suicide. Judas betrayed Jesus. Peter denied Christ. The list goes on and on. This shows the undeniable setback of humanity.

The very essence of humanity and our proneness to sin caused this brokenness and barrier between God and us. We can see how God began to regret that He even created humans because we ended up going so far away from His original intentions—we became wicked. God wanted to destroy us—and did so during the time of Noah. Thank God for His grace, that He was willing to spare the family of Noah to start again. Instead of wiping us out completely, He preserved a few of us that were found to be pleasing or worthy enough to maintain the continuation of humanity. Even with the preservation of Noah and the creatures of the earth, to have a clean slate and start again, the problem of the separation between God and man still existed. Sin was still present. The disconnect was still there, so God had to come up with a plan...some type of resolution to restore the relationship between God and man. We needed reconciliation with God.

The ultimate solution was sending His Son, Jesus Christ, the One who was without sin, to die for our sins, paying our debt in full so that we can have access to God. But before He did that, He needed a temporary solution for that moment. The temporary solution was to bring the order of heaven to earth by building a tabernacle so that God could dwell among man again. There would also have to be a mediator between God and man—someone to be the middleman set apart for the service of God only. This temporary solution was not quite the same as the Garden of Eden because man did not have direct access to God as they did before because there was a veil that now separated God and man.

Since God could not look at sin, this man was to accept sacrifices and offerings and present them to God on behalf of the sinner, so that person's sin could be forgiven. It was a serious task, and that person had to be holy and pure, which came through daily rituals of washing of the feet and hands. Only a chosen vessel could go behind the veil into the holy of holies within the tabernacle where God's glory was, which was only once a year and took a great deal of preparation from that man to get to that point. That middleman...that mediator...that one who was to be set apart for the service of God for such an important task, was the high priest. Only the high priest was able to get to the holy of holies. The priest was one whose inheritance was the Lord Himself. The priest was to work and care for the place where God would decide to dwell, which was the earthly tabernacle. This was the pending point and the temporary solution to fill in the gap until the Great Mediator, the Great High Priest and Great Redeemer, who we know as Jesus

Christ, came to break the barriers once and for all.

Through the resurrection of Jesus, we are now new creatures and have been called to be priests due to the new covenant, meaning to be of service for the kingdom. Since we are called to be priests in the new day, it is pertinent that we understand the priest of the old days.

CHAPTER 7

SPIRITUAL COMMUNICATION TEMPORARILY RECONNECTED AT THE TABERNACLE

All this is from God, who reconciled us to himself through Christ and gave us the ministry of reconciliation; that God was reconciling the world to himself in Christ, no counting people's sins against them. And he has committed to us the message of reconciliation. We are therefore Christ's ambassadors, as though God were making his appeal through us. We implore you on Christ's behalf: Be reconciled to God.

2 Corinthians 5:18–20 (NIV)

Reconciliation was needed in a world because humanity lost communication and a connection with the One and Only True God. God is a God of mercy and grace. Although He was disappointed with the way man turned away from Him, He still is merciful enough to give us a way out. But how was this to be done? How could all this disorder be fixed? He had to find a way for the order of heaven to be introduced on earth to show man the right way and get them back on track to holiness, righteousness, and purity. A resolution was necessary. What He decided to do was to reestablish order of having access to His presence by way of the tabernacle and by assigning holy ones to work and care for that tabernacle. This would be a sanctuary that God would dwell in. This was a place that would be set apart for Him and His order. This place would give mankind the grace and opportunity to bring blood sacrifices so their sins could be forgiven and so they could find atonement with God. The tabernacle was going to be a place where blood would be shed on a continuous basis to be reconciled with God. God had to choose someone to get the tabernacle built. God's chosen vessel was none other than Moses.

God gave Moses instructions to show him how to build the tabernacle to mirror the heavenly tabernacle. This was a tent constructed and set apart for God's dwelling. God provided the specifics of how to construct the tabernacle so that we can understand heavenly protocol.-

After the tabernacle was built, there had to be someone there to work and care for it. Just as God needed someone to work and care for the Garden of Eden before the fall, God needed someone to do the same for the tabernacle, which is why God assigned people set apart for this place to do so. He called priests to fill in this void.

This further allows us to have a fear, holy reverence, and opportunity to have access to His presence by learning the steps to take just as the priests did in the times of old. In the Word of God, it says that we are a royal priesthood, meaning that you and I are priests. Only priests were allowed to have access to God's presence, to intercede, to burn the sacrifices, and be purified constantly by the washing of hands and feet for the benefit of the people of God and one's own self, who wish to get closer to God.

The priests were chosen by God as ones who were holy to perform godly tasks at the tabernacle. Priests stood as a representation of God to the Israelites; priests also stood as a representation of Israel to God. It also says in the Word of God that our bodies are a temple. We can also apply anything that God instructed in the tabernacle and temple of ancient times to our bodily temple.

Since there is a connection between the heavenly and earthly tabernacle, let's take a trip to the tabernacle to find out more. It is important to know that the Lord gave instructions to build a tabernacle here on earth in the Old Testament as a representation of what is in heaven. In actuality, the tabernacle is a blueprint of the order of heaven. God wants us to understand the pattern of heaven so that we can follow it here on earth. Now that Jesus died and was resurrected, our bodies have become the new temple. That is, through the name of Jesus, we can apply what God is saying about the temple to our bodily temple.

The tabernacle was a tent that was portable and was moved during the travels of the Israelites as the Lord directed them. It consisted of different parts: the outer court, the inner court, and the holy of holies. The tabernacle was a place where man was to get close to God through their offerings and sacrifices dedicated to God, with the priest making the sacrifice on their behalf. In the tabernacle, there were plenty of items that had significant purposes, from the lampstand, the table of shewbread, and much more.

The tabernacle is deeply tied into the functions and daily tasks of the priests. To have a deeper understanding of the priest, we must first understand the importance of the tabernacle. As mentioned before, the tabernacle is an earthly representation of God's temple in the heavens. That is why the Lord instructed His servants in the days of old to construct the tabernacle in such a meticulous way. It is important to note that before the tabernacle was built on earth during the times of Moses—there was a pre-tabernacle. One may wonder what the pre-tabernacle may be. The answer is the

Garden of Eden, which stands to be the first tabernacle made on earth in representation of what is in heaven. The first tabernacle on earth (pre-tabernacle) was built directly by God, without man helping with the construction of it. God built the Garden of Eden, not by hands, as one would think, but by the sound of His voice.

As previously mentioned, the priests were given the task to work and care for the tabernacle. This very task was given to Adam in the Garden of Eden. According to Genesis 2:15 (NIV), *"The LORD God took the man and put him in the Garden of Eden to work it and take care of it."* This reveals that Adam was the assigned priest for the pre-tabernacle. God was revealing the heavenly order here on earth, even from the time of creation.

During the days of Moses, God assigned Aaron, his brother, a Levite, to be a priest in addition to his sons to serve as priests at the tabernacle. Also, it was only the Levites that could care for the sanctuary. Numbers 3:5–10 (NIV) says:

> *The Lord said to Moses, "Bring the tribe of Levi and present them to Aaron the priest to assist him. They are to perform duties for him and for the whole community at the tent of meeting by doing the work of the tabernacle. They are to take care of all the furnishings of the tent of meeting, fulfilling the obligations of the Israelites by doing the work of the tabernacle. Give the Levites to Aaron and his sons; they are the Israelites who are to be given wholly to him. Appoint Aaron and his sons to serve as priests; anyone else who approaches the sanctuary is to be put to death."*

Aaron and his sons became the first assigned priests after the fall of Adam. The priesthood then continued through his lineage of the Levites for a long period of time (until Jesus died and rose again, shifting the priesthood to His line). Priests had a high level of responsibility on their shoulders to take care of the sanctuary.

Only the Levites were appointed to take care of it, and it had to be in an orderly fashion, in accordance with the instruction given by God to Moses. They had to follow protocol and understand the necessities for the maintenance of God's tabernacle while also serving the people of God. Anyone else who attempted to perform priestly tasks that were not appointed was put to death. This shows how crucial and how serious it was for the order to be maintained. Common treatment and familiarity of God's tabernacle were dealt with in a harsh manner. God wanted man to understand that there was holy protocol that must be followed; He is not a common God. Respect, honor, and reverence had to be maintained. Anytime the Israelites started moving away from holy protocol of the One and Only True King, we can see that rebellion was present, which led them away from His presence and into exile. God made it known that His house, which was His tabernacle, must maintain holy order.

God was able to make a connection to His people again by way of the tabernacle. The tabernacle was a dwelling place for His presence that was evident for man to see due to the cloud of smoke that ascended from the tabernacle. The layout of the tabernacle spoke volumes of the protocol God expected from His people for them to have access to Him. The access required the shedding of blood from something that was of high value, without spot, wrinkle, or blemish. God wants us to understand how to communicate with Him the right way through holy protocol, which we can find through the layout and the duties of the tabernacle.

With this in mind, let's dissect the three parts of the tabernacle into the holy furnishings and priestly duties that were performed in each section.

The Tabernacle, the Blood, and the Priestly Responsibilities

The tabernacle was a dwelling place for God on earth; it is a place where God's Shekinah Glory resided. It is a place created by the instructions of God. God instructed Moses to build a sanctuary in a tent-like manner in Exodus chapter 25 as a solution to restore the loss of a relationship with man due to the sin of Adam. The tabernacle was built to give man a chance to be able to have access to God again and to preserve the priesthood that God originally gave to Adam. This access could only come through blood sacrifices of certain animals so that man could receive forgiveness and mercy for their sins. These sacrifices had to be free from defect. The people who made these sacrifices had to come with repentance. It was also instructed by God that the ark of the covenant be built and placed within the holy of holies, the holiest place of all three sections within the tabernacle.

Later in the word of God, it was placed within David's heart to build a permanent structure for the sanctuary of God to reside here on earth. This permanent structure became the temple, which was built during the reign of David's son Solomon. This temple was called "Solomon's temple."

The design of the tabernacle was specifically given to Moses by God. The tabernacle served as an earthly sanctuary for God for 485 years. After that period, the temple was built under the ruling of Solomon and completed around 960 BC. Solomon's temple was known as the first temple of Jerusalem. It followed the same pattern of the tabernacle. It was destroyed in 586 BC by the Babylonians, but a second temple (the original second temple), which was smaller in size, was rebuilt by Zerubbabel, governor of Judah, through the allowance of King Cyrus. Zerubbabel's temple was completed in 516 BC. It was then expanded by King Herod in 20 BC but later destroyed by the Romans in AD 70.

As we move forward in our studies, it is important to note that although the tabernacle and temples provided a way for the people to have access to God again, they did not have direct access; it had to be done through the priests. There were three sections found within the tabernacle and the temple: the outer court, inner court, and holy of holies. Each section contained specific furnishings that the priests used to perform holy services, tasks, and rituals.

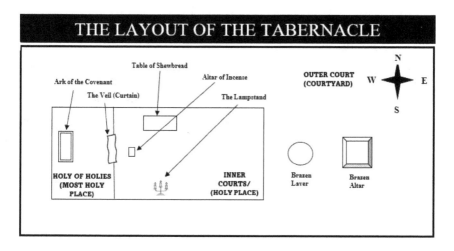

Although these sections are found in both the tabernacle and temple, we will stick to the study of the tabernacle only for easier understanding and to refrain from jumping back and forth. Let's now move into the layout of each section of the tabernacle, the furnishings, and the activities that were performed in each section. We will begin first by discussing the outer court found outside of the tabernacle; then, we will make our way inside the tent.

The Outer Court (the Courtyard)
(Exodus 27:9–19)

The first section of the tabernacle is the outer court, also known as the courtyard. The courtyard was surrounded by a fence of linen curtains so that the tabernacle and the holy activities could be set apart from the regular dealings of the land. This curtain was a representation of the separation between God and man. The entrance of the courtyard was made of blue, purple, and scarlet linen containing silver bands and hooks with bronze bases.

- Blue represents priesthood, heaven, divinity, revelation, and the Holy Spirit.
- Purple represents royalty, majesty, and kingship.
- Scarlet represents the blood of Jesus and His saving grace.
- Silver means reconciliation, atonement, and the price of redemption.
- Bronze represents God's judgment.

In the courtyard, there were sacred furnishings and sacred activities performed. The sacred furnishings consisted of the brazen altar and brazen laver. The brazen altar was closest to the courtyard entrance. The Israelites were able to enter the courtyard through the entrance known as a gate to bring their offerings and sacrifices. The gate represents Jesus.

"Very truly I tell you, I am the gate for the sheep. All who have come before me are thieves and robbers. But the sheep have not listened to them. I am the gate; whoever enters through me will be saved" (John 10:7–9a, NIV).

The priests would bless the animals of the Israelites as they would arrive through the entrance of the courtyard. The Israelites could go to the brazen altar, but they could not go any further than that. Only the priests were able to pass this point, which was to the next sacred item known as the brazen laver. This area was set apart for the cleansing of the priest, so they could purify themselves before entering the inner court of the temple and for making sacrifices on behalf of the people. It was important for the purification process to take place because God gave the priests divine protocol to adhere to so they could have access to the tabernacle and furthermore into His presence. In short, the brazen altar was used specifically for burning sacrifices and offerings, and the brazen laver was specifically used to maintain the purity of the priests. Let's first discuss the details of the brazen altar.

The Brazen Altar
(Exodus 27:1–8)

The brazen altar, also known as the *bronze altar* or *altar of burnt offering*, was located near the courtyard entrance. It was the first sacred item to be seen upon entering the courtyard and the largest piece of furniture within the setup of the tabernacle. This demonstrated that to approach the Holy God of Israel...sacrifice was required. The altar was square in size, and its measurements were seven and a half feet square and four and a half feet high. It was made of acacia wood (wood means flesh biblically) and was overlaid with bronze. As mentioned earlier, bronze means judgment; this altar was a representation of the judgment of God over sin. There was a necessity for the altar to be portable. Because of this, the altar contained two carrying poles, which were held by rings, each attached to longest sides of the altar so that the priests could move it at the appointed time. It also contained four horns on the four corners of the upper part of the altar. From the altar, smoke and fire would ascend into the heavens, which were hidden from no man demonstrating the power and holiness of the Almighty God. This place showed heaven and earth coming together. All people were able to witness and smell the sacrifices made at the altar. It was at this place the man began the process of reconciliation.

This altar was a place where sacrifices were made to bring forth reconciliation to the people, and those who were bringing their sacrifices of flesh and grain had access to the altar, but as mentioned before, the people could not pass this point. The Hebrew word for "altar" is *mizbeach*, which translates to "a place of slaughter."[11] At this place, sacrifices were made, and judgments were issued. The sacrifices could be one of the five types of offerings: burnt offering, sin offering, guilt offering, peace offering, or grain offering. Five means grace, which is what God granted to us when He sent His only-begotten Son. What exactly is grace? Grace is free to all; it is the undeserved favor of God granted to man by God through the gift of salvation to sinners. Below you will find the description of the five offerings, the Hebrew word for the offering, an additional translation of the Hebrew word for clarity, and the Bible passage where the specified offering can be found.

- Burnt offering—*"Olah"* translates to *"ascent, to go up"*— was an offering that was burnt up to provide atonement. The smoke that came from the offering ascended into the heavens and was received by God. This, in turn, provided atonement for the Israelite, who provided the sacrifice. This offering represented consecration, dedication, and surrender as unto God (Leviticus chapter 1).

- Sin offering—*"Chata'at"* translates to *"condition of sin, guilt of sin"*—the word "Chata" means "to sin, miss the way, go the wrong way, incur guilt, forfeit, purify from uncleanliness."[12] This was an offering that dealt with payment for sins that we have committed against God. This offering also provided atonement for the Israelite, which canceled out his sin (Leviticus chapter 4).

- Guilt offering—*"Asham"* translates to *"offend, be guilty, to trespass, commit an offense, do injury."*[13] This was an offering dealing with the sins that were committed against others or that others may have committed against them. All of which requires forgiveness to either give it or receive it (Leviticus chapter 5).

- Peace offering (fellowship offering)—*"Sh'lamim"* means *"peace,"* which translates to being *whole or having a sense of completeness.* "Shalom," a related word that may be more apropos, also means peace. This symbolized receiving peace from God and fellowship with Him. This helped the Israelite to cast all cares upon the Lord; in so doing, they would relinquish their anxieties and burdens and receive God's peace (Leviticus chapter 3).

- Grain offering (meal offering)—"*Minchah*" ironically translates to "*meat offering*," even though meat was not a part of this offering.[14] This offering consisted of grains, which came in the form of wheat or barley. It was then mixed with oil and frankincense without yeast or honey in it. It was the most holy in reference to the food offerings given. God had no stipulations for the amount given to Him. A portion would go to God and the remainder to the priests. The Israelite was able to give the amount out of free will. It represented thankfulness, worship, and praise for God's provision. The Israelite would give to God because God has given to them. Everything that belongs to the one who offered this gift is recognizing that everything they have comes from God (Leviticus chapter 2)

For the purpose of this reading, we will focus on the sin offering because this ties into the sacrifice that Jesus made for us. When a sin offering is made, an Israelite would bring their sacrifice as an offering to the priest in the courtyard to have their sins forgiven by God. The priest would then take the sacrifice and make sure that it is free from flaws and imperfections. It had to be something valuable to be accepted as a true sacrifice. If the offering was found to be valuable, the priest would approve it.

After the priest's approval, the Israelite would place the animal upon the brazen altar and bind it to the horns of the altar. The Israelite would lay his hand upon the head of the animal, and the animal would then be accepted on his behalf as an atonement for the Israelite. The sacrifice would take place by having the Israelite slaughter the animal. The priest would catch the blood of the sacrificed animal in a basin and splash the blood around the sides of the altar. The Israelite was required to skin it and cut it into pieces; the priests would then burn it upon the altar. The aroma of the sacrifice would ascend to the heavens as a sweet-smelling aroma that was pleasing to the Lord. That blood was a payment for the sin of the Israelite, and the sin would be forgiven.

"In fact, the law requires that nearly everything be cleansed with blood, and without the shedding of blood there is no forgiveness" (Hebrews 9:22, NIV).

Keep in mind, this was a ritual. To receive forgiveness, a sacrifice had to be made by the people. It was not a once and for all kind of act; it had to be done continuously to maintain forgiveness from sin. Unfortunately, at the time, these rituals had to be performed for man to stay connected to God since we no longer had direct access…all due to sin. Sin is not something to be taken lightly. To get access to God, a man must be free from sin and have repentance within his heart. The brazen altar helped bring resolution, but keep in mind this was a temporary solution.

In general, what does this mean?

Jesus came as the ultimate, perfect, pure, and holy sacrifice as the final payment by the shedding of His blood, giving us all access when He came to earth, giving His life as the Lamb who was slain. His sacrifice is the largest and most important part of what it takes to have access to God. He was One who was undeserving of taking on the sins of humanity. His passion and love for us gave us forgiveness for our sins, saved us from the death penalty that comes from our sins, and gave us life more abundantly if we just believed in Him. No longer is our communication with God the Father severed. Jesus' sacrifice, which came by the shedding of His blood, has given us the access to communicate directly with the Father. There is no more separation between God and man because the blood of Jesus has reconnected us. However, we must take note that our access can only come through Jesus—there is no other way.

The Brazen Laver
(Exodus 30:17)

The *brazen laver* (*also known as the bronze laver*) is a place located at the southeast corner of the tabernacle, where the priests would go to wash their hands and feet ceremonially to make sure they were cleansed before performing the sacrifices. The brazen laver was a circular basin made of brass that held water. The material used to construct the brazen laver came from women who served at the tent of meeting and who offered the brass from their mirrors that were brought from Egypt.

"They made the bronze basin and its bronze stand from the mirrors of the women who served at the entrance to the tent of meeting" (Exodus 38:8, NIV).

The brass from these mirrors were polished so well that their reflection could be clearly seen, which made the brass from their mirrors symbolize vanity. These offerings were considered as a notably large sacrifice to self. The priest would also wash his hands and feet again after making any sacrifices before entering the holy place (inner court). Only the priests assigned for that day would use the brazen laver. The hands and feet washing of the priests in the waters of purification would take place before starting their morning duties. This cleansing was done as a ritual and for symbolic reasons. The priests made sure to cleanse themselves before performing the following duties:

- Before they approached God by entering the tabernacle.
- Before performing sacrifices on the altar.
- This was to help them with their conscience to make sure they were cleansed of anything of where their hands and feet were beforehand. It was important to do so with proper protocol and proper procedures in a sanctified manner…because if not—they could die. They knew they were serving a Holy God, so their duties must be done

with reverence; their mind and heart had to be free and clear of sin.

Then the LORD said to Moses, "Make a bronze basin, with its bronze stand, for washing. Place it between the tent of meeting and the altar and put water in it. Aaron and his sons are to wash their hands and feet with water from it. Whenever they enter the tent of meeting, they shall wash with water so that they will not die. Also, when they approach the altar to minister by presenting a food offering to the Lord, [21] they shall wash their hands and feet so that they will not die. This is to be a lasting ordinance for Aaron and his descendants for the generations to come."

Exodus 30:17–21 (NIV)

The question is, why did God make the washing specific to their hands and feet? Hands represent our works and service. Feet represent our destination, meaning our walk with Christ. When the priests followed the proper protocol by ceremonially cleaning themselves, they were demonstrating that they must be cleansed from the things of this world. Their hands must be cleansed daily from their own fleshly works and sinful nature. Their feet must be cleansed daily from their own ways and own destination so that their walk with Christ can be cleansed and purified. This means that self was put to the side, and God was to be glorified. We can also see that in the book of Revelation, it describes the feet of Jesus being bronze.

"To the angel of the church in Thyatira write: These are the words of the Son of God, whose eyes are like blazing fire and whose feet are like burnished bronze" (Revelation 2:18, NIV).

Remember, His feet were pierced as a representation of our walk with Christ. His pierced feet brought the judgment of God for our sin. At the same time, His grace given to us through His holiness and the shedding of His innocent blood brought purification to our walk, which canceled out the judgment that comes from our sin. He has paid our debt in full.

In general, what does this mean?

Our brazen laver experience can represent Jesus surrounding who we are in this walk with Him, meaning as we are continually renewed and cleansed through the reading of His word, we are more like Him, and we become reflections of Him. Although we are in this world, we are not of this world. Priests walked barefoot, and their feet would undoubtedly get dirty. Their hands got dirty as well from their daily service. The dirt was unavoidable. We are in this world, and the dirt that comes from us walking on this earth and dealing with daily situations can cause us to sin. Our daily walk in this world is unavoidable, and the filth that comes with it is unavoidable. That is why it is imperative that we cleanse ourselves daily through repentance, obedience, and the washing of His Word. This is a necessary part of communication with God. We, as modern priests, must make sure to maintain holiness and purity from sin by staying in communion with Him by maintaining a clean walk, which can only come by the power of the Holy Spirit through Christ Jesus.

Inner Court/Holy Place (East Side of the Tabernacle Tent)
(Exodus 26:1–36)

The inner court was within the tabernacle tent. It was the first room that the priest entered in after going into the entrance of the tent. The outer portion of the tabernacle tent was covered with layers of curtains to the specifications of God's instruction so that it could be one unit. Ten curtains made of linen, eleven curtains of goat hair, a covering of ram skins dyed red, and over that, a covering of leather that can withstand wear. The colors of the curtains contained various colors, including blue, purple, and scarlet. The curtains had the image of cherubim woven into them. The upright frames and crossbar frames of the tabernacle were to be made of acacia wood and overlaid with gold with silver bases. The entrance of the tent contained a curtain (also known as the veil) with gold hooks and acacia wood posts overlaid with gold with bronze bases. Inside the inner court, palm trees were carved into the doorposts.

Before entering the inner court, also known as the holy place, the priest had to go through the veil. The veil separated the outer court from the inner court. Upon entrance of the inner court, one had to be cleansed and purified at the brazen laver first. Within the inner court, a different level of holy activities would take place. The public was not able to enter here. Only the priests could go in. In this part of the tabernacle, it became quieter, and the lighting was not from the outside but instead from within. In this part of the tabernacle, the holy furnishings consisted of the lampstand, the altar of incense, and the table of shewbread. Each holy item was maintained by the priest through specific instructions given by God. The holy place is where the priests would worship. Through observations, we can see that the furniture outside the courtyard of the tabernacle was made of bronze or overlaid in bronze. However, inside the tabernacle, the furniture was overlaid with gold only. This was symbolic of being closer to the presence of God. There is no need to crucify or sacrifice an offering again because this has already been done. Therefore, judgment is not necessary from within the tabernacle.

In general, what does this mean?

The inner court experience represents being set apart and free from the distractions of this world. The courtyard is easily accessible by all men, but the inner court can only be accessible by the priest. It is a place that requires purity and cleansing before entering. Unlike the courtyard, its light was to be cared for and maintained by the obedience and reverence of the priest. Additionally, the entrance of the tent contained cherubim on it, whereby the courtyard entrance did not. Cherubim symbolize the presence of God because they guard His presence. Due to this, there is a higher level of responsibility required of the priest because they have now entered the dwelling place and sanctuary set apart for God. Something that is not to be taken lightly.

Since there were ten curtains, let's look at the number ten. "Ten" spiritually means "responsibility," symbolizing that the priest must be responsible by making sure he is clean before entering a place where God dwells. The priest was also responsible for maintaining the holy place by caring for the items and serving within it as specified by God, which represented staying in communion with Him. This is a place of relationship. The layers of curtains that hovered over the tent with various materials represented God's sanctuary being a place of covering.

When we work for God and do His will in accordance with His ways, we get closer to Him, but it must be maintained for the relationship with Him to remain clear and free from distraction. The curtains of white linen mean being cleansed, made new, and set apart. The next layer of eleven curtains of goat hair represents the judgment that comes with the old nature. "Eleven" means judgment, and the goat hair represents our flesh. Hair represents our crown and glory. It tells who we are as a person. Since the curtain was made of goat hair, we can view the hair of a goat as a significant representation of our old nature...who we are in the flesh, and the eleven is the judgment that comes with it. The next curtain layer of the rams' skin dyed red is our new nature, covered in the blood of the Lamb. According to studies, "The ram skins dyed red covering represents the ransom sacrifice, which covers our imperfect humanity. It is over the goat hair covering to show that it covers our flesh with its imperfections."[15] The last covering of leather that went over the ram skins was a representation of being covered through all seasons of life, whether good or bad, rain or shine, darkness or light. It is a covering that is durable, that can stand the test of time, and that is God Himself. The palm trees carved into the doorposts are a representation of victory. By serving God, we are automatically engrafted into His Kingdom and become recipients of His promises, which means we, too, have been given the victory in our lives if we follow and serve Him.

The Golden Lampstand
(Exodus 25:31–40)

According to the word of God, the lampstand was hammered out of one piece of gold with six branches extending from the lampstand, three on each side. This came to a total of seven cups made to hold the oil and give light. The lampstand provided light within the inner court. The oil used to maintain the flames was only that of the purest and clearest olive oil. The priests were instructed to maintain this light both day and night; it was important that the light never went out.

In general, what does this mean?

The lampstand represents the light within us. As followers of Christ, we must maintain our fire and be a light in this world of darkness. The olive oil represents the Holy Spirit. The Holy Spirit is the fuel that helps us to maintain the fire. We, as the now priests (royal priesthood), must make it priority to keep our fire for God burning continuously according to Leviticus 6:13; only then will we be able to see the way to God and maintain a relationship with Him. The centerpiece of the lampstand containing the cup of light is Jesus Himself. He is our foundation, and we are to live by His example. He is the only way to get to the Father; He is the bridge and the foundational key to connect God and man. The six branches represent man, "humanity"; we are connected to Him so we can get to the Father. John 15:5 (NIV) says, "I am the vine, you are the branches. If you remain in me and I in you, you will bear much fruit; apart from me you can do nothing." Our life is completely dependent on Him. Just as a vine supplies nourishment to the branches that are connected, so too do we receive spiritual nourishment when we are connected to Him. It is because of Jesus that we have gained access to be engrafted into the Kingdom of God. It is because of Jesus that we become joined heirs of Christ. He is the Light of the World, and if we belong to Him and He lives in us, we are to become that light to others. This all comes through the help of the Holy Spirit. It is incumbent that we maintain the fire, stay connected by being of service to Him and maintaining communication through His Spirit, and live a life of holiness so that we can be effective as we remain active for Him in our daily service as royal priests.

Table of Shewbread
(Exodus 25:23–30)

The table of shewbread was made of acacia wood and overlaid with gold. This table contained four gold rings on its corners so that the carrying poles could slide in it for the purpose of travel. It was placed on the northern side of the holy place. In this place, the priests would perform rituals and worship. The table of shewbread was maintained by the priests by keeping fresh bread on the table weekly. They also sprinkled frankincense on the bread, which came from the offering of the people. There had to be twelve loaves on the table, representing the twelve tribes of Israel. The twelve tribes represented God's covenant to the people of God. The loaves also symbolized Jehovah Jireh, the God who provides for His people. Only the priests were able to eat this because the bread was holy.

In general, what does this mean?

The bread represents Jesus. He is the Bread of Life that we may never hunger again, meaning that He provides for us. He has given us life so we can have life more abundantly. We eat the bread during communion as remembrance of Him to recognize that He sacrificed His flesh so that we may live. This is a sign that we are in a covenant with Him—which is the new covenant. Before Jesus was crucified on the night He was betrayed, He sat down with the twelve disciples, which can be referred to as the Lord's Supper, which can be found in 1 Corinthians 11:23–33. The twelve disciples had bread, which represented the body of Jesus. They had wine, representing the blood of Jesus. In the present time, when we take communion, we remember and recognize that Jesus died for us and that He will one day return to us. As we partake from the bread and the wine, it symbolizes that we are one with Christ. We are also maintaining fellowship with Him by this simple act.

Altar of Incense
(Exodus 30:1–10)

The altar of incense is also known as the golden altar. This holy item was made of acacia wood overlaid with gold and placed near the entrance of the most holy place. It was dedicated for burning incense twice a day, which meant that smoke came from this altar. God provided a specific recipe reserved only for the altar of incense. This recipe was not to be used for anything else other than this purpose and this specific item. If anyone used the ingredients that were specified for the altar of incense outside of the purposes of the altar of incense at the tabernacle, they would die.

"Do not make any incense with this formula for yourselves; consider it holy to the Lord. Whoever makes incense like it to enjoy its fragrance must be cut off from their people" (Exodus 30:37–38, NIV).

The priests would burn the incense, and a sweet aroma would ascend, filling the room with smoke. The smoke released was particularly good for the priest because it blocked them from being able to see into the most holy place, which was a place where the very presence of God dwelled. Remember, at those times, if anyone saw the face of God, they would surely die. With this knowledge, it was beneficial to the priest not to have easy access to see inside the most holy place until the appropriate time.

In general, what does this mean?

The altar of incense represents our intercession and prayers. When we think of intercession and prayer, we can view them as being our actual communication with God. When we intercede, we are communicating to God on behalf of someone. When we pray, we are conversating with God, bringing forth our concerns, supplications, exhortation, adoration, and so forth. This is our phone line, our time of talking with Him one on one. The specific recipe that was given to the priests for this holy item, and only this holy item means that there is a specific way to communicate with Him. In God, there is always protocol and order. Intercession and prayer must be done through the name of Jesus and by the guidance of the Holy Spirit.

How we communicate with Him is set apart for Him. He is not common, so we should revere Him and communicate with Him in an honorable way and through the name of Jesus. What we do for God should be for Him and Him only. The way we commune with Him should be holy.

Recipe for Prayer
(Matthew Chapter 6 Model of Prayer)

In Matthew 6:9–13, Jesus provided a specific model of prayer that we can use as we communicate with Him. We don't necessarily have to say this prayer word for word, but He wants us to understand the concepts to use during prayer. Below you will find a simple explanation of the *Matthew chapter 6 model of prayer*. We can also see that the tabernacle is demonstrated within the model of prayer, which will be notated as well with an asterisk.

"Our Father in heaven, hallowed be your name" (Matthew 6:9b, NIV).

- First, you give honor to God. Recognize Him for who He is. Give Him praise, honor, glory, and thanks for who He is and what He has done. Only He alone is to be worshiped.

- "Your kingdom come, your will be done, on earth as it is in heaven" (Matthew 6:10, NIV).

- This is when we ask for His will in heaven to be done in us on earth. We are to be reflections of Him. This is also when we make declarations speaking forth what is done in heaven also be done among us.

*Matthew 6:9–10 represents the *holy of holies*—because it is not about us, but about Him only. It is where His commands are issued (which is a demonstration of the Ten Commandments). It is also the place where His will is done through us (which is a demonstration of the staff within the ark). As we give Him honor for who He is and what He has done, we are referring to the manna found within the ark. The ark, His Shekinah Glory between the cherubim, and His mercy seat in the tabernacle on earth are a representation of His will on earth being done as it is in heaven.

"Give us today our daily bread" (Matthew 6:11, NIV).

- God is always the supplier at our present time of need; that is why it says, "Give us today." He gives us our daily provisions, which signifies our daily bread. This is when we make our requests known to God. God has given us the authority to do so. He is our Father who promises to provide. At this point, we come boldly before His throne and bring to Him our concerns through prayer and intercession. This also represents us relating with Him, where we stay in communion with Him through fellowship, prayer, devotion, and worship on a daily basis.

*Matthew 6:11 represents the *inner courts*—because the bread within the inner courts had to be replaced regularly on the table of shewbread. Here the priests would fellowship and partake from the bread that was provided from the offerings of the people. It is also where the altar of incense was located, which represents our prayers and requests to Him.

"And forgive us our debts, as we also have forgiven our debtors" (Matthew 6:12, NIV).

- This is when we repent and ask for forgiveness for our sins, transgressions, and iniquity. We must live a life of repentance to stay in communion with God. We must also use this time to forgive those who have hurt us so we can receive forgiveness from God. This helps us to be in right-standing with God so we can maintain our relationship with Him and maintain the relationships we have with others.

"And lead us not into temptation but deliver us from the evil one" (Matthew 6:13, NIV).

- This is when we ask for God to lead us as we follow Him because the enemy always is on his post, trying to kill, steal, and destroy us. If we pray for God to help us, the Holy Spirit will guide our footsteps in the right direction.

*Matthew 6:12–13 represents the *outer courts*—because this is the place where the sacrifice of flesh is made to receive forgiveness. This is also an area that is exposed to the world that is not under the covering of the tabernacle tent. At this place, we are in the presence of our neighbors, meaning where relationships are created, maintained, and sometimes broken if we are not mindful of taking the right actions. It is a busy place that is accessible to all. This is also where the enemy can tempt us due to our exposure to the world, which distances us from God's protective covering of the tabernacle tent. However, with the help of the Spirit of God and through the blood of Jesus, we can be delivered from the grasp of the evil one.

If you notice, God's viewpoint is different from ours. He starts communication from the holy of holies because He is Spirit, and it is where He dwells. Mankind, however, must begin communication from the outer courts because we are fleshly beings. To get to His Spirit, we have to shed our flesh first.

As we can see, the model of prayer is specific and helps us to know exactly what is necessary for our prayers to be effective. We should not use this recipe of prayer for anyone else other than Him. He is the Holy God and the Only True God—we should pray to no one else but Him.

The Veil

The veil stood to represent the fact that humanity did not have free access to God; there was a separation between God and man. Sacrifice and purity were necessary to enter in. The veil was made of white linen and had cherubim woven into it with the colors purple, scarlet, and blue. The cherubim showed that God's presence was guarded and protected. This veil was large, thick, and heavy. It hung on four posts made of acacia wood covered in gold. To enter the most holy place, the veil would have to be moved.

Holy of Holies/Most Holy Place (West Side of the Tabernacle Tent)

The holy of holies is also known as the most holy place. It was the second room within the tabernacle tent. It was the smallest room within the tabernacle, set apart specifically to house the very presence of God, and was separated from the holy place with a veil. This room contained the most precious piece of furniture, which is the ark of the covenant, and upon this was the mercy seat. The mercy seat had two cherubim with wings that enthroned the glory cloud.

The High Priest

Only the high priest could enter this area. Not only that, but the most holy place could only be accessed by the high priest once a year to bring sacrificial blood from the brazen altar and burnt incense to serve as atonement for the people. This day was recognized as the Day of Atonement. *Atonement* is the act of making a sacrifice for the sins of man to reconcile man back to God.

The high priest would go here to make sacrifices on behalf of the people as well as himself for their sins, which took much preparation, consecration, and sanctification. He would sprinkle blood on the mercy seat in between the cherubim. The high priest would even avoid sleeping the night before to make sure to avoid any possible impure dreams to remain holy and pure. The most holy place was so holy that the high priest had to do everything possible to make sure he was holy and pure enough to enter. If he was not—he could die upon entrance.

The High Priest's Garment

He was clothed in a special blue robe over a white linen tunic with a gold chest piece that contained the stones of the twelve tribes of Israel, four rows and three stones in each row, and the name of the tribe within the stone. The twelve tribes of Israel were: Zebulun, Issachar, Judah, Gad, Simeon, Reuben, Benjamin, Manasseh, Ephraim, Naphtali, Asher, and Dan. The gold chest piece, known as the breast piece of decision, which contained these names, was to be over the heart of the high priest as a continual memorial before God. This symbolized that the high priest would bear the responsibility over his heart for the Israelites as a means of making decisions on their behalf. The high priest's robe contained gold bells and pomegranates of blue, purple, and scarlet hemmed on the bottom of it. The bells and the pomegranates were placed upon the robe in a pattern that alternated. Over the blue robe was an ephod that contained the colors of blue, purple, and scarlet with a girdle that he would tie around his waist. On the right and left shoulder of the ephod contained an onyx stone with the name of Jacob's twelve sons engraved into it by order of birth—six on each side. Reuben, Simeon, Levi, Judah, Dan, and Naphtali on the right shoulder. Gad, Asher, Issachar, Zebulun, Joseph, and Benjamin on the left shoulder. These stones also signify the covenant that God has with His people. He would also wear of turban of fine linen for his head with the words "Holy to the Lord" engraved upon a plate of pure gold within it like a seal. The gold plate was fastened to the ephod by a blue cord on the front of the turban. According to Exodus 28:38 (NIV), *"It will be on Aaron's forehead, and he will bear the guilt involved in the sacred gifts the Israelites consecrate, whatever their gifts may be. It will be on Aaron's forehead continually so that they will be acceptable to the LORD."* The garments of the high priest were designed specifically by the Lord to set them apart to be consecrated for the service of the priestly call.

As one can see, the high priest has a heavy and serious call to minister to the Lord on behalf of the people. He had to wear sacred garments as God directed for his consecration, so he could serve as a high priest and follow strict protocols as he performed his chiefly duties. He had to stay clean and pure as the God directed to effectively be of service to God and the Israelites. Only the high priest could officiate the rituals necessary for the Day of Atonement into the tent of meeting. Only the high priest could make sacrifices, intercede, and conduct any ceremonies within the most holy place, which took place on the Day of Atonement, a day that happened once a year. Regular priests were given sacred garments as well for their consecration to give them "dignity and honor" (Exodus 28:2) and had to follow the Levitical priesthood protocol as directed by God for their daily priestly services, but not to such a high degree and account as the high priest. The high priest was appointed to be over the regular priests and had charge over the complete priestly order. Aaron was called as the first high priest, and any high priest that followed thereafter had to be descendant directly from Aaron and come from the tribe of Levi. The tribe of Levi was the only tribe set apart for priestly duties. Becoming a high priest during this time was not by choice but instead, by the regulations that God set for the Levitical priesthood. To obtain the office of a high priest, it had to be inherited.

Again, only the high priest could enter the most holy place specifically for the Day of Atonement, a day set apart for the cleansing and forgiveness for the people of Israel. He had to make atonement for his own sins, his household, and for the people of Israel. It was a serious task.

Ark of the Covenant

In the most holy place resided the ark of the covenant. This sacred furnishing was set apart to house the presence of God. The ark of the covenant was made of acacia wood and overlaid with gold both inside and outside. It contained four gold rings on the feet so that carrying poles could be inserted within the rings. The carrying poles were to remain in the ark and not be removed. God would speak to the high priest within the most holy place after holy protocol was followed. This was a place that was exactly as it is called "Most Holy"; sin could not thrive there, flesh could not survive there, only the very presence of the Almighty could stand. That is why it was imperative for the high priest to take all necessary steps to remain holy in mind, body, spirit, and soul. The high priest had to go through the process that God required. If not…he would die. The high priest had to be aware of the requirements that God set for the priestly duties and follow them to the maximum level to get to this holy place. It took honor, sacrifice, and repentance.

The ark of the covenant contained three sacred items that were placed inside of it: the budding staff of Aaron, the two tablets containing the Ten Commandments written by the finger of God, and a golden pot of manna.

The *budding staff* of Aaron represented God's selection. God selected Aaron and anointed him specifically to be the high priest. It also served as a reminder of the power of God due to the miracles He demonstrated during the times of Moses and a reminder of how God delivered them from Egypt. This was a sign that no other god could stand beside Him. He is the only true God, and all others must submit to Him. The *two tablets* containing the Ten Commandments represented God's law and that He is the Supreme and Holy God. This was God's method of communication to the people of Israel to serve as reference and direction to live a holy life as unto Him. This was written word to show right from wrong and emphasized who He is and His desire to be first within their lives: "Thou shalt have no other gods before me" (Exodus 20:3, KJV). The *golden pot of manna* shows His promised provision for His people.

The Mercy Seat

Seated on the top of the ark was an atonement cover made of gold, known as the *mercy seat*, which included two cherubim facing one another. The presence of God was as a cloud of glory, which was enthroned by the cherubim. The mercy seat is where the high priest would sprinkle the blood as atonement for the sins of the people. Because the people were in desperate need of His mercy due to their sins.

In general, what does this mean?

God wants us to understand that we have access to Him through Jesus, but we must maintain reverence for Him. He wants us to know that He is a Holy God that should not be approached in a presumptuous manner but also must be bold coming before His throne by knowing who we are in Him through the authority given to us by Jesus. The holy of holies (the most holy place) is the smallest room in the tabernacle, yet the most important room that houses His presence. Since only the high priest could enter it back in the days of old, it means that this is a quiet place set aside for Him and us as an individual only. We must be chosen by Him, meaning one who hears the call and answers His call through honor, sacrifice, and reverence to enter His presence. This place is not accessible by the unbelievers, the rebellious, or those who do not honor His presence. It is a place of intimacy with Him for those who are holy and righteous through Jesus, where we can be one with Him in that secret place.

In this place, we can be in His presence and be free from the cares of this world. In this place, flesh cannot stand. This place is reserved only for the spirit, where it is no longer about you and me but all about God. This is a place of complete surrender and complete honor. In this place, we find God's direction, which is a representation of the Ten Commandments. Here we are given the unction to follow His precepts and commands through His law that is no longer followed in our own strength but by His Spirit. His law is now written upon our hearts. We find God's manna, which is His provision and covenant. He provides us with everlasting life through the life of Jesus, which is an everlasting covenant. We also find Aaron's staff, which represents remembrance of God's mighty acts to demonstrate His power and the one who He chooses to be the high priest for His people. Back then, God chose Aaron and his line to inherit the priesthood, but now God's eternal choice is Jesus, who has rightfully taken the position as the ultimate High Priest once and for all to pray and intercede for us in the more perfect tabernacle. The blood sprinkled on the mercy seat was a sign of Jesus and that through Him, we are given access to the Father, in addition to grace and mercy from the Father, even though we are undeserving of it.

The Cross Formed at the Tabernacle

We now have a basic understanding of the history of the tabernacle as well as the first and second temples. As we focus more on the tabernacle, we can see that it was extremely significant in the word of God because it signifies the reconnection back to God through ceremonies and rituals necessary to receive atonement for sins. But more importantly, it mirrors the blueprint of the sanctuary of heaven. The tabernacle also shows us the power of the cross. We can see that the promise of the saving grace that comes through the cross was there all along.

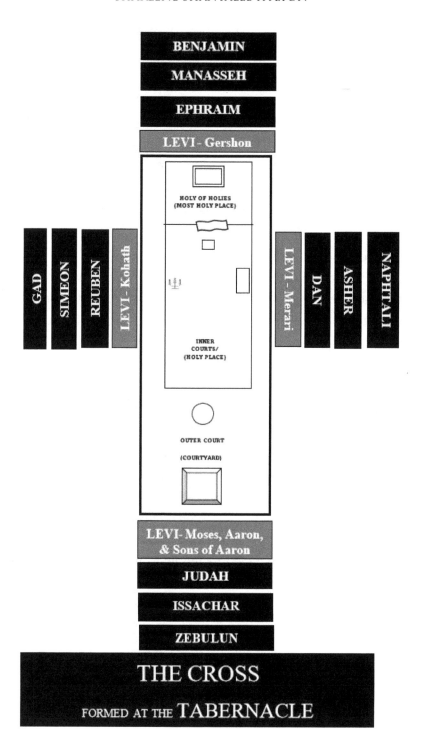

If we examine the formation of the tabernacle, we can see that the complete makeup of it (which includes the positioning of the tribes that surround it) creates the formation of the cross. As we know, our Savior was sacrificed on a cross. The blood that He shed on it ultimately led to the reconnection of humanity back to God the Father. It is important to know that the cross is symbolic of our connection to heaven. It can be seen as our phone line, our gateway, our door, and our access back to God.

We must also note that the cross Jesus died on consists of two pieces of wood; one that is horizontal, and another that is vertical. Wood represents the humanity. As we know, although we are spiritual beings, we are still humans made of flesh while on this earth. The horizontal wood is symbolic of our earthly works and relationships. If you notice, this is where the hands of Jesus were stretched out on. Spiritually, hands represent our works. He shed His blood for the works of our hands, and through His blood, we have received payment and mercy for the sins that our hands have committed. This can also symbolize our horizontal relationships and communication with others here on earth.

The vertical wood symbolizes communication to God; this is our relationship from earth to heaven. Jesus' head with the crown of thorns rested upon the vertical piece of wood, symbolizing His blood shed for the renewal of our mind. If you notice, the feet were on the lower part of the vertical wood. Feet represent our destiny and our walk in this life. God created us to worship Him in hopes that by our free will, we will come to find Him and live a life for Him, walking specifically for His purpose. Our purpose is our God-given destiny.

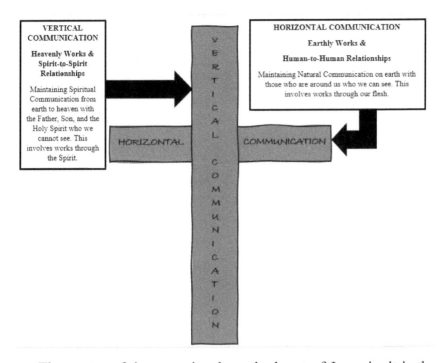

The center of the cross is where the heart of Jesus is; it is the center of everything. His love for us connected us to the love of the Father through His sacrifice. His shoulders also rested here, shoulders representing authority and government. Jesus had the governmental authority to be the bridge to cover the gap that was created between man and God due to the sin of humanity. This gap was covered by the sacrifice of His blood on the cross. This cross was a marker of the journey made by Jesus, which shows the fulfillment of the requirements necessary to mend heavenly and earthly communication through the tabernacle. All of this was done by Him being the ultimate sacrifice as the Lamb of God who was slain for our sins.

The cross is in remembrance of Him; the tabernacle layout was a foreshadowing of Him. The cross also represents the victory He has given to humanity by following the priestly duties within the heavenly tabernacle to save us from the judgment of God. Through the cross, which symbolized the tabernacle fulfilled, we have been granted access to be reconnected to God.

CHAPTER 8

SPIRITUAL COMMUNICATION PERMANENTLY RECONNECTED IN THE HEAVENLY SANCTUARY/ THE MORE PERFECT TABERNACLE

Now that we have discussed the tabernacle, the priests, and the high priest, we can apply that knowledge to the heavenlies. We talked about the earthly sanctuary of the Old Testament, which was the tabernacle; now we will focus on the heavenly sanctuary.

God has a pattern, a heavenly blueprint of the heavenly sanctuary, which is discussed in the book of Revelation. The heavenly blueprint is what God made available to show us the way to connect with Him. Jesus came as the High Priest to stand in the gap for humanity as one who had the authority to connect God to man and man to God. Jesus came as the Lamb to save humanity from the judgment that was due to us for our sins. How awesome it is to have our God come to fulfill all things necessary to make sure the heavenly blueprint was operating and functioning as it was ordained to according to God's original purpose in heaven and on earth. Only the Son of God could come as the High Priest once and for all, one who was worthy and pure enough to pray for us and one who was Holy enough to be heard by God. Only the Son of God could come as the one to be the actual sacrifice, becoming the sacrificial Lamb, one who was Holy enough and free from defect to be accepted to identify with us as an atonement for our sins so that we can be forgiven and be at one with God. Jesus came and took on the role of both the High Priest and the Lamb to gain victory over death and reconnect humanity back to God. Additionally, He stood as the actual door, He became the entry point and the access for God and humanity to reconnect again. This was the key to permanent communication between humanity and God.

Jesus, the Lamb Who Was Slain

Throughout the study of the tabernacle, we see that it takes a pure sacrifice to be able to begin the process of communicating with God. It takes a sacrifice that is acceptable to be able to enter into the presence of God. A sacrifice is what the Israelites needed to receive atonement, and a sacrifice is what the priests used to perform their priestly duties. In Exodus chapter 12, we see the sacrifice of a lamb and the blood of the lamb smeared across the sides and tops of their doorframes that protected the Israelites from God's judgment. It was the blood of the lamb that stood as a sign to the Lord to pass over the homes of the Israelites when He sent the plague on the firstborn of every family and livestock of Egypt. It was the blood of the Passover lamb that kept the Israelites from the judgment of God and saved them from death. The Lord allowed this day to make a clear separation between Egypt and Israel. It then became a celebration for generations thereafter and a Jewish custom to celebrate the Passover. The blood of the lamb represented in this scenario was a foreshadowing of the blood of Jesus, the

Lamb of God.

In all things, we can see that God placed a high emphasis on sacrifice to bring God and man together again. So, if this was necessary on earth, we know that it has already happened as a necessity in heaven. This shows us that a sacrifice was necessary in heaven. That is why God had to send His Son to earth to bring humanity and God back together. Jesus became the sacrifice of God. His sacrifice for mankind was pure, without fault or sin, and worthy to be the one to bring all things together once and for all. As it says in the word, He went as a lamb to be slaughtered willingly for our sins so that we may receive forgiveness for our sins, have life more abundantly, and be protected from the judgment that comes from our sins. We see that Jesus is represented in Revelation chapter 5 as the Lamb who was slain. The Lamb of God signifies that an altar exists in heaven because we know that it is at the altar that sacrifices are made. We previously learned that the earthly tabernacle is a replica of what is in heaven; with that in mind, let's review the heavenly tabernacle.

The Outer Court

There is a reference to the *outer courts* in Revelation 11:2a (NLT) when it states, *"But do not measure the outer courtyard, for it has been turned over to the nations..."* In this chapter, John was given a measuring rod to measure the temple and the altar but was told not to measure the outer courtyard due to the timeframe of forty-two months, whereby the Gentiles will trample on the holy city. As we previously learned, the outer courts in the earthly tabernacle were accessible to the Israelites. There was no need for the Israelite to go through rigorous steps of cleansing before making his way to the outer court because he was given access to enter in as he was and provide his sacrifice. In the heavenly sanctuary, we can see that the Gentiles had access to it; there were no restrictions.

In the reference above, we can see that John was foretold that the nations would even trample this area. However, the outer courts were not a place of concern for measurement.

How awesome it is that Jesus came and fulfilled the priestly protocols necessary for humanity to have access to God by giving of His life as the Lamb of God. His life demonstrated the walk-through of the tabernacle from the outer court all the way into the holy of holies. He entered this world as a baby through a human being made of flesh and bone. He walked this life as a man and experienced but did not succumb to the temptations of the world, which is a representation of entering in through the *outer courts*. He was chosen to be a sacrifice to take on the sin of man. He is the One who was slain and undeserving of such a death; He was sinless and yet took on the sins of humanity by shedding His blood on the *brazen altar* of the cross. His blood covers all sins of all men. He paid a high cost for us by His death and through His blood, which paid our debt of sin in full—once and for all.

Hebrews 9:26b–28a (NIV) says, "But he has appeared once for all at the culmination of the ages to do away with sin by the sacrifice of himself. Just as people are destined to die once, and after face judgment, so Christ was sacrificed once to take away the sins of many..."

Brazen Altar

We can also see the *brazen altar* represented in the heavenlies in Revelation 11:1, where the angel measured the temple and the altar, and in Revelation 6:9–11, when the souls of the martyrs were under the altar crying out.

Revelation chapter 5 discusses who was found to be worthy to open the scroll. He is being celebrated as the Lion of the tribe of Judah, but as John looked to find Him, Jesus was standing instead as the Lamb of God at the center of the throne, with seven horns and seven eyes. Horns showing that He has complete power and authority as the Lamb who was slain. One would think that He would reveal Himself as the Lion, roaring with power and strength, and one who is known to be King of His territory, a fearless creature, and a conqueror over everything. But as the Word of God says, God uses the foolish things to confound the wise. He presented Himself not as the Lion but as the Lamb instead, with horns demonstrating His power. A lamb is humble, helpless, and meek, which are the complete opposite traits of what we would find in a lion. Jesus, as the Lamb who was slain, speaks powerfully in so many ways because it is the slain Lamb that gained power and authority over death and the grave. It was necessary for Jesus to conquer and complete the protocol necessary to go through each part of the more perfect tabernacle as the Lamb.

It was only the sacrifice of the Lamb that could be accepted as payment for our sins. The sacrifice of a Lion could not fulfill the requirements necessary for sacrificial blood within the tabernacle. This was not the custom, and the custom had to be completed. God is a God of order, and He Himself had to follow protocol, for He is a man that cannot lie, and His word cannot return to Him void. God knew He had to have a lamb as the sacrifice according to the order of the steps necessary for reconciliation. So, He came to perform what was required to complete the old so that the new could begin. Yet, at the same time, He is so awesome that He allowed the Lamb who was slain to come from the tribe of Judah. The sacrifice of Jesus as the Lamb of God is forever recognized upon the brazen altar in heaven. The sacrifice does not need to happen again and again because when He died as the Lamb of God—it was finished. Though Jesus appeared as a Lamb in Revelation chapter 5, He is also the Lion of the tribe of Judah. They are one and the same, for He is the Great I Am.

Brazen Laver

Next, we can see the *brazen laver* identified in Revelation 22:1 as the river of the water of life, which flows from the throne of God. At this place, the thirsty will be able to drink freely and will be victorious. The brazen laver represents the cleansing fountain that comes as a gift from Jesus. His blood has cleansed us from the sins that make us so filthy. He is also the Word, which through His word we are renewed daily. He also demonstrated on the earth that He took on the call of taking the sins of the world by getting baptized by water. Being baptized is a proclamation that is only reserved for those who are sinners, which is humanity. Even though He is the Son of God, free from sin, He was humble yet bold enough to take this step of being baptized in preparation of what was to come because of His purpose as the Savior of the world. His sacrifice washed us whiter than snow and has given us the opportunity to get close to God through our acceptance of Him, through our repentance, through a walk set apart for Him, and through His Spirit.

The brazen laver was also represented on the Body of Jesus as He died on the cross. When they pierced His side, water came gushing out of it. This was a miraculous sign that His sacrifice was unique. Just like Eve was made from the rib taken from Adam and became bone of His bone and flesh of his flesh, so too is the church, which is the Bride of Christ, made from the sacrifice of Christ. As the second Adam, His sacrifice gave us the ability to be forgiven for our sins and reborn through Him by becoming one with Him by water. This water gushing from His side is the gift of living water that gives us eternal life. This is a representation of the Spirit of the Living God within us, the essence of who we are and the life within us.

The Brazen Laver is a fountain that is continuously providing cleansing to those in the heavenlies making all within heaven always whiter than snow. There is no need to go to this fountain in heaven over and over again performing ritualistic cleansing in our own strength because it is a continuous flow from the throne of God freely given and poured out to all. He has given us the gift of the Holy Spirit, who is the Living Water.

Jesus, the Door

In Revelation chapter 21, the new Jerusalem is described, which is the Holy City. This is the heavenly sanctuary coming down to earth. In this place, God has made all things new, where we no longer must go up to Him and He come down to us. Instead, God will live among His people. His sanctuary is within the Holy City made of gold, favoring the transparent glass in heaven, containing high walls made of jasper and precious stones, with twelve gates made of pearl, twelve angels at each gate, with the names of each tribe of Israel written on the gates. Three gates faced four directions, three north, three east, three south, and three west. The twelve gates had twelve foundations, with the twelve apostles' names upon the foundations, and the streets were made of pure gold. The twelve gates are a representation of Jesus as the door. Since it is twelve gates, this gives further assurance that Jesus is the one who holds governmental authority and rulership. He is the only one who has the authority to be the door that gives us access to the Father...no one can come to the Father accept through Him. All things must go through Him. As the door, Jesus is the access to clear communication with God.

To get into the place of the Father, it takes the blood of the Lamb as the only key to enter in. To enter something, there must be an entrance to that something. In other words, a key is an item specifically used to lock or unlock a door of a restricted area. In this case, the door is Jesus Himself. One cannot enter the presence without a sacrifice made first, which calls for blood. One cannot enter in the presence without first going through the door, which is the actual access. Which goes back to Jesus being the door. Jesus confirmed this when He said, *"I am the way and the truth and the life. No one comes to the Father except through me"* (John 14:6, NIV). Jesus is the way to get to God. He is the Word of God, who is Truth. Due to the access given to us through Jesus, we now can have access to eternal life in Him. As we enter in through the Door, we can see the heavenly things that can only come through Him.

Jesus, the High Priest

Jesus came as the ultimate sacrifice and forever stands as the ultimate High Priest once and for all. Hebrews 4:14–16 (NIV) says,

> *Therefore, since we have a great high priest who has ascended into heaven, Jesus the Son of God, let us hold firmly to the faith we profess. For we do not have a high priest who is unable to empathize with our weaknesses, but we have one who has been tempted in every way, just as we are—yet he did not sin. Let us then approach God's throne of grace with confidence, so that we may receive mercy and find grace to help us in our time of need.*

As previously mentioned, in the past, the high priest had to pay the price by offering sacrifices for his own sin in addition to sacrificing for the sins of others. However, Jesus came to fulfill all things as the High Priest by sacrificing His own body and shedding His blood once and for all as the ultimate sacrifice free of sin. He was not appointed by man to do so but instead appointed by God. According to Hebrews 7:17 (NIV), God speaks of Jesus by stating, *"You are a priest forever, in the order of Melchizedek."* To be in such a rank as Melchizedek shows that it is the highest of the highest rank that really could not be matched by anyone. This shows the true high power and authority of Jesus.

If you are familiar with the background of Melchizedek in the book of Genesis, we can reflect on how he had a dual duty. He not only operated as the king of Salem, meaning king of peace, but also as a priest. The meaning of Melchizedek is "king of righteousness." Being both a king and priest at the same time was extremely rare. Abraham gave a tenth of what he had to Melchizedek because he realized that he was lower in rank to Melchizedek. Collecting a tenth from the people is symbolic of the law that was set apart for the priests of God. This gesture made by Abraham demonstrated that he acknowledged Melchizedek as a priest. The giving of a tenth to a priest was a foreshadowing of what was to come in the tabernacle after the Aaronic priesthood was established. The priests were given a tenth of what the people earned because their inheritance was the Lord, so the Lord was their provision. The priests and tabernacle were provided for by the sacrifices and offerings of the Lord's people.

Melchizedek was also believed to be the preincarnate Jesus. Melchizedek presented bread and wine to Abraham and his men, who grew weary after battle. This is like what Jesus did for the Last Supper when He broke the bread and poured the wine for the disciples as He taught that it should be done in remembrance of Him. When Melchizedek presented the bread and wine to Abraham, the bread was a foreshadowing and representation of Jesus' flesh that would be sacrificed for us. The wine was a representation of Jesus' blood that would be poured out for the remission of our sins in the new blood covenant. At the Last Supper, which included the breaking of bread and drinking of wine, we can also see that this was a time of fellowship and communion with one another. Jesus, as the High Priest, shows that through the sacrifice of His body and pouring out of His blood, we can remain in fellowship and communion with God our Father. Melchizedek was a foreshadowing of Jesus Himself without beginning or end, who stands as both a king and high priest. Christ became the source for salvation eternally because He is alive forever more. In priesthood, it required a man to be birthed into it due to their forefathers being in the priestly line. But it is written that Jesus was not born into the Levitical priesthood because He came from the tribe of Judah. Instead, He became a priest by the oath of God Himself.

"The Lord has sworn and will not change his mind: 'You are a priest forever'" (Hebrews 7:21, NIV).

Jesus will always serve as the High Priest because He has defeated death with triumph and lives forevermore. Meaning He will never die, so the position of the High Priest will always belong to Him. Even as He was on the cross, He began to act in the role as High Priest when He prayed and interceded on our behalf, saying, "Father, forgive them, for they do not know what they are doing" (Luke 23:34a, NIV). In Hebrew 7:25 (NIV), it mentions that Jesus always "lives to intercede" for us. "...for he bore the sin of many, and made intercession for the transgressors" (Isaiah 53:12b, NIV). A High Priest takes on the role of making a sacrifice on behalf of the people. Jesus was giving His life as a sacrifice for the people of the world. He is now in heaven, and we can get to God only through Him, Jesus Christ, who is the High Priest.

In heaven, the Son of Man is seated at the right hand of God, interceding on our behalf. As it states in Romans 8:34 (ESV), *"Who is to condemn? Christ Jesus is the one who died—more than that, who raised—who is at the right hand of God, who indeed is interceding for us."* Jesus has earned His position to be at the right hand of God and intercedes on our behalf with authority because of the price He paid for us and now serves as the one and only high priest.

Not only is Jesus the High Priest, but He can also understand us because He has been faced with temptation to the highest degree. He understands what it feels like to be tempted, and He was able to overcome all these temptations by avoiding sin. He is blameless and pure. Jesus understands. Keep in mind that understanding is an important part of communication. We learned about understanding in the fifth concept, known as "decoding," when we discussed the seven concepts of communication. Decoding is the process of interpreting and understanding the message being sent to the recipient. Without "understanding," the process of communication is incomplete. For the recipient to be able to receive the message, whether it be through verbal, nonverbal, written, or visual, he or she must first understand it.

God had to come down to earth in the form of flesh as the Son of Man so He could understand us. It was important that He understands to be able to pray for us with compassion and without unfair judgment but instead with all fairness. He understands how it is to feel weak due to the weakness that He felt when He lived among men as a human being, which makes Him have empathy for us when we face our daily trials, tests, and unfortunate circumstances. Therefore, He more than fits the position of serving as the high priest in the heavenly sanctuary. Due to this, we can come before the throne of God with complete assurance that God will come to our rescue through Jesus when we need help.

According to Hebrews 8:1, it says that Jesus is the High Priest, seated at the right hand of God, who serves in the true sanctuary. This means that Jesus stands as the high priest in the heavenly sanctuary. It also mentions that the priests here on earth serve at a sanctuary that is only a copy, a shadow of what is in heaven (Hebrews 8:5). This demonstrates that the earthly temple is really a copy of the heavenly sanctuary. The word of God emphasizes the importance of the priests throughout the Old Testament but reassures us that Jesus is the High Priest making all things before obsolete.

Inner Courts

He was rightfully able to enter the inner courts of the perfect tabernacle through His priestly service here on earth to the people and for the people while also living a life of worship to God.

Golden Lampstand

He became the light of the world, which is the *golden lampstand* found within the heavenly tabernacle. The *lampstand* is identified in Revelation 21:23 (NIV), "The city does not need the sun or the moon to shine on it, for the glory of God gives it light, and the Lamb is the lamp."

Table of Shewbread

Jesus is the bread found on the *table of shewbread* because He is the Bread of Life. The twelve loaves represent twelve as a governmental number and represent authority, which solidifies His lordship. As the Word states, "...the government will be on his shoulders..." (Isaiah 9:6, NIV)

Altar of Incense

The altar of incense is represented in Revelation 8:3–4 in the heavenly tabernacle.

Jesus went to the *altar of incense* and sprinkled His blood upon it and prayed for us, which became a sweet-smelling aroma to the nostrils of God. According to Hebrews 5:7 (NIV), "During the days of Jesus' life on earth, he offered up prayers and petitions with fervent cries and tears to the one who could save him from death, and he was heard because of his reverent submission." He lived a life of prayer and obedience unto the Father, which helped Him to stay on the right path in His purpose. His obedience caused

Him to fulfill the call by giving His life as the purest sacrifice.

The Veil

The veil represents the barrier between God and man due to sin. However, the sacrifice of Jesus' life ripped the veil from top to bottom. Meaning heaven has given access to God through the blood sacrifice of Jesus.

"...since we have confidence to enter the Most Holy Place by the blood of Jesus, by a new and living way opened for us the through the curtain, that is, his body..." (Hebrews 10:19–20, NIV)

His body has now become the veil because we must go through Him, the new curtain for entry into the most holy place in the heavenlies.

Holy of Holies/Most Holy Place

As a High Priest, He was able to enter the *holy of holies* in the heavenlies with His blood sacrifice as payment for us so that we may now commune with God. Our God is so merciful that He completed the walk through the tabernacle by shedding His own blood. In the holy of holies in heaven, we can find ark of His covenant and the mercy seat.

Mercy Seat

His own blood was used as atonement for our sins and sprinkled upon the *mercy seat*, where His own Father is seated, within the more perfect tabernacle within the heavenly sanctuary. Where the Father is seated is where the presence of God is. He is the Glory!

"For Christ did not enter a sanctuary made with human hands that was only a copy of the true one; he entered heaven itself, now to appear for us in God's presence" (Hebrews 9:24, NIV).

Jesus fulfilled His call on earth as purposed by God. He is now seated at the right hand of God, having gained authority through God. He has the authority to be the high priest for us and appear before God on our behalf. We are now joint heirs with Christ and have received the mercy of God and forgiveness of God because of His blood that paid for our sins and connected us to His Father, who is also our Father. Not only is Jesus the High Priest, but He is the Lamb who was slain. Not only is He the Lamb who was slain, but He is the Horn of Salvation that His own blood was sprinkled on in the outer court and the inner court and upon the mercy seat in the holy of holies. The appointed high priests in the Old Testament had the chief role of overseeing the regular priests and the priestly order. This is the chief role that Jesus, as the High Priest, has over us as the royal priesthood of this day and hour. Jesus was chosen by God to serve as the High Priest forevermore, and He intercedes for us as the regular priests in this day and hour.

He prays and intercedes on our behalf and gives us the access to get to God, but we must be clean to enter. This access only comes through the blood of Jesus; we need that to obtain God's mercy and grace, which takes responsibility on our part. We must understand that He made a way for us. He is the way for us to get God through the shedding of His blood, but at the same time, we must not take His sacrifice for granted. If we are repentant, humble, cleansed daily from sin through the reading and washing of His word, and avoid blatant sin, then we can enter in.

We must understand that we are now a royal priesthood, meaning that we must adhere to the holy protocol to get to God. A royal priesthood means that we are different than the average priest; we are priests that come from royalty, which is God Himself. We are priests that serve under the ruling of a King, who is the King of kings. Not only are we royal, but we are also priests that belong to Him. We must stay righteous, pure, and holy. To do so, it takes staying in communion with Him by remaining clean through the washing of His word and being of service for Him while here on earth. All of this must be done through maintaining communication with the King of kings.

There is a process for clear communication with God, and Jesus is the gateway each time. Jesus can't be overlooked or avoided; we must get to God only through Jesus. This communication cannot come through our own strength; we need to stay covered. We need God's continual mercy and grace. That's when Jesus, the High Priest, comes into place in our lives.

Ark of the Covenant in Heaven

It is only through Jesus that we can be royal priests, and only through Jesus can we gain access to His throne in heaven, which is where the ark of the covenant resides…this is the place of the Holy City…where the presence of God dwells.

In the heavenly sanctuary, there is a great throne, which is the highest place where God is seated. It is the throne of all thrones. At His throne, God issues His commands, and the angels act to these commands. He communicates to let His will be done. This is the Holy City of our God. As He sits on the throne, Jesus, the Lamb, is by His side, where the angels and elders worship them. We can also see that there is no temple in this Holy City, "…because the Lord God Almighty and the Lamb are its temple" (Revelation 21:22b, NIV). This is the place where the new covenant is housed, which is the ark of His covenant, and the place where consistent communication between God and His creation will be.

CHAPTER 9

WE, THE ROYAL PRIESTHOOD— MAINTAINING SPIRITUAL COMMUNICATION THROUGH OUR BODILY TABERNACLE

Since we, as new creatures, are to follow the pattern of heaven, we must know that we are also called to be priests in our bodily tabernacle. Again, I must emphasize the word "called." Meaning, we must answer and respond to the call of Jesus, accept it, and walk according to the ways of God in holiness, righteousness, and purity. We must live a life of repentance, obedience, and submission unto Him so that we can be in right standing with God.

First Peter 2:9 (NIV) states that we are called to be a "chosen people, a *royal priesthood*, a holy nation, God's special possession, that you may declare the praises of him who called you out of darkness into his wonderful light."

As we take hold of the promise found in 1 Peter 2:9 by hearing the call and answering His call, we become God's royal priesthood, which comes with accountability. As we say yes to the call, we must stand firm and let our actions match up to the "yes." As we take on this responsibility through Jesus, we must know the authority we hold. As priests, we are to work and care for God's temple, which is now our body, maintain the holy fire within it, and keep in communication with God as He keeps communicating with us.

Did you catch that? Even though we are talking about priests, it still makes a full circle back to keeping communication with God, and in so doing, He will keep communicating with us. God wants us to understand that everything in His Word connects specifically when it comes to communication with the Father of Heaven. We are to follow Jesus' example by serving in our earthly temple. We serve through our bodily temple by being obedient to His commands through the help of the Holy Spirit, which comes through a maintained healthy relationship with Him, sacrificing, cleansing ourselves daily through the reading of His word, prayer, and intercession, keeping the fire burning on the altar, and reverencing His presence. So that one day, after much preparation and consecration, we can ascend by entering the holy of holies. In this place, we can experience His glory, where flesh is no more, and be able to receive His direction and discipline (which is the staff). We can receive His commands and law (the two tablets of the Ten Commandments), which is now written upon our hearts; we can also receive His Word, Jesus Himself (which is the manna).

We are priests in our bodily tabernacle. If you were to look in a full-length mirror and stretch out your hands, you would see that you form the shape of the cross. The actual tabernacle is in the shape of a cross and bears witness that access to God came through the sacrifice of Jesus on the cross. Our body shows us that we are living testaments of the remembrance of what Jesus did for us on the cross. We are walking tabernacles that also house the presence of God. But our tabernacle must stay pure and maintain oneness with God through a life of repentance with Him, which takes consistent conversation with Him.

Since we are a royal priesthood, we must stay in communion and be in right standing with God. We are priests of our current temple, which is our body. All that pertains to the priests of old, such as: how they functioned, how they performed their daily tasks and duties, how they communicated with God, and how they utilized the horn, pertains to our bodily temple now. The main difference is that we no longer have to depend on mere man that serves as an earthly priest to make a sacrifice for us to gain access to the Father. We now have direct access to God through Jesus, our High Priest.

As previously mentioned, it is important that we stay in communion with God to succeed and have a purposeful life. We were once privileged to automatically have the God connection and clear communication with Him because that was His original plan. However, the sin of humanity changed everything causing a disconnected spiritual phone line between God and man. Positively, God brought the temporary resolution in the Old Testament through the tabernacle and then later the temple. Then to God be the glory, the permanent solution was sealed in the New Testament with the new covenant when Jesus came and died for the sins of man and stepped in as the High Priest forevermore.

We are a royal priesthood, meaning we are present-day priests of this hour. What should we do as priests? Live a life of repentance. Live a life of sacrifice. Live a life set apart for God. Live a life of servanthood and ministry for God. Live a life of continual communication with God through intercession and prayer. Live a life of submission to God with reverence and fear. Listen for the response of God, take heed to His instruction, and follow His directions. We can apply what we learned from the tabernacle and the priests who worked within it to our present-day lives. Priests worked daily and followed the protocols of God daily. We, too, must do the same to maintain a holy and healthy walk with Christ.

While we are on that note, we will take a look at the process of communication to God the Father through Jesus and by the power of the Holy Spirit as we travel through the tabernacle as a royal priest in the present time. Let us begin.

Outer Court

We must first go to the entrance of the outer courtyard spiritually. That is by making the effort to leave the things of this world. The gate of the outer courtyard is what separates the priests apart from the world. No one can force you to leave this world and enter the life of sanctification with Christ; it is a life choice that is made specifically by the individual. One must have the desire to give of yourself as a living sacrifice unto God through repentance, submission, and obedience. You must also enter His gates with praise and thanksgiving. Giving honor to God for what He has done for you and your family. As we communicate daily, we must always remember to give God glory.

Brazen Altar

The next thing is to acknowledge what Christ has done for you. He died on the cross, which is the brazen altar, and shed His blood for the remission of your sins. Remember, the brazen altar is a place of fire, where blood is shed, and the sacrifice is burnt by the fire of God. Jesus did His part by shedding His innocent blood as payment for our sins, which burns away our sins and the judgment that is due unto us. But we must do our part by confessing our sins, turning away from our sins, and seeking forgiveness. It is a requirement to sacrifice the things that so easily beset us on the altar as well. This includes the sacrifice of our flesh. In exchange, we accept His purpose for our lives, walking completely committed to Him. In Revelation 6:9–11, we can see those who gave their lives for the cause of Jesus; their souls were under the altar in heaven, representing their sacrifice is remembered.

"When he opened the fifth seal, I saw under the altar the souls of those who had been slain because of the word of God and the testimony they had maintained" (Revelation 6:9, NIV).

The martyrs sacrificed their lives physically because they were killed due to their faith in Jesus. As this applies to us, we don't have to literally be killed to be a sacrifice for God. As we give our lives to Christ, we are giving our lives to Him spiritually. We become living sacrifices for Him.

"Therefore, I urge you, brothers and sister, in view of God's mercy, to offer your bodies as a living sacrifice, holy, and pleasing to God—this is your true and proper worship" (Romans 12:1, NIV).

As we begin to give up our own fleshly desires and our own will so that God's will may be done, we are making a sacrifice at the brazen altar of our bodily tabernacle. This is when we give our heart to God, making it pliable for Him to use by coming before Him. It must be broken, humble, and contrite so that He can have His way. As He has His way, we are sacrificing our flesh because it is more of Him and less of us. Our sacrifice of flesh becomes a smell pleasing to His nostrils. This becomes our worship that is true, holy, and acceptable unto Him.

Brazen Laver

We have to stay in the word of God continuously, which washes us from our sins. Our hands and our feet must be cleansed because we still must walk through this world, even though we are not of this world. Due to the daily challenges of this world that can easily taint us, it is necessary to maintain cleansing through His word. Think about it, at the brazen laver, the priests had the ability to see themselves in a reflection through the mirrored bowl and through the water that was in it. We are supposed to reflect Him, so as God reveals Himself through His word, it cleanses as He exposes what is not like Him within us. We are to be reflections of His image. As we take in more of Him, our fleshly ways become less and less. Our feet, meaning our walk, is purified daily through the reading of His word. Our hands, meaning our works, are cleansed and purified daily so that we may work according to His plans and purpose. The brazen laver in our daily walk is necessary to hear God clearly. We must be cleansed to have clear transmission within our communication with God.

The Door

The next step is entering into the holy place. A place that is not accessible to all. It is only for those who have earned the right to enter. In our walk with Christ, we go to another level when we accept Him, learn more about Him through His Word, which causes us to do more for Him. Which is to give service to Him and minister before Him. We can only get there through the door, which is Jesus Christ Himself. The only way through the door is through our repentance, sacrifice, obedience, consecration, and reverence.

John 10:7 (KJV), "Then Jesus said to them again, Verily, Verily, I say unto you, I am the door of the sheep."

Inner Court

Once we have gone through all necessary steps required by God to enter the holy place in our walk, that means we have dusted off everything from the world. We are now able to go into the inner court. This is where we serve God and minister before Him. This is a place where all the noise and the busyness of the world stops, our flesh is submitted, and the light from the outside is no more. Any light we see is from the fire that we must maintain. In this place, we have moved from the natural…into the supernatural.

The Golden Lampstand (Menorah)

The golden lampstand represents Jesus being the light of the world. As a current royal priest, it is our duty to be joined to Him by maintaining the fire with clear and pure oil. Remember, the golden lampstand has a main piece in the center, which is Jesus; we represent the branches of the lampstand. He is to remain the center of our lives. As we do this, we are one with Him and have been grafted into the Kingdom of God with Him. The oil in the cups of the lampstand is a representation of the Holy Spirit. It is by the Spirit of God that we can understand God more. The Holy Spirit brings the revelation and light to the Word of God. He helps us with our daily walk and convicts us of our wrongs so we can get things right with Christ. He directs us on the path that we should go, giving us wisdom and counsel. He helps us to maintain our relationship with Christ if we allow Him by not quenching Him. At this place, the fire must be maintained, and we must avoid quenching the fire, which is the Holy Spirit. The golden lampstand was also mentioned in Revelation 4:5 (NIV) when it said, "From the throne came flashes of lightning, rumblings and peals of thunder. In front of the throne, seven lamps were blazing. These are the seven spirits of God." The menorah is a representation of the seven spirits of God, which can be found in Isaiah 11:2.

1. The Spirit of the Lord,
2. the Spirit of Wisdom,
3. the Spirit of Understanding,
4. the Spirit of Counsel,
5. the Spirit of Might,
6. the Spirit of Knowledge,
7. the Spirit of the Fear of the Lord.

The seven spirits of God are the Holy Spirit. Isaiah 11:2 explains simply what comes from the Holy Spirit. As we accept Him into our life and into our walk with Christ, the seven spirits listed are what we supernaturally obtain from Him as we connect to His Holy Spirit. The Holy Spirit helps us to maintain our heavenly relationship through the seven spirits that come from Him. He is the "Spirit" that maintains our *Spirit*ual communication.

Let's look at each of the seven spirits and break it down to simple means for our understanding. The *Spirit of the Lord* is the Holy Spirit given supernaturally to us by God. This is when we are baptized by the Spirit and where we operate not by our own strength, which comes from flesh, but instead by the Spirit, which can be found in Acts chapter 2. The *Spirit of Wisdom* comes from the Holy Spirit. He guides us to think wisely and to act wisely spiritually, which manifests naturally. The Holy Spirit is the *Spirit of Understanding*; He gives us the ability to gain understanding from what God is revealing to us. He brings insight into the hidden mysteries of heaven. The Holy Spirit comes as the *Spirit of Counsel* by giving us direction. He allows us to view situations from a heavenly perspective by guiding our path and pointing us in the way we should go and giving us warning when we need it. The Holy Spirit comes as the *Spirit of Might* because He is the power part of the Trinity. He empowers us to serve God, and with our vessels, He can do mighty exploits through us, such as moving in signs, miracles, and wonders. The Holy Spirit comes as the *Spirit of Knowledge*, giving us the ability to be educated through heavenly means. The *Spirit of the Fear of the Lord* comes from the Holy Spirit. He teaches us to fear God, not by means of being terrified of God. But instead, by showing us to reverence God. He helps us to revere God as being Holy, Sovereign, and Powerful; therefore, He shows us how to not treat Him as being common. As the Holy Spirit helps us to revere God, we are careful to do what is right and just before Him.

The seven spirits of God, which is the Holy Spirit, are also the seven eyes found upon the Lamb of God in the book of Revelation.

> *Then I saw a Lamb that looked as if it had been slaughtered, but it was now standing between the throne and the four living beings and among the twenty-four elders. He had seven horns and seven eyes, which represent the sevenfold Spirit of God that is sent out into every part of the earth.*

Revelation 5:6 (NLT)

The seven eyes represent Jesus having the ability to see and have knowledge in a complete way. This demonstrates that Jesus is all-knowing. With the authority He holds as the Lamb of God, He was able to send His Spirit in fullness and completeness to the world so Jesus can be revealed to them by the knowledge granted to them by the Holy Spirit. It also demonstrates how the Spirit and Jesus operate together; the eyes being connected to the Lamb shows the Holy Spirit being connected to Jesus as the light in the darkness. Jesus is the light of the world, and the Holy Spirit is the oil that lights the fire and keeps it burning in the darkness. The spiritual significance of the eye is a lamp of the body.

According to Luke 11:33–36 (ESV),

> *"No one after lighting a lamp puts it in a cellar or under a basket, but on a stand, so that those who enter may see the light. Your eye is the lamp of your body. When your eye is healthy, your whole body is full of light, but when it is bad, your body is full of darkness. Therefore, be careful lest the light in you be darkness. If then your whole body is full of light, having no part dark, it will be wholly bright, as when a lamp with its rays gives you light."*

The lampstand is very important in our walk with Christ, as this is a representation of staying on fire for God. It is symbolic of our consistent connection to God. As we remain connected with God by the direction of the Holy Spirit, we remain complete in Him. As we stay connected, our fire continuously burns and shines in this world of darkness. Just as Jesus came as the light of the world, we are to be lights in this world and let our light shine for Him. That is why God told the priest to make sure the fire must continuously be lit with pure oil. He does not want our fire to go out. The fire within our bodily temple must always be burning. Why? Because He lives in us. To be effective, communication with Him is necessary. Think about the seven spirits of God. "Seven" means completion. This ties back in with the seven key concepts of communication that were discussed earlier in this book. Remember, the seventh concept of communication is a response, which begins the loop of communication. The seventh concept does not always happen in communication. But as I mentioned earlier in this book, it is the goal to always make it to the seventh concept because this is what determines and signifies healthy communication because that ensures there is communication between both parties...the sender and recipient. That loop shows there is two-way communication... from sender to recipient, then from recipient to sender, and back to sender to recipient, etc. It is not always promised that the recipient will respond. If there is no response, that means there is a dead end in the communication process, preventing a loop from taking place, therefore, resulting in an end to the conversation. But God wants that loop between man and God to remain to ensure a healthy relationship. All of this comes through the Holy Spirit, our maintainer of communication. With that said, the Holy Spirit is necessary in our walk with Christ. He is the oil, and He is the fire. He is the breath that awakens, empowers, and brings life to our walk with Christ. He is our helper and empowers us to keep us connected.

Table of Shewbread

This place is where we see God's provision, remember His promises, and fellowship with Him as well as with others for the cause of the kingdom. It is so important that we sit and sup at the table with others, that is, through doing everything in remembrance of Him. We worship Him and minister to Him, singing songs of praise, delighting in His word, taking of His communion, and acknowledging Him for His goodness with others in the Body of Christ. This is the place of discipleship, where we are discipled, and depending on your call, we can also disciple others. This is where the church comes in; we are among others for one purpose and one cause, which is to give God glory and advance His kingdom. The twelve loaves also represent the authority God has given us as priests to do what He has called Him to do through ministry.

"When Jesus had called the Twelve together, he gave them power and authority to drive out all demons and to cure diseases, and he sent them out to proclaim the kingdom of God and to heal the sick" (Luke 9:1–2, NIV).

As current-day priests, we take on the name of Christ. We are now ambassadors for Him, representing Him through our walk. As we connect to Him, we inherit the kingdom. This means we have power and authority to do here on earth what He did here on earth, even to a greater magnitude. Before Jesus went to sit at the right hand of the Father, He said to us greater works we shall do. He has given us the power and authority to do great things for His Kingdom all through the power of His name...Jesus.

Altar of Incense

We go to the altar of incense daily by sending up our prayers, praise, and intercession. All of this should be done perpetually. God wants us to be able to pray to Him and make requests to Him with belief that He will answer. He also expects that we intercede as well as our priestly duty. It is expected of us to think beyond ourselves and our own personal situations by praying for others. This place is where we labor in the kingdom; in other words, work for Him on behalf of others. Priests were called to do that, to be the middleman, standing in the gap for others and bringing the needs of others before God.

Moses interceded for the Israelites when they did wrong by worshiping a golden calf. He did not want the judgment of God to strike them, and God heard His prayer. Abraham interceded on behalf of the people by conversating with God and negotiating with God so that He would not destroy the city if there were a few good people that lived within the city. David prayed for the Israelites when the angel began striking them for his sin of taking a census. He interceded by admitting that it was his sin and not that of the people. He asked that the hand of God fall on him and his own family. The list goes on, but this was just to name a few.

We are to keep praying and interceding as a means of serving and laboring in the kingdom; this also demonstrates the cross within us. When we pray to God, it demonstrates the vertical connection. When we pray for others, it demonstrates the horizontal connection. As this happens, there is a spiritual connection in the center binding heaven and earth together, forming the shape of a cross. This is the cross of spiritual communication. Matthew 6:10 (NIV) says, "Your kingdom come, your will be done, on earth as it is in heaven," which shows the agreement between heaven and earth. As a reminder, there is a recipe for prayer in Matthew 6:9–13, which we discussed earlier in this book, that you can feel free to revisit as a refresher. The altar of incense is a place that represents our direct communication to the Father.

The altar of incense stands high and is the furniture that is closest to the holy of holies. Only the veil separates the altar of incense from His divine presence. The closeness from this piece of furniture to the holy of holies shows the importance of this altar. The height of the altar of incense within the holy place demonstrates the effectiveness of this furniture. Although it is the smallest piece of furniture, it is the piece that reaches the heights of heaven through the voice of our prayers and intercession. The fire from the brazen altar is used at the altar of incense to burn the incense. The fire at the altar of incense must continuously burn, which means that it is important that we maintain the fire in our walk with Christ; this fire maintains the communication. The horns of this piece of furniture are symbolic of the power of prayer and intercession.

There is a slight difference between the brazen altar and the altar of incense. As we learned earlier in the study of the tabernacle, the smoke of the brazen altar ascends to the heights of heaven through the sacrifice of our sins, which is the smell of the burning flesh of an animal and sometimes grain offerings. The smoke of the altar of incense, on the other hand, is a sweet aroma that comes from special ingredients specific for incense at this altar. No flesh is involved here; this sweet aroma is different from the outside smoke and ascends as a pleasing fragrance to the nostrils of the Father. This aroma symbolizes the collection of our voice making its way to the Father.

The altar of incense has a voice! Which can be your voice. This is a place of our communication with God, where your voice is counted and heard. This is where your voiceprint is made in the heavens. As your voice ascends through your prayers and intercession, which can also represent your cries, it is caught in the heavenlies, becoming a voice from the altar in heaven.

The incense and smoke that comes from the altar of incense create another layer of protection that keeps us, as priests, from being too close too soon to the most holy place. The smoke created at this place helps us to adhere to protocols of God. Yet, at the same time, it is received by the Father and makes room for us to get closer to Him. Our voice makes room for us and makes our presence known to the Father before we enter in. It ascends to the Father in corporation with incense, and He hears our voice in heaven.

This is also a place where angelic visitation can take place. We can see this in the story of Zechariah, a priest who was the father of John the Baptist. Before John the Baptist was even born, God revealed to Zechariah that John would be born. This happened when Zechariah went to the temple to burn incense to perform his priestly duties. As he was ministering at the altar of incense, an angel appeared before him to reveal that his wife would bear him a son. "Then an angel of the Lord appeared to him standing at the right side of the altar of incense. When Zechariah saw him, he was startled and gripped with fear" (Luke 1:11–12, NIV).

This simply shows the power of prayer and how it causes the angels to take action. Even as we look at the book of Revelation, it shows that an angel took the prayers of the saints together with incense and stood at the altar of incense in heaven before the throne of God.

"Another angel, who had a golden censer, came and stood at the altar. He was given much incense to offer, with the prayers of *all* God's people, on the golden altar in front of the throne" (Revelation 8:3, NIV).

We are God's people, which means all of our prayers are ascending and being caught in the heavenlies. Remember, what is done on earth should be as it is done in heaven. Just as the altar of incense stands before the holy of holies, where God is enthroned in the tabernacle, we know that it is a copy of the golden altar (of incense) that stands in front of the throne of God. This brings us more revelation to what Jesus said when He was teaching the disciples how to pray in Matthew 6:10. This demonstrates that what is done on earth should reflect what is already in heaven. During the construction of the tabernacle, God emphasized the importance of following His instructions so that nothing is overlooked. God's desire was to replicate the heavenly sanctuary on earth because He wanted to give humanity the opportunity to have access to Him through the instrument of our voice, just as it is in heaven.

Revelation 8:4 (NIV) goes on to say, "The smoke of the incense, together with the prayers of God's people, went up before God from the angel's hand."

The voices that came from the prayers of God's people ascended were just as real as the smoke that ascended from the altar of incense. These prayers were heard by the Father, and the angel took action. The angel filled the censer with fire from the altar, and the prayers of God's people caused an explosive answer from heaven. This came through thunder, lightning, and an earthquake. This goes to show the power of prayer and how God's angels, known as servants of flaming fire, present themselves and are activated to work on our behalf at the altar of incense. We can see that there is power when heaven and earth come in agreement. So, it is important that we know our prayers, as long as they are true to the protocols of God, can make changes when God and heaven stand in agreement.

Again, I must reiterate how much of an important part the altar of incense plays in our walk with Christ. It is the place of communication with Christ through conversation. It is also important to note that the Holy Spirit is our helper at this point. He goes beyond our flesh and prays the heart of the Father through unknown languages. He sees what we cannot see and moves beyond the limitations of our earthly language and bypasses our minds.

In the same way, the Spirit helps us in our weakness. We do not know what we ought to pray for, but the Spirit himself intercedes for us through wordless groans. And he who searches our hearts knows the mind of the Spirit, because the Spirit intercedes for God's people in accordance with the will of God.

Romans 8:26–27 (NIV)

It is critical that we pray and intercede through tongues of the Spirit of God. If we do not speak in tongues, it is highly recommended that we covet this good gift and ask Him to grant us with the gift of tongues. With this in mind, we are taken to a higher level in Christ and are more equipped to tap into areas and realms within the Spirit through prayer and intercession.

Once we make our prayers and supplications to the Lord, we can move to the next step, which is to enter the holy of holies. To enter the holy of holies, we must go through the veil first.

The Veil

The veil is what originally separated us from God's presence and His Shekinah Glory. Remember, after the fall of Adam, man was exiled from the presence of God (the Garden of Eden), and the cherubim were given the orders to guard the gates that separate man from God with flaming swords. That barrier between man and God remained there until God sent the permanent solution. This barrier is a representation of the veil that separated man from God in the tabernacle and temple.

However, when Jesus died on the cross, that veil was ripped from top to bottom. Meaning the hands of God in heaven ripped the veil of separation; man had no part in this matter. The guardians and throne-bearers of the presence of God, known as the cherubim, were given the okay by the Father to open the gates because of the blood of Jesus—which is the key to the gates. Because of this, we have gained access by God's approval because of the blood sacrifice of the Lamb of God. We can now enter in through the blood of Jesus that came through the sacrifice of His body, which is the new veil. We may boldly enter the most holy place because we have been made new through Christ and His blood that saved us all.

As current-day priests, this place of spiritual communication is when we have reached a place of being clear from sin after we have sacrificed the flesh, asked for forgiveness, washed ourselves through His Word, and come to God through thanksgiving, prayer, and supplication through the acknowledgment of Jesus and through the name of Jesus. At this place of communication, we must have a heart that is softened and a body that is pure and cleansed through repentance. This is a place that still involves us because we are still praying about ourselves and our surroundings, and we are still ministering before Him with our works of service to Him. This is where we speak, and God listens. So, communication with the Father is not at the maximum level just yet, where it is only about Him.

Once we get past all these things, we now have eyes to see and hear what the Spirit is saying. The flesh represents a natural veil that spiritually blinds us, so we must get beyond this in order to access the Father. Flesh must have no part to move forward to the next level of spiritual communication. When we get past the flesh, we can enter through the spiritual veil that rightfully gives us access to God, which comes through the Body of Jesus. When we have done this, we know that we can boldly enter the presence of God Almighty. We can now enter in through the veil.

Holy of Holies

In this place, it is all about Him. This is a place of stillness where the presence of God dwells, resides, and inhabits. God's presence lights this place, so there is no need for natural light. His glory, meaning His Shekinah, is the light! This is where man can be in complete communication with God. As priests, we can see God in His holiness, splendor, and power. This is the place where

God is connected to man. It is such a holy place that we cannot enter in a common manner but instead with the highest degree of reverence. This is where we find the instruction of God. It is where God speaks, and we listen. But to get here, flesh cannot stand. We must get past the veil first.

As current-day priests, we get to this place by setting time aside for God alone through sacrificing of ourselves by giving Him our time, thoughts, heart, mind, undivided attention, and most importantly, through our obedience. Sometimes, it takes being closed away, even turning away the plate by fasting and praying. At this place, we are in His presence. In His presence, all good things exist because we are in the presence of the Great I Am. Meaning, whatever we need at that present moment, He comes as the Great I Am to be just that.

The Ark of the Covenant

As we know, the ark of the covenant is the only piece of furniture that is found within the holy of holies. *The mercy seat* covers the ark of the covenant, demonstrating that God, the One seated upon the throne, is a forgiving God and merciful God, even though we are undeserving of it. It is by the blood sacrifice of Jesus that serves as atonement for our sins to give us the ability to receive the mercy of God when we initially were supposed to get judgment by death. But to God be the *glory*, we can receive God's mercy and grace as we enter the most holy place by the blood of Jesus, where God is seated between the cherubim. We, in turn, can behold the beauty of His majesty and give glory to Him.

Upon the mercy seat, which is the actual cover to the ark of the covenant, are cherubim with their wings stretching over the presence of God, which came in the form of a cloud of glory. His presence is the Shekinah Glory and the *Glory Cloud* made of smoke. Where there is smoke, there is fire. Where the presence of God is...the fire will always be. This Glory Cloud is God, and from which His voice speaks.

As we look into the contents of the ark of the covenant, we can see how it connects to us as the royal priesthood. The ark contained the manna, staff of Aaron (God's chosen vessel for the priesthood), and the Ten Commandments. *The manna* shows us that God is our provision. We can find what we need in Him at this place. If we need healing, He is there to provide it. If we need hope, He is there to provide it. If we need peace, He is there to provide it. The list is never-ending because He is the forever present, all-powerful, and all-knowing God. The staff represented in our bodily tabernacle demonstrates God's delivering power and knowledge that God has chosen you to commune with Him. *The staff* also shows us that He has given us access to dwell with Him and deliver others just as Moses did. In this place, we come out changed for the better. We come out equipped because as we communicate with Him here, He speaks to us. He gives us instruction to do mighty exploits for Him. The staff also shows that He is there to give us guidance through love and correction. The *Ten Commandments* also show us that He is giving us instruction to do His will. "Ten" meaning responsibility. When we get instruction from Him, we are held responsible and accountable for that information. We are enlightened by His direction and gain insight by His voice. The voice of God is released in the holy of holies. This is where we get a response back from God after giving Him ourselves as a living sacrifice. Jesus has given us access to do so.

When the time comes to exit His presence, we come out changed, renewed, enlightened, emboldened, and empowered by the Most High for the benefit of enhancing and advancing His Kingdom. Think about it, when Moses went up to Mount Sinai after fasting for forty days and forty nights, He was able to go into the presence of God, which was in the form of a dense cloud on the mountain, found in Exodus chapter 19. This mountain was set apart as holy as directed by God. God warned them about the limits set up to keep the commoner from getting too close; if they did, they would die. God required consecration. The cloud that was upon this mountain was a representation of the Glory Cloud in the holy of holies. That is where He heard the voice of God and communed with God. He was given direction by God and heard the heart of God. This is where God spoke and where Moses listened. God gave Moses tangible instructions to give to the Israelites.

This is an excellent example of what a relationship between God and man is like. God and Moses were conversating, in communion with one another, and communicating. Not only that, but Moses was also radiant with the glory of God on his face because he was in the presence of the Almighty God. It caused people around him to be afraid; this was holy fear. The glory of God shining on the face of Moses was simply a manifestation of the empowerment granted to Moses by God Himself. Remember, where the presence of God is, the fire is also. The glory that was shining on the face of Moses was the fire of God! He was on fire from the empowerment of God.

The same applies to us as current-day priests. When we are in His presence, we come out empowered and shining with light of God. When God empowers you—you have gained authority by Him. There is no need to make an announcement that God is with you—it is made obvious. We begin to look like Him because we are connected to Him. That is when people can see and recognize the God in you. Which brings holy fear to the people for God's glory. We are empowered not for selfish means or gain but for the glory of God to be effective in the Kingdom of God as directed by Him. We are sent out to increase and advance the Kingdom of God. To share what He has given us in His presence as a benefit to the people in this world so that they may follow Him. The holy of holies is a place of fire and is the ultimate place of communication; this is where God communicates with us. The fire shows that the communication between God and us is live and active. This is the place of response! It is a process to get to this place, but it is well worth it.

Everything we do daily in this walk with Christ is to get to the final place of clear communication where the actual loop of communication takes place...which is the place where He responds. This is a place where we are on fire for Him because we are connected to the God who answers by fire. We are radiant with His fire. At this place, we look like Him, smell like Him, and shine like Him. This is where the spiritual phone line is reconnected through Jesus Christ and sparked by His fire.

This final and complete place of communication could only come by the sacrifice made by Jesus Christ. He came forth as the Horn of Salvation, the Heavenly Horn, and the Horn of all other Horns, with power to save us all. By His saving grace, our relationship and communication with God the Father have been restored.

Now that we have that understanding, let us not forget that we discovered that horns are connected to the spiritual communication between God and man. With this in mind, let's review spiritual communication by understanding the significance of horns. In the next chapter, we will discuss what horns signify in reference to the tabernacle and communication.

CHAPTER 10

THE SIGNIFICANCE OF HORNS

We now have a detailed understanding of the tabernacle and how it connects with the spiritual communication between God and man. We have also gone into great detail about horns and communication. God revealed that horns are pivotal to communication in the heavens through mouths made of horns in the heavenly vision. We discussed the meaning of Jesus as the Horn of Salvation. We understand that God is the Hornist of heaven who is the Voice of the Horn. We see the Holy Spirit is the Breath of the Horn. We also discussed how a horn functions in the spirit and nature, but do we truly understand the meaning behind a horn in general?

Let's start with the basics by looking at the word "horn" in the Hebrew language, which was the language of Jesus when He walked the earth. The Hebrew word for horn is "*qeren*," which alludes to something that projects in an outward manner to shine, brightness, or send out rays; it is also used to describe the radiant face of Moses after being in the presence of God in Exodus 34:29. These rays can be likened to horn-like projections because Moses' face was shining outwardly, projecting light outwardly, and sending out rays. Just as horns project from the head of a horned animal, the radiance of God was projecting from Moses' face. Habakkuk 3:4 connects the light and brightness to horns, which signifies power. Exodus chapter 34 signifies the power that was given to

Moses as He stood in the presence of God and received direction from God. Moses was chosen by God, and God granted Moses with power to lead His people. This passage signifies that Moses was empowered by God, who is the source of all power!

Horns are significantly important and symbolic in the Word of God. In the Bible, we can see horns represented in multiple ways. It is a must for us know the various meanings of the horn so we can comprehend the message God is sending us in reference to spiritual communication. Horns are evident throughout the Bible and throughout the tabernacle, but why? Let's first begin by looking into the meaning of a horn.

What do horns represent in the Bible?

Horns represent power, strength, honor, glory, dominion, and protection. They are also used literally as instruments.

It is always good to get the background of a subject for foundational knowledge. We see horns mentioned in the word of God, and although the horn is mentioned all over the Bible, it is important to note that these references are not the same. We must understand the context behind how the horn is mentioned. The horn can be represented as instruments known as a ram's horn, known as the shofar, a trumpet, a bugle, etc. It can also be seen as actual horns that protrude from something, such as horns at the altar, horns on the Lamb, horns sprouting from the beast, etc. It can also be used figuratively as an exalted horn. The horn is also used when referring to Jesus as the Horn of Salvation, as we discussed earlier in this book. This shows that there are so many references, but all are very different from one another.

With that in mind, we will look at the significance of the meaning of the horn biblically, metaphorically, spiritually, naturally, and symbolically. These findings were highly influenced from the study of horns within Holman's Bible Dictionary 2003 version.

Let's see the breakdown below:

- Biblically, we can see that "horns are used as trumpets, vessels, and as symbols," which were used literally and figuratively.[16]

  - We can see that different people within the Bible used trumpets and horns of rams to release sounds for various purposes. We also see the horn being used as a vessel to hold anointing oil. As previously mentioned in this book, we see the ram in the thicket caught by its horns to serve, as a replacement sacrifice, during the time Abraham was about to sacrifice his son Isaac in the book of Genesis chapter 22. This was symbolic of Jesus Christ taking the place of us (humanity) as a living sacrifice.

- In a metaphorical sense, horns represent strength, honor, and victory.

  - For example, we see within the word of God, it talks about the horn of a person being exalted in multiple places. This symbolizes the strength and honor of a person being positively lifted from their status or situation. An exalted horn shows that there is victory and success in the life of the person whose horn has been exalted. Oppositely, if there is a cut-off horn, this means there is defeat in the life of that person. The word of God also demonstrates the fate of an exalted horn and a cut-off horn. "All the horns of the wicked also will I cut off; but the horns of the righteous shall be exalted" (Psalm 75:10, KJV). A cut-off horn is also symbolic of being weakened and humbled.

  - Another example is Jesus as the Horn of Salvation, representing the strength, honor, and victory that He holds as Lord.

- Spiritually and naturally, we can see that horns represent strength and protection.

  - Horned animals use their horns as a weapon for protection and for attacking, to dig, and to mark their territory. This demonstrates the fighting strength of the animal and clearly shows that its horn is where its glory resides. Horns (for the most part) do not branch out like antlers. Instead, horns on an animal are symmetrical in shape and made up of a protein known as keratin, which serves as a covering over a bony core that is living. We are familiar with keratin because that is what hair and fingernails are made of. Horns are connected to the skull of the animal by bone and do not shed like antlers would on a yearly basis. If a horn is cut off an animal—(for the most part), it does not grow back. That is why animals with horns are not afraid of having their horns disconnected during an attack because it is a part of their skull—a place of strength.

- In the book of Psalms, it talks about the strength of a wild ox. To see this, we must look at different translations for an easier breakdown.

  - In the New Living Translation Version, the word clearly states, "But you have made me as *strong* as a wild ox. You have anointed me with the finest oil" (Psalm 92:10).

- This scripture talks about the strength of a wild ox. As we know, oxen are noted for their horns. Additionally, a wild ox is symbolic of "the strength of Israel." As we know, God's favor is with Israel and His chosen people. This shows us that whoever has an exalted horn is who God has also favored and chosen. Also, in the second part of the scripture, it further says, "You have anointed me with the finest oil." If someone has been anointed, that means they have been chosen by God, not only that "the finest oil" represents that they are set apart and given the best of the best. In other words, they are blessed.

- We also know that oil represents the Holy Spirit. So, this scripture also represents the Holy Spirit being present while being anointed with this strength from

God.

- In the New King James Version, it says, "But my horn You have exalted like a wild ox; I have been anointed with fresh oil" (Psalm 92:10).

- In the scripture above, we can see that "you have made me as strong" is replaced with "my horn you have exalted," which denotes that they are one in the same meaning. Just as horns are the strength of an animal in the natural, this scripture backs up that a horn is a representation of strength spiritually. Since these sayings are interchangeable and both compared with that of a wild ox, we can clearly see the meaning behind an exalted horn. An exalted horn means being a strengthened vessel of God, one that has been blessed, highly favored, and chosen by the Lord.

- *Symbolically*, in addition to what we already know, *horns are an emblem of dominion, authority, kingship, glory, and power.*

  - Horns are used as a symbol of prophecy. In the book of Daniel chapter 7, horns are mentioned, which stand as a representation of actual kings. Since horns represent kings, then we can search deeper into what kings represent. In general, kings are known to have dominion, glory, and power over a kingdom or kingdoms. In the book of Revelation 17:12, we can also see that rising horns are a representation of kings and their power. The only difference here is that they have not yet received their kingdoms but will soon get their hour of authority along with the beast. The mention of the horn in the books of Daniel and Revelation connects to what we know as the end times.

- *Topographically, the horn represents peaks and hills, more so in Palestine* on a topographical map.

  - Research shows that the vegetation within the Palestinian hills strongly supports the growth of olive trees. The oil from olive trees is a representation of the Holy Spirit. This is extremely important because, throughout the Word, we can see that the Holy Spirit is connected to the horn. We know that the Holy Spirit is the "breath within a man that gives him understanding," according to Job 32:8. So with this in mind, let's now overlook the connection of the Holy Spirit to that of a horn, even topographically regarding peaks and hills. If one takes the time to think about breath, it connects us to life. Reason being, is that everything that breathes has life. Visually we can think about a human being connected to a heart monitor. The EKG shows a line that is connected to the heartbeat of the human. As the heart beats, the heart monitor captures it and creates "peaks and hills" within that line for every heartbeat, which ranges in size. The heartbeat is also a representation of existing life. If there is no more heartbeat, the line on the monitor flatlines, which represents a problem—a lack of life and no breath. The peaks and hills represent the life of God—His breath—which is His Holy Spirit. Not only does the oil from the olive tree represent the Holy Spirit, which points to life, but the olive tree itself represents life. Anytime a tree is depicted in the word of God, we can automatically conclude God is referring to life, fruitfulness, and multiplication. This amazingly shows that even topographically, the connection of the horn and God's precious Holy Spirit is still made evident.

Now that we have discussed the meaning of the horn in various ways, let's take some time to discover the meaning of the horn in the tabernacle. We can utilize the information we just learned from this chapter and apply them to the next chapter if necessary.

CHAPTER 11

REVISITING THE TABERNACLE BY WAY OF THE HORN

The use of horns was evident throughout the entirety of the tabernacle and the temple. Horns were found in the outer court and inner court but not in the holy of holies. There is a meaning behind the horns in the tabernacle that God wants us to be able to understand as it applies to communication.

The tabernacle has everything to do with communication with God and the requirements necessary to communicate with God. We are going to see how the horn fits into this. Earlier, we discussed the tabernacle in detail, but it was by no accident that the horns were not mentioned; there was a purpose behind it. I believe that it was necessary to set the horns apart in a chapter for itself, so we can have a study dedicated specifically to the horns only. Remember, the purpose of this book is to connect the horn to spiritual communication. Due to this matter, we are studying from this unique angle. The horns in the tabernacle will be our primary focus for this chapter, so we can see how it connects to communication. It was important that we knew the basics of each part of the tabernacle regarding the furnishings and rituals that were done there to be able to see how the horn fits in to the function of each part of the tabernacle. As we study this, we will see the bigger picture as it pertains to horns, spiritual communication, the tabernacle, and the revealed secret that was there all along. The horns were represented on three pieces of furniture in the tabernacle...one piece of furniture per section. This includes the brazen altar, found in the outer court, the altar of incense, found in the inner court, and the ark of the covenant, located in the holy of holies.

Horns on the Brazen Altar

The brazen altar, which was in the outer court of the tabernacle, was built specifically with the directions from God Himself, with dimensions that were 7.5 feet by 7.5 feet wide and 4.5 feet tall. The brazen altar was the largest furnishing of all sacred items that were within the tabernacle. The altar was set apart for the sacrifices and offerings of the people. God made sure of it that horns were built on the four corners of the altar. Meaning there were four horns included on this large piece of furniture, one horn for each corner. Not only were they a part of the altar, but they were also used as a main part of the sacrifice that was given by the Israelite.

The Israelite had to lift their animal sacrifice to put it on the altar, which had weight, representing the weight of sin. Keep in mind that these animals would resist. They have feelings too and obviously did not want to be sacrificed. It took strength, focus, determination, and the help of others to get the animal on the altar. This is something we go through in life as well. It is not easy to give up sins, sometimes, the flesh wants to overtake the spirit, but it takes perseverance to overcome the resistance that comes from the satisfaction of our flesh.

Once the animal was on the altar, the Israelite would tie it with rope to the horns to make sure it was secured. Think about it, if the animal sacrifice had to be stretched out on this altar and bound by rope or cords, that means its limbs were stretched out across the altar. This is like our Lord and Savior, Jesus Christ, being stretched out across the altar of the cross. He was bound by the nails in His hands and feet as He was sacrificed.

As we learned earlier, the horns represent strength, kingdoms, and power, among many other things. In this case, the horns represent the power of Jesus, which came through His death on the cross. The priest would catch the blood from the sacrifice in a sprinkling bowl and sprinkle the blood upon the horns. Blood symbolizes life. Sprinkling the blood on the horns shows that the blood and the horns are now one, symbolizing atonement. It is through the blood of Jesus that we have become one with God because the blood canceled out the penalty of death for our sins and has given us life. The blood of Jesus has power to save us, deliver us, and set us free from the power of sin. The power of Jesus supersedes any other power. When the sacrificial blood of atonement meets the horns on the altar, we are seeing the Horn of Salvation being demonstrated. This is a depiction of Jesus Himself. Jesus sacrificed His life, shed His blood, and delivered us from sin, giving us saving grace and access to God.

We must also take note of the fact that there are four horns on the brazen altar. Four represents the world, which has four points, north, east, south, and west, which are the four corners of the earth. This is a representation of Jesus on the cross, the cross having four points, He was the sacrifice in the center. Meaning that Jesus has given His life to save the people of the world. If they repent and if they recognize and believe that He died for them and rose from the grave, then they will be saved from their sins.

According to studies, the four horns at the altar have the power to provide the following four provisions to the sinner:

1. "Propitiation—Romans 3:25, 1 John 2:2—mercy seat Hebrews 9:5

2. Substitution—Isaiah 53:6

3. Redemption (Ransom) —Colossians 1:13–14

4. Reconciliation—Leviticus 8:15, 2 Corinthians 5:18."[17]

All of the above is what Jesus, as the Horn of Salvation, has provided to prevent us from receiving the judgment of our sins. Remember, the brazen altar is a place of judgment and also a place of sacrifice in exchange for our sins. "Altar" meaning *lifted up*; we give our sacrifice, and in turn, Jesus is lifted up. When Jesus is lifted up in our lives, we receive the mercy of God through *propitiation*. Meaning we are avoiding retribution from God Almighty, the One who judges. The horns of the altar represent Jesus coming as a *substitution* for us. He came as the Lamb of God and took on the iniquity that belonged to us. He was sacrificed in our place so that we may have life instead of death. We have received *redemption* for our sins. We were once held captive in the darkness of sin, but through Jesus, we have been redeemed and received forgiveness from this place and brought into His light. Lastly, through the sacrifice of Jesus, we have received *reconciliation* with the Father of heaven. We are now made one with God through the power of the blood of Jesus.

We now clearly see that the horns on the brazen altar are a depiction of Jesus and what He did for us. This shows His cause and His cost. His cause was to come to earth in the form of flesh to teach us His ways, understand our ways, save us from death, and join us back to God, the Father. His cost was to give of Himself as a living sacrifice. He paid the price through the shedding of His blood. As the priests sprinkle the blood upon the horns of the altar, we are seeing the power of the blood of Jesus through His death.

Horns at the Brazen Laver at the Temple (Not the Tabernacle)

We described the brazen laver earlier in the book when discussing the tabernacle. Please keep in mind that the horns were not represented at the brazen laver at the tabernacle. However, there were horns represented at the temple. Although we are not focusing on the temple in this book, I believe it is worth briefly discussing the horns in the temple since we are discussing the subject matter of horns. To discuss this, we must look at the entirety of what the horns were a part of before we dive into the study of horns on this sacred piece of furniture. We will start by discussing the main part, which was the bowl that held the water for ritual cleansing.

The bowl of the brazen laver rested upon the backs of twelve bronze oxen that faced the north, east, south, and west by threes. "Three" representing life and perfection, which is what Jesus brought to the people of the world when He died for us. "Twelve" meaning kingdom authority and governmental authority, which shows that He is the one and only true God who has authority over all kingdoms and all governments. Since the bowl of this brazen laver rested upon the backs of twelve bronze oxen, *we can acknowledge that oxen have horns.* We know that horns mean power, but as discussed previously, an ox represents the strength of Israel. The bowl of water resting upon the backs shows the strength of Jesus, who has true authority and that He has power to save. Since there are three oxen facing each direction, we realize that the strength and power of Jesus are perfect and give life to the people of the earth. The fact that the bowl is upon the backs shows that He has exalted us with His power by cleansing us with His blood. When we accept Him, we are strengthened, cleansed, and renewed by His blood and become reflections of He who lifts us up. The word "back" translates to the Hebrew word "achor"—which is "hind side" and "the back part"—God said, "...you will see my back" (Exodus 33:23, NIV), which was the "after-glow of the divine radiance" that followed God after He passed Moses by.[18] This brings us back to the brazen laver being a place of reflection; the bowl of the laver is mirrored and holds water. As the priest looks into the water as he is cleansed and purified through the washing of his hands and feet, he sees his reflection, which should reflect God as he surrenders himself for the service of God. Just as Moses' reflected the glory of God on His face after being in His presence, so too should the priests reflect God's presence. Remember, we are the current day priests, so this means we should reflect Him. Even though the oxen were not represented in the tabernacle, Jesus is still represented at this place because of what the brazen laver represents, which is His cleansing power. His cleansing must be done continuously to keep in communion with a Holy God. It is our duty to maintain the cleansing by staying in His word, which keeps us washed daily.

The oxen are not represented in the tabernacle, more than likely because the tabernacle was a place that was always in movement; it did not stay in a permanent place. If there was too much weight, it would have been hard to move. The temple was made in likeness of the tabernacle. That means all could not be lost, only advanced. It may be possible that the oxen could also be a representation of the twelve tribes of Israel. The horns on the oxen could represent the power granted to the tribes because God set them apart for His purpose. During the times of the tabernacle, the twelve tribes surrounded and camped around the tabernacle at their designated spot. There were three tribes on the east side of the tabernacle, three tribes on the north, three tribes on the south, and three tribes on the west. Since the tribes did not literally camp around the temple, this could be a possibility of why the twelve tribes could be represented by the oxen to serve as remembrance for the covenant promised to the tribes and the generations thereafter if they follow the commands of the Lord. This comes through serving God, acknowledging He is the one and only true God, and maintaining true repentance and true sacrifice unto Him, which in turn keeps the holy, clean, and pure. This promise is for us as well because we have been grafted into His family once we acknowledge Jesus as our personal savior and walk a life of true repentance.

Below the rim of the bowl, there were 300 gourds. Gourds, in a biblical sense, according to research, symbolized "fertility, new life, the arousal of the High God (whose emblem was the Sun) and hope for bodily resurrection."[19] This can represent Jesus surrounding who we are in this walk with Him; we are given new life from Him, "the Son," who was resurrected. We are continually renewed and cleansed through the reading of His word; we are more like Him and are reflections of Him. We can also take note of the number 300. Three hundred is the number God chose when He used Gideon to fight thousands. He downsized the army of Gideon from 22,000 to 300 to demonstrate that their victory could in no way be by the hands of man but only by God Himself. He wants to always get the glory and will share it with no man. He is the only true God who has power to save. He is the High God who stands as God over all gods. Our strength comes from God…not man.

Horns on the Altar of Incense

The altar of incense was the only piece of furniture in the inner court that contained horns. There were four horns on this altar, one horn for each corner. The horns of the altar were touched with blood by the priest when a sin offering was made on behalf of himself and the people once a year. The rest of the blood was poured at the base. The horns of this altar, and the blood sprinkled upon it, were a representation of how the power of the blood of Jesus has given us access to pray to God the Father. We are no longer separated or inhibited from praying directly to Him. Praying is communication from man to God. However, again, we must keep in mind that this access is only granted through Jesus. His blood is the key. The horn is Jesus as the vessel, and the blood is the cost of Jesus giving up His life as a living sacrifice, paying the debt of our sins in full. Through Him, we can be reconciled with God and can communicate in and through the name of Jesus.

Now, as previously mentioned, the altar of incense has a voice. Do you know that the voice comes from the horns of the altar in heaven? Revelation 9:13–15 (NIV) confirms this voice: "The sixth angel sounded his trumpet, and I heard a *voice coming from the four horns* of the golden altar that is before God. It said to the sixth angel who had the trumpet, 'Release the four angels who are bound to the great river Euphrates.' And the four angels...were released..."

It is a mystery as to whom this voice belongs to. We learned earlier that the voices of the martyrs came from under the altar. But this scripture is somewhat different. It says "a voice," which is singular. This shows us that it is different from the many voices of the martyrs. The singular voice in this scripture obviously had the power to loose the angels that held the trumpets. That goes to show this voice belongs to someone who holds high authority in the heavens. Since the altar represents a place of God's judgment, I believe that this may be the voice of judgment. We know that God is Judge, so this may very well be the ruling that comes from God as Judge. The word of God supports this in Isaiah 33:21–22 (NIV):

> *There the Lord will be our Mighty One. It will be like*
> *a place of broad rivers and streams. No galley with*
> *oars will ride them, no mighty ship will sail them.*
> *For the LORD is our judge, the LORD is our lawgiver,*
> *the LORD is our king, it is he who will save us.*

Everything that comes from God has life. This reveals that even the altar of heaven has life. Since it represents His judgments, and since God is the Great I AM, this place can represent Great I AM as the One who judges. In this scripture, we see the Lord is Exalted. Keep in mind that the altar means "to lift up." This can help us to see that the altar of incense is a place of exaltation for our God who judges, where the coal used from the brazen altar is also used to burn incense at the altar of incense; it is also where sacrifice of prayer is released and God is lifted up. As Judge, He has the power to loose what has been bounded. In this case, His orders of judgment were released from the four horns of the altar, loosing the angels bound in the river of Euphrates. Going back to the original thought that He is the voice from the four horns of the altar. This also goes back to what was discussed in the beginning of the book when it comes to the horns of heaven. Remember, God the Father is the Hornist. It is God's mouth that is placed upon the horn (the wind instrument of heaven) to initiate the communication. But the horn itself is Jesus, the Horn of Salvation.

"And I heard a *voice from the altar*, saying, 'Yes, O Lord God, the Almighty, your judgments are true and just'" (Revelation 16:7, NLT).

Now, if we look at this scripture, we see that there is a voice represented in a different way from the altar. It is important to look at the difference between both scriptures. In Revelation 9:13, it says there is a voice from the four horns of the altar, but in Revelation 16:7, it says, "...a voice from the altar." Meaning this is a different voice. This is obviously not the voice of God the Father who judges because this voice is responding to the Lord God Almighty and coming in agreement with God by saying His judgments are true and just. Since we already ruled out that this is not the voice of God, this can be one of three voices, it can either be the angel that stood at the altar, the voice of the martyrs joined together as one voice, or even the prayers of the saints as one voice. Remember, we discussed that there is an angel assigned to the altar of incense in heaven, the one who has the censer and hurled it to the earth after combining the incense with the prayers of the saints. We also previously discussed the martyrs who stood under the brazen altar in heaven. All three representations had a voice at the altar.

The purpose of this chapter is to focus specifically on the horns of the altar. To avoid error and confusion, we briefly looked into the difference between the *voice from the four horns of the altar* as opposed to the *voice from the altar*. The voice from the altar, which represents the angel, the martyrs, or prayers of the saints, is not our focus at this time; we simply discussed this to get clarity. The focus is the power behind the horns of the altar. My belief is that the voice from the four horns of the altar is the voice of God as Judge, and the four horns of the altar are Jesus as the Horn of Salvation to the world.

No Horns at the Ark of the Covenant (He is the Horn)

The ark of the covenant, as previously mentioned, was in the holy of holies. This most holy and sacred piece of furniture contained an atonement cover, but there were no horns in this place. Now keep in mind, the priest would sprinkle blood upon the horns of the brazen altar and the altar of incense. One would think that the ark of the covenant contained horns to place the blood on as well since the high priest would come to this place once a year, bringing forth the atonement blood. Although the high priest would bring the sacrificial blood in the holy of holies, there were no horns to place it on in the most holy place. Instead, it would be sprinkled on the mercy seat that was on top of the ark of the covenant. There was no need for the representation of horns on the ark because He is the Horn; He represents Himself at this place. The mercy seat on the ark is where the Horn of Salvation is seated, and this is where God's presence resides. God's presence is between the cherubim at the ark of the covenant. Covenant, meaning the promises of God, is ever-present. Now through the sacrifice that Jesus made, He is now *seated* at the right hand of God, granting us with *mercy* to protect and prevent us from the judgments of God. We received atonement through and by the blood of Jesus, meaning we are now "at one" with God through the power of the Horn of Salvation, who is seated at the mercy seat. Hallelujah!

As one can see, the horns were represented in each section of the tabernacle, meaning the only way to move forward and get closer to the presence of God (which resided within the holy of holies), there had to be a step-by-step process. Each section required blood on the horns. This means that we can only enter each section through the blood of Jesus. We cannot enter in presumptuously; there is protocol that requires a key. That key is Jesus. When we see the horns, we see Jesus, the Horn of our Salvation. The catch is that we not only have to see and recognize the symbolism of the horns, but we also must take heed to the order of gaining access to get closer to God. Meaning, the blood is necessary to be sprinkled on the horns. It is one thing to see the horns, but it is another thing to sprinkle the horns with blood. We must acknowledge that Jesus came and died for our sins; the shedding of His blood paid the way and paved the way for us to enter in. We must take action on our part to access God, which requires repentance and our sacrifices. We must follow the process of communication through Jesus, which begins in the outer court. We can only get into the inner court after repenting, making a sacrifice that is acceptable in the outer court, and using the name of Jesus. We can only get into the holy of holies if we maintain repentance, make a sacrifice of our prayers and supplication, and recognize that Jesus is the only way.

CHAPTER 12

HORNS USED BY THE PRIESTS (THE WORSHIPERS AND INTERCESSORS)

In addition to working and caring for the temple, priests were also given the task to use an instrument. The instrument utilized by the priests was none other than the horn. Traditionally, they used horns of rams (shofars) and silver trumpets (bugles). Please keep in mind that shofars of the present day are not limited to rams only; they can also be horns of wild goats known as an ibex or wild antelope also referred to as a kudu, etc. It is important to note that shofars cannot come from the horns of cows or anything in the likeness of it. Reason being, is that cows are a reminder of the idol worship that the Israelites performed during the time of Moses. They built a golden calf and began to worship it, which was detestable in the sight of the Lord. The priests would use horns for various purposes. Why? It was a commandment issued by God Himself.

"The sons of Aaron, *the priests, are to blow the trumpets*. This is to be a lasting ordinance for you and the generations to come" (Numbers 10:8, NIV).

If you notice, God didn't say the priests are to clang cymbals, beat drums, or play the harp or lyre, but instead, He said to "blow the trumpets." Now, if God selected the horn/trumpet as an instrument set apart for the priests for service by His instruction and commands, we can know this is an instrument of great importance in the heavens. Remember, the temple on earth is a representation of what is in heaven. God is telling us that the horn is of great significance in the heavens. Since God is highlighting this instrument, it would be best to find out the functions of what the horn was used for by the priests. As we begin to study the functions of the horn by the priests and the tasks and duties performed by the priests with the horns, we will get to understand the significance of the horn through an earthly perspective. This will cause us to further understand the importance of the power of the horn in a heavenly perspective. With this in mind, let's look at how priests used horns.

Horns of Rams Were Used
for Spiritual Purposes

In the Word of God, we can find that the priests used horns at different times for different purposes, like anointing someone. This act could involve using a natural instrument created from God Himself as opposed to an instrument made from man. The priest used the horns of a ram as a vessel to contain anointing oil to anoint people. A ram's horn is also known as the shofar. We can find this specified use in the book of Samuel.

"The LORD said to Samuel, 'How long will you mourn for Saul, since I have rejected him as king over Israel? Fill your horn with oil and be on your way; I am sending you to Jesse of Bethlehem. I have chosen one of his sons to be king'" (1 Samuel 16:1, NIV).

"So Samuel took the horn of oil and anointed him in the presence of his brothers, and from that day on the Spirit of the LORD came powerfully upon David" (1 Samuel 16:13, NIV).

God used Samuel to anoint David as king with a ram's horn, which was different from when he anointed Saul. In the Word, it says that Samuel anointed Saul as king using a flask of oil (1 Samuel 10:1). If we compare the two anointings, we can see that Saul walked in the ways of the Lord temporarily. The Spirit of God departed from him when he allowed the sin of pride to step in. Saul never repented from this sin. On the other hand, David continually walked in the ways of God, fearing Him continuously. David sinned, but the difference is he repented to God so that the Spirit of the Lord would not depart from him. The oil used to anoint Saul was from a vessel that was molded and decorated by man known as the flask. The oil used to anoint David was from a vessel designed and molded by God because it came from His creation, which is the horn of a ram.

Zadok was another priest that used a ram's horn to anoint Solomon, the son of David, as king.

"Zadok the priest took the horn of oil from the sacred tent and anointed Solomon. Then they sounded the trumpet and all the people shouted, 'Long live King Solomon!'" (1 Kings 1:39, NIV)

One may wonder, "Out of all the horns of various animals that could be used for blowing as an instrument, why use the horns of a ram?" Well, God has a special purpose for rams, and the background of this can be found in the book of Genesis through the life of Jubal. Jubal was used in the book of Genesis to advance the culture of humanity through music.

"His brother's name was *Jubal*; he was the father of all who play stringed instruments and *pipes*" (Genesis 4:21, NIV).

Let's stick a pin in the name Jubal because this connects back to rams and horns. The Hebrew meaning of the name Jubal (also known as *yovel* and *yuval*) is "ram's horn." As we can see, God introduced instruments to humanity in the early part of the Bible to Jubal, who stood as the "father of all who play stringed instruments and pipes" (Genesis 4:21b, NIV). Pipes are wind instruments and horns fall under the category of wind instruments. God was hinting from then that the very man He chose to father those who played stringed and wind instruments would have a name that meant ram's horn. With that in mind, we can reread this as "the ram's horn" stood as father of all who play stringed and *wind instruments*. A father is known as someone who is superior, a chief, a patriarch, a founder, a male head, and an authoritative figure. Since stringed and wind instruments were the first instruments introduced to mankind, this demonstrates that this family of instruments ranks the highest of all other instruments. Of this family, the ram's horn is the superior and chief instrument. Due to the backstory of Jubal, we can call the ram's horn the "father of all instruments." With that in mind, we can conclude that the ram's horn is not only the superior and chief of the highest-ranking family of instruments but father of all instruments created. The ram's horn is an instrument that is exalted above the rest. The ram's horn is known as the horn of jubilee or trumpet of jubilee. The root word of "jubilee" is Jubal, which goes back to the name Jubal, who serves as the father of these instruments.

The word "ram" has a meaning as well. Ram means "high, exalted, and supreme." This helps us to further understand that the horn belonging to that of a ram is just that. It is the high, exalted, and supreme instrument because it represents the maker of the horn, Who is our High and Exalted God. He is the Supreme God and Father over all fathers.

The second mention of the ram's horn can be found in Genesis chapter 22. This is when Abraham was on the cutting edge of sacrificing his son Isaac as unto the Lord at Mount Moriah. As he was about to do this, the angel of the Lord stopped him and provided a substitute sacrifice. That substitution happened to be a ram in the bush caught by his horns. Out of all animals that could have been provided in substitution for his son, God chose a ram that happened to be caught by his horns. This was not coincidental but instead intentional as purposed by the Lord. The ram in the bush was symbolic and a foreshadowing of the Lamb of God, Jesus Christ, who would come as our substitute to die for our sins.

As we can see, God holds the ram's horn to a higher standard. That is why it is the God's chosen instrument used by the priests for specific services. It was mentioned earlier that a ram's horn could also be referred to as a shofar. The Hebrew translation of shofar means to have "a sense of increasing, cutting into or burning into," and the root word of it means "beauty," signifying the "beauty of the burning and cutting away that takes place in the heart and soul of man."[20] When the shofar sounds, it draws and pulls on our hearts and soul and catches our undivided attention. It is a sound that calls the soul to a place of repentance. Just like the Word of God cuts away at anything that is unlike God within us through the sword of the Spirit, the sound of the shofar does the same through beauty. The "sense of increasing" is the feeling of urgency, conviction, and alertness we feel within our hearts and soul as the sound of the shofar is released.

The ram's horn that is used to make the shofar is not straight but instead shaped with a curve that signifies a heart that is pliable, moldable, contrite, and humble.

According to research, it is stated that "On Rosh Hashanah the more a person bends his mind and humbles himself by bending in prayer, the better. Therefore, a curved shofar is sounded as an illusion to our bent minds and bent bodies" (Talmud Rosh Hashanah 26b).[21]

Keep in mind that a straight horn is symbolic of leadership and one who has power. This can come in the form of a person, a thing, a kingdom, or a nation. That is why the ram's horn is a chosen instrument of God for the priests because it is where God wants us to be when it comes to humanity. He wants our hearts to be pliable, moldable, contrite, and humble to remain connected to Him. The voice of the shofar causes us to do just that.

Silver Trumpets Were Used for Natural Purposes

As mentioned earlier, the silver trumpets were used as well. The priests used them to call the people to assemble, to warn, to gather leaders, to celebrate, to make way, to set out, and to cry out. Silver trumpets were made by man, but a ram's horn was made by the Creator, God Almighty. Since God chose silver trumpets to be used by priest in addition to the horns of a ram, we know that it must be for a reason. I pondered on why God chose silver as a metal used for the making of the man-made trumpet. I came to find out that silver is malleable. Malleable means that it is a material that can be hammered, beaten, and molded into a different form without cracking or breaking. In other words, it is pliable. Silver was also the most valued metal that was found to be precious in the east, and it could resist oxidation. Gold, on the other hand, must be melted into form without harm. As we know, "bronze" represents judgment, so this meaning doesn't quite fit the purpose of the trumpet for all seasons. God chose silver as the metal used for the man-made trumpet because of its pliability, which parallels with that of the ram's horn; both are pliable. God is emphasizing that He wants pliable vessels and pliable hearts. We must also note that silver trumpets were limited to certain purposes and not made for spiritual warfare or to contain anointing oil, this was set apart for the shofar instead.

In this section of the reading, we have come to understand the importance of the ram's horn (shofar) and the silver trumpets. We discussed why these were God's selected instruments for the priests and the purposes set apart for each instrument. We also know different calls can come from these instruments. Each call has a specific sound. The sounds and calls of the horn are interesting to learn about and will be discussed later.

CHAPTER 13

HORNS USED BY THE WATCHMEN (THE PROPHETS)

While we understand that priests were appointed to use horns during their duties, it is important to note that ram's horns were also assigned to the watchmen as well. Watchmen are those appointed as guards to protect towns, cities, military stations, and kingdoms by keeping a lookout to foresee any coming danger or threats, therefore, keeping those they are guarding safe from potential harm. The Hebrew word for watchman is "*tsaphah*," which means to "look out or about, spy, keep watch, behold, espy, look up well, wait for, to lean forward, to peer into the distance, to observe, await, and watch."[22] All of these are descriptive characteristics of what a watchman does. In short, their assignment is to keep watch and send warning if they have identified danger. In biblical times they were stationed in specific areas that gave them access to see from a higher perspective and to be able to see things from afar; such areas include watchtowers and tall walls. The position of the spiritual watchman is depicted in Habakkuk.

"I will stand upon my watch, and set me upon the tower, and will watch to see what he will say unto me, and what I shall answer when I am reproved" (Habakkuk 2:1, KJV).

In the natural, watchmen are trained with an eye to discern when there is a friend or foe on the horizon. They have to stay alert, vigilant, and are required to communicate what they see quickly without delay. It is the responsibility of the watchmen to send warning by blowing the trumpet to alert the people so they have a chance to protect themselves. If they do not blow their horn to give the people a chance to protect themselves, and the people end up getting harmed, the watchman is held accountable for their spilled blood. There is a plethora of examples of active watchmen in the Bible. Let's look at a watchman on duty to get an idea of their role during the times of King David:

> *While David was sitting between the inner and outer gates, the watchman went up to the roof of the gateway by the wall. As he looked out, he saw a man running alone. The watchman called out to the king and reported it. The king said, "If he is alone, he must have good news." And the runner came closer and closer. Then the watchman saw another runner, and he called down to the gatekeeper, "Look, another man running alone!" The king said, "He must be bringing good news, too." The watchman said, "It seems to me that the first one runs like Ahimaaz son of Zadok." "He's a good man," the king said. "He comes with good news."*

2 Samuel 18:24–27 (NIV)

As we can see, the watchman mentioned above made sure to look out and positioned himself in a high place so he could see ahead, which was the roof of the gate by the wall. He made sure to keep the king aware. We must also understand that the watchman is not always a literal guard on a physical city wall but also a spiritual guard for the people of God's spiritual walk, which we know as prophets, God's seers. Ezekiel was one who was called by the Lord to be a watchman and an actual prophet to God's people. The same way a physical watchman was held accountable for the safety of the people against physical attacks is the same way the prophets, who are watchmen over the souls of God's people, are held accountable if they don't give them God's warning. But if the watchman gives the warning, and the people don't take heed to the warning, the watchman has done his/her job and will not be held accountable if the people choose not to listen. God explained this in detail to Ezekiel before God sent him to give warning:

> *The word of the Lord came to me [Ezekiel]: "Son of man, speak to your people and say to them: 'When I bring the sword against a land, and the people of the land choose one of their men and make him their watchman, and he sees the sword coming against the land and blows the trumpet to warn the people, then if anyone hears the trumpet but does not heed the warning and the sword comes and takes their life, their blood will be on their own head. Since they heard the sound of the trumpet but did not heed the warning, their blood will be on their own head. If they had heeded the warning, they would have saved themselves. But if the watchman sees the sword coming and does not blow the trumpet to warn the people and the sword comes and takes someone's life, that person's life will be taken because of their sin, but I will hold the watchman accountable for their blood.' "Son of man, I have made you a watchman for the people of Israel; so hear the word I speak and give them warning from me."*

Ezekiel 33:1–7 (NIV)

Watchmen over the souls of the people are required to warn the people of their wickedness so they may repent before they are punished with the judgment of God. When they make a warning, they are blowing their trumpets sounding an alarm for the people to act by turning from their wicked ways. The sound of the trumpet from the spiritual watchman is a call to obey the Lord. God always gives warning before judgment, and He uses the prophets, who are the spiritual watchmen, to get the job done.

"I appointed watchmen over you and said, 'Listen to the sound of the trumpet!' But you said, 'We will not listen'" (Jeremiah 6:17, NIV).

That is why it is imperative that the spiritual watchman is in right standing with God, so he can hear the warnings of the Lord for the people who belong to God and sound the trumpet to alert them. That way, they can turn from their rebellion, receive grace and mercy, and live. A watchman can only be effective if he is awake, aware, alert, prepared, and in position. So that when the time comes to give warning, the watchman can do so quickly by blowing the trumpet without delay. In so doing, the people can hear the call and have the chance to obey.

Keep in mind that the use of the trumpet was not limited to priests and watchmen only. The trumpet was freely used by other servants of God within the Bible as well, which we will discuss soon.

CHAPTER 14

THE CALLS OF THE HORN AND THE TRUMPET

Now that we have discussed those who were assigned to blow the trumpets in the Bible, let's discuss the calls that come from the trumpet as they sound it. There are different sounds that come from the horn and different times the horn should be used. The reason being, is that each sound that is released carries a purpose. God gave directives of how to blow for these purposes. In the book of Numbers 10:1–10 (NIV), God gives Moses instructions about two silver trumpets:

> *The LORD said to Moses, "Make two trumpets of hammered silver, and use them for calling the community together and for having the camps set out. When both are sounded, the whole community is to assemble before you at the entrance to the leaders—the heads of the clans of Israel—are to assemble before you. When a trumpet blast is sounded, the tribes camping on the east ae to set out. At the sounding of a second blast, the camps on the south are to set out. To gather the assembly, blow the trumpets, but not with the signal for setting out.*

> *"The sons of Aaron, the priests, are to blow the trum-*

pets. This is to be a lasting ordinance for you and the generations to come. When you go into battle in your own land against an enemy who is oppressing you, sound a blast on the trumpets. Then you will be remembered by the LORD your God and rescued from your enemies. Also at your times of rejoicing—your appointed festivals and New Moon feasts—you are to sound the trumpets over your burnt offerings and fellowship offerings, and they will be a memorial for you before your God. I am the LORD your God."

To simplify what we just read, we can break it down into a bullet point format. In this scripture, God explains when and how to blow the trumpets for specific calls, which include but are not limited to the following:

- When both trumpets are sounded—it is the call to assemble the community at the tent of meeting entrance.
- When a single trumpet sounds—it is the call for leaders and the head of clans to assemble only.
- When a trumpet blasts—it is the call for the tribes and the camps to set out.
- In addition to what is listed in Numbers chapter 10, the horn can make a sound/call to represent the following:
- A sound of rejoicing, celebration, victory, liberty, and freedom.
- A sound to confuse the enemy.
- A sound to remember God's provision and protection.
- A sound to bring breaking.
- A call of going into battle.
- A sound to signal the conclusion of a battle.
- A sound of deliverance.
- A call for people to gather and pray.
- A call to praise and worship.

- A call to awaken.
- A call of returning to God.
- To make way for the Day of the Lord.
- The call to come to safety behind the walls of the city.
- There is a sound that is set apart for calling the people to assemble.
- There is a sound that is set apart to give warning and an alarm.
- There is a sound of the horn that sends a command from the general to the army he leads.
- A sound for a king's coronation and his crowning.
- A sound preparing or making way for God's presence/entrance.
- A sound announcing God's presence is among us.

Rosh Hashanah (The Feast of Trumpets)

In our present day, the trumpets are sounded when the Jews celebrate Rosh Hashanah, which is the Jewish New Year. This time of celebration can also be referred to as Yom Teruah, which is translated to the "day of shouting" and "day of shofar blowing." Rosh Hashanah means "head of the year" and is celebrated for two days. It is said that what a person does during Rosh Hashanah, which is the start of the year, highly depicts what will happen the remainder of the year. It is a time of judgment. Rosh Hashanah is set apart for self-improvement, a time of reflection, and also for prayer. It is set apart as the birthday of the universe, the anniversary for the creation of Adam and Eve, and a time of proclamation, coronation, crowning, and celebration of God as King of the universe.

"with trumpets and the blast of the ram's horn—shout for joy before the LORD, the King" (Psalm 98:6, NIV).

It is also a time of remembrance and importance of the ram's horn (shofar) during the time of Abraham when God provided the ram in the bush in place of his son Isaac because of his obedience. This was done because Abraham was willing to give up what he clung to and thought was important to him because of the love he had for God. Abraham's obedience demonstrated that He wanted to do what God wanted. God's will was more important to him than his own will. Sounding the shofar helps the Jews to remember that time and more.

The sound of the shofar during Rosh Hashanah is a time of repentance, a time to ask Him to grant His mercy and grace from the His judgment, ask for His forgiveness, with the hopes of returning to Him with a whole and complete heart. It is important to understand the sounds of the shofar that are released on this day for the Jews, which consists of four distinct sounds:

- *Tekiah*—one pure sound, one note that is unbroken, or one blast of the trumpet, which represents being whole and complete. It is a strait sound and a note that calls out. This sound causes us to search our hearts, ask for forgiveness, and repent. It is a sound of summoning to come before God and listen.

- *Shevarim*—is three short sounds that resemble trembling; it is the "sigh-like," which is a sound of a cry and sadness. It recognizes any hurt, brokenness, and tears from within or brokenness that we have caused within others. It is a broken sob. A sound that brings someone to a place of recognizing their faults and a longing and willingness to change. To turn from our wicked ways and return to God. Even though it is three short blasts, it is one sound.

- *Teruah*—this comes with nine short wave-like staccato sounds. It is a sound of breaking apart/breaking away and/ or causing damage to something. This is a place of being shattered as pain or hurt overwhelms us. It is a signaling sound and a sound of awakening. It is a wailing. *Teruah* means "shout." To be more specific, it means "a shout or blast of war, a battle or war cry, alarm, or joy."[23] Shouting is something done with one's own voice, and this is the shout of the shofar. In the story of Joshua, the priests and troops gathered, releasing a shout of the voice with the shofar to cause the walls of Jericho to come tumbling down.

- *Tekiah Gadolah*—a single long blast that is uninterrupted, unbroken, and gets louder; this is when we work through the hurt, mend our lives, and get to a place of healing for the hurt we have caused others. It is the place of sincerity of heart and atonement. This is when we reach a place of healing and become whole again. This is the hope of deep-rooted healing where our cry has reached the heavens.

Although some of the sounds released on this day seem to be many sounds and notes, such as *shevarim* and *teruah*, all four sounds are one sound. *Tekiah* is one sound. *Teruah*, a sound of nine short sounds, is one sound. *Shevarim*, three short sounds are one sound. Lastly, *Tekiah Gadolah*, a long unbroken blast, is one sound. All of this shows that our sound and our cry is our voiceprint to God, which comes from our heart, representing ourselves as an individual, an individual that desires to be one with God.

Below you will find some amazing quotes that will help bring more understanding about the meaning of Rosh Hashanah.

The following quote by Rabbi Lewin, a teacher and lecturer on Judaism, explains what takes place within service during Rosh Hashanah. He discusses the number of blasts for each sound and then goes on to explain the themes of each sound as they blow the shofar during each session:

On Rosh Hashanah, one hundred blasts are released, all four sounds are one blast. The notes are divided into five sets. First thirty before Mussaf, ten for Malchuyot, ten for Zichronot, ten for Shofarot, forty at the end of service. Rosh Hashanah has three major related themes:

> *Malchuyot—crowning Hashem King of the World;*
>
> *Zichronot—Hashem remembers our actions and judges us;*
>
> *Shofarot—the day is called Yom Teruah, the day of sounding the Shofar.*
>
> *For each theme, the shofar is sounded.[21]*

The three major themes that Rabbi Lewin describes can help us to go beyond by having the comprehension of how a sound can have significant meanings. By first crowning God as King, then remembering Him as the God who not only acts but also judges. Lastly, by recognizing the day of making sounds with the shofar.

The next quote is provided by an educator by the name of Prof. William Kolbrener of Bar-Ilan University. He explains Rosh Hashanah in a more intimate way as it pertains to him, or better yet, humanity as they make their sounds and cries to God. He goes into what goes on within us and the feelings we have but can't really say by words. He describes being able to release that inner cry through the sound of the shofar:

> *Rosh Hashanah is the day of revelation, God reveals Himself to us through the Shofar, reminds us of the shofar that blew at Mount Sinai, and the Great Shofar that is going to blow at the end of days. It reminds us at that initial blast of air, that God inspirited into man when He created him. So not only do we remember Jewish history, we remember our connection. I've heard people say Shofar gives them shivers, it resonates, it internalizes. The Shofar is supposed to get inside us. It's supposed to remind ourselves of our desire for God. Sometimes we find ourselves in our lives disconnected from ourselves. Feeling just despair about the various commitments that we make*

and the various things that we do that seem to have no real relationship to who we are. And the call of the Shofar is like that feeling of awe or anxiety that we feel in synagogue. That's just a reminder that there is something beneath all of that…

It draws me close to God.

It draws me close to myself.

They must happen at the same time. To get close to God, must first get in touch with myself. So those two things come together and Shofar brings them together. It's in Rosh Hashanah that God encourages us through this Mitzvah of blowing the Shofar to access that part of myself. The sages say that speech went into exile when the people of Israel were in Egypt, at a time when you are enslaved, when you are feeling depressed, when you have no other means, you can't talk, you cry out. So, the cry of the shofar in some sense parallels the cry that an individual feels. As Rosh Hashanah approaches and we anticipate hearing the voice of the Shofar, perhaps we also anticipate hearing our own inner voices. with anxiety and depressed and can't talk. The cry of the Shofar is the cry that the individual feels with the anticipation that we hear our own inner voices.[24]

The shofar is used to sound the voice that we ourselves cannot express in words. It helps us make a sound from our spirit, which is the sound of our heart and the sound of our inner man. Through this section, we should now have a basic understanding of the various calls of the trumpet, how it sounds, and what each call signifies.

Covenant Established through God's Trumpet at Mount Sinai

The first actual sound of the trumpet in the Bible was made by God Himself at Mount Sinai in Exodus 19:16–19. This was when God descended upon the mountain with fire after He had the Israelites prepare for His coming. As He descended upon the mountain on the third day, there was thunder, lightning, fire, smoke, and a loud blast of the trumpet.

"As the sound of the trumpet grew louder and louder, Moses spoke and the voice of God answered him" (Exodus 19:19, NIV). Usually, when a human blows a trumpet, they can only hold a note for so only so long because eventually, they must stop to take a breath. This differentiates from the sound of the trumpet on Mount Sinai. The fact that the sound of the trumpet got louder and louder and did not die out demonstrates that this sound was from a superior being, God Almighty. The sound of the trumpet at Mount Sinai was the sound of God's voice. In the beginning of the book, we discussed God's voice as thunder, but He is not limited to just that; His voice is also the sound of the trumpet. As He blew the trumpet at Mount Sinai, He was making a call to come so He could teach the Israelites His ways.

The trumpet blown on Mount Sinai signified three things:
1. God's never-ending covenant with the people of Israel,
2. the announcement of the union between God (the Bridegroom) and Israel (the bride),
3. the coronation and celebration of God as King over Israel.

This was a place of commitment, where Israel became betrothed to God in hopes that Israel (His bride) would be faithful to Him as their covering. This is similar to when Abraham sent His servant to find a wife for Isaac. The servant found Rebekah for Isaac and gave her a gold nose ring and gold bracelets, promising that her soon-to-be husband would arrive for her. She became betrothed to Isaac once she accepted this offer. This was the announcement of the God as the Bridegroom and stood as a historical moment for the Jews. What took place on the third day at Mount Sinai was the establishment of the covenant between God and Israel. God provided His commandments and promises as the sender and initiator of this covenant, and Israel accepted the covenant as the recipient. Which goes back to the concepts of communication that we learned at the beginning of this book. God as the sender and initiator of the covenant was bound to honor His promises as long as Israel (the recipient) agreed with them and honored them by following the terms and commands within the covenant.

Remember, the shofar automatically alerts and catches the attention of those who hear it, pulling, cutting, and burning into the hearts and souls of the people. His voice as the Bridegroom through the sound of the trumpet on Mount Sinai caught the people of Israel's attention and initiated a response. God gave His commands to them, and they accepted. The people were first terrified due to His power, might, and holiness, but they answered the call with one voice as a bride of the Bridegroom saying, "Everything the LORD has said we will do" (Exodus 24:3b, NIV).

Since God came as the Heavenly Hornist at Mount Sinai, releasing the power of His voice through the trumpet and as thunder, proposing to the soon-to-be bride, and establishing His covenant, He was also setting an example for us here on earth. That means, when we blow our trumpet, we are remembering His covenant and releasing our voice as a response and cry out to Him. We are responding to His covenant that He initiated with us. We are communicating with Him all of our needs because we responded to His call, submitted to Him as our Bridegroom, which demonstrates that we are now under His canopy and submitted to His spiritual authority. The promises He gave us remain true as long as we stay faithful to Him and remain pure.

With this knowledge, we can come boldly before Him, making requests to Him as our provider and covering all things. What concerns us concerns Him as our Bridegroom. That is why we can mirror what He does; we, too, can use our trumpets as an instrument to communicate with Him. Each sound that we release to Him from our earthly trumpet, He will hear and remember His covenant and respond from heaven. But it is all conditional—that condition is to love Him with your whole heart and soul, be faithful, serve Him, and obey Him. That is why He said,

> *"Hear, O Israel: The LORD our God, the LORD is one. You shall love the LORD your God with all your heart, with all your soul, and with all your strength. And these words which I command you today shall be in your heart."*

> **Deuteronomy 6:4–6 (NKJV)**

> *And now, Israel, what does the LORD your God ask of you but to fear the LORD your God, to walk in obedience to him, love him, to serve the LORD your God with all your heart and with all your soul, and to observe the LORD's commands and decrees that I am giving you today for your own good? [...] Circumcise your hearts, therefore, and do not be stiff-necked any longer.*

> **Deuteronomy 10:12–13, 16 (NIV)**

Jesus emphasized this again in Matthew 22:37–40 (NKJV),

> *"Jesus said to him, 'You shall love the LORD your God with all your heart, with all your soul, and with all your mind.' This is the first and great commandment. And the second is like it: 'You shall love your neighbor as yourself.' On these two commandments hang all the Law and the Prophets."*

In the natural, a bride and the bridegroom make a wedding vow to one another before making the final commitment to say "I do," which is:

"I, ____, take you, ____, to be my lawfully wedded (husband/wife), to have and to hold from this day forward, for better, for worse, for richer, for poorer, in sickness and in health, until death do us part."

This vow demonstrates that as a husband and wife unite as one, they are promising to uphold their vow to one another for the rest of their lives. They are promising to be there alongside their spouse through the good and the bad, regardless of what situations may arise. They have become one in all situations. Well, just as the bride and the bridegroom make this promise in the natural, so too do we become one with God in all situations spiritually once we decide to be joined to Him. The commandment found in Deuteronomy 6:5 (NIV), "Love the Lord your God with all your heart and with all your soul and with all your strength," is our vow to God, our Bridegroom. We are saying to Him that when things are great, we will remain faithful and true to Him and love Him no matter what. We are also saying when things aren't so great, we will still remain faithful, true, and love Him with all of our hearts, souls, and strength…no matter what. We then seal the vow by saying the powerful words of commitment to our Lord by saying, "I do."

Once we have made this vow to God by accepting His commandments and come under His canopy of authority as our Bridegroom, we can now come boldly before Him making our requests to Him. We have become one with Him, which causes us to automatically receive His protection and His provision as His bride. We have come in alignment with Him and His covenant that He has given us. When we go before the Lord making our requests to Him, we are staying in communion with Him. As we pray and intercede for others, we are making our voice be known to God. In other words, we are blowing our trumpets to the God who keeps His covenant. You may be wondering what that covenant may be; let's take a deep look at this in the next section.

Remembering the Covenant as the Horn Is Blown

So, what exactly is God's covenant with us? Throughout this chapter, we have gone over the many meanings, sounds, and calls of the horn. The hearer of that horn that we blow is the covenant-keeping God. Due to this matter, we are going to take time to focus on the horn being a sound remembering His covenant. Multiple studies say there are different numbers of covenants that God has given us, varying from five to eight. There is no argument of how many there are. It is all in the eyes of the beholder. I will go ahead and list seven that may be familiar to the masses:

1. *Edenic Covenant (Garden of Eden).* A conditional covenant based on obedience. If Adam obeys by eating only from the permitted fruit, he will live. If he disobeyed by eating from the forbidden fruit from the tree of knowledge of good and evil, he would die (Genesis 2:16–17).

2. *Adamic Covenant (the Promise to Adam and Eve).* An unconditional covenant based on the result of Adam and Eve's disobedience. This was when God spoke to the serpent, Eve, and Adam. The serpent would be made low, crawling on his belly, and will be enemy of Eve (the woman/the church/Bride of Christ) forevermore. The woman will have labor pains during childbirth, and the husband will be her master. The man (Adam) will have to work to eat until the end of his days, and he will return to the dust from which he came (Genesis 3:14–19).

3. *Noahic Covenant (the Promise to Noah).* An unconditional covenant between God and the living creatures of the earth (mankind and animals) based on the result of the flood. He will never again send a flood to destroy all life (Genesis 9:1–17).

224

4. *Abrahamic Covenant (the Promise to Abraham)*. An unconditional covenant between God and Abraham and his descendants. This promise includes the three S's. The *Seed* (he will be father to the nations), the *Soil* (the land that God would give them), and the *Savior* (all the families of the earth will be blessed through him because of Jesus Christ, his descendent, who will serve as the Savior of the world) (Genesis 12:1–3).

5. *Mosaic Covenant/Sinai Covenant (the Promise to Moses)*. Also known as the Law of Moses—a conditional covenant between Israel and God based on their obedience. If the people of Israel obey God's voice, Israel will be God's treasured possession, a kingdom of priests, and a holy nation (Exodus 19:5).

6. *Davidic Covenant (the Promise to David)*. An unconditional covenant between God and King David and Israel based on the faithfulness of God. He will make David's name great; He will give the Israelites a home for themselves where wicked people will no longer oppress them and give them rest from their enemies. He will establish a house for David, raise up his offspring who will build a house for God, and God will establish the throne of his kingdom forever. The house of David and his kingdom will endure forever (2 Samuel 7:8–16).

7. *New Covenant (the Promise to Us through Jesus)*. An unconditional covenant between Jesus and mankind who believe in Him. This covenant is superior to the old covenant, therefore making the old covenant obsolete. In this new covenant, He will write His law upon the hearts of man. He will be their God, and they will be His people. Upon accepting and partaking of the cup representing the blood of Jesus that has been poured out for us (Luke 2:20), He will forgive their sins and remember them no more (Jeremiah 31:31–34), grant them with the Holy Spirit, and receive an eternal inheritance and live forevermore because of the death of Jesus that redeemed them from their sins (Hebrews 9:15).

For the purpose of this book, let's briefly look into God's covenant with us through the Mosaic covenant and the new covenant.

Mosaic Covenant

The Mosaic covenant is about the promises of God that the people of God shall be His treasured possession; they shall be a kingdom of priests and a holy nation.

> *Then Moses went up to God, and the Lord called to him from the mountain and said: "This is that you are to say to the descendants of Jacob and what you are to the people of Israel: 'You yourselves have seen what I did to Egypt, and how I carried you on eagles' wings and brought you to myself. Now if you obey me fully and keep my covenant, then out of all nations you will be my treasured possession. Although the whole earth is mine, you will be for me a kingdom of priests and a holy nation.' These are the words you are to speak to the Israelites."*

Exodus 19:3–6 (NIV)

These promises belonged to them if they obeyed God fully and kept His covenant. This goes to show that the Mosaic covenant had stipulations and conditions; in other words, it was a conditional covenant. God's promise would only be fulfilled if the Israelites obeyed Him completely. The Israelites were to obey His commandments and the establishment of God's law through the Ten Commandments and additional laws, which can be found in Exodus chapters 19 to 24.

The covenant is also expounded in Deuteronomy chapter 11, which discusses that if they love and obey the Lord, they will have strength to take over the land and possess it. He swore that they would live long in the land promised to their ancestors, and it would be given to their descendants. This land was known to be flowing with milk and honey; it is a land that is cared for by God Himself and the rains of heaven. Grain, new wine, and olive oil, and their cattle will be provided for, and they would have much to eat. All these promises were for the Israelites to grab hold of...*if* they loved and obeyed Him.

> *So if you faithfully obey the commands I am giving you today—to love the LORD your God and to serve him with all you heart and with all your soul—then I will send rain on your land in its season, both autumn and spring rains, so that you may gather in your grain, new wine and olive oil. I will provide grass in the fields for your cattle, and you will eat and be satisfied.*
>
> **Deuteronomy 11:13–15 (NIV)**

As you can see, the covenant of God stood strong and if they were faithful, obeyed Him, loved Him, and served Him with all their heart and soul. God continuously reminds them, which is also reminding us, that we must love Him and obey Him with our hearts and souls. When everything is summed up, we can see that it all goes back to staying in communion with Him, being in a one-on-one relationship with Him. If we love Him, then we obey Him; if we obey Him, then we will serve Him. All this really stems from our hearts. If we give Him our complete heart and complete soul, we will be at one with Him. If we are at one with Him, we can't help but continue to communicate with Him.

To communicate with a Holy God, who is our Bridegroom, we see that it takes sacrifice and obedience and remaining free and clear from sin. It is all about the heart, which is why God said that He wants a circumcised heart, where the wall of fleshly ways is removed, and our heart is free from the sin that comes from the flesh. In Psalm 51, David prayed a prayer of repentance after he sinned. He is one who had a relationship with God, and he did not want his relationship to be broken with God due to his sin. Out of desperation, he cried out to the Lord to have mercy on him, to wash him and cleanse him; he acknowledged his faults and asked to blot out his transgressions and iniquity. He did not want the Holy Spirit to be taken away from him, so he pleaded with God not to take His Holy Spirit from him. He also realized that he could have been cast out of God's presence, so he asked the Lord to not do this to him. He also realized the key to receive mercy, forgiveness, and a restored relationship with God was a broken spirit in addition to a broken and contrite heart. He realized that the heart was the connection.

> *Create in me a pure heart, O God, and renew a steadfast spirit within me. [...] You do not delight in sacrifice, or I would bring it; you do not take pleasure in burnt offerings. My sacrifice, O God, is a broken spirit; a broken and contrite heart you, God, will not despise.*
>
> **Psalm 51:10, 16–17 (NIV).**

New Covenant

The new covenant is about the law being fulfilled through Jesus; it is unconditional for those who believe in Jesus. The ministry of Jesus serves as a superior covenant over the old one and includes promises that are far better than the former covenant. He came as the ultimate High Priest of the new covenant. This can be found in Hebrews 8:6–13 (NIV):

> *But in fact the ministry Jesus has received is as superior to theirs as the covenant of which he is mediator is superior to the old one, since the new covenant is established on better promises.*
>
> *For if there had been nothing wrong with that first*

covenant, no place would have been sought for an-
other. But God found fault with the people and said:

"The days are coming, declares the Lord, when I will
make a new covenant with the people of Israel and
with the people of Judah. It will not be like the cov-
enant I made with their ancestors when I took them
by the hand to lead them out of Egypt, because they
did not remain faithful to my covenant, and I turned
away from them, declares the Lord. This is the cov-
enant I will establish with the people of Israel after
that time, declares the Lord. I will put my laws in their
minds and write them on their hearts. I will be their
God, and they will be my people. No longer will they
teach their neighbor, or say to one another, 'Know
the Lord,' because they will all know me, from the
least of them to the greatest. For I will forgive their
wickedness and will remember their sins no more."

By calling this covenant "new," he has made the first
one obsolete; and what is obsolete and outdated will
soon disappear.

I also think it is important to add what Jesus said as He made
the promise of the Holy Spirit, who serves as our engagement ring
until the Lord returns to come back for His bride on that wonderful
day. Jesus promises He will return one day, and the Holy Spirit living within us serves as solid proof that He will keep His promise if
we love Him and keep His commands. We belong to Him, and He
is our Beloved One. He will not go back on His word. The words
of Jesus can be recognized as Covenant as well because He is the
Son of God:

"If you love me, keep my commands. And I will ask the
Father, and he will give you another advocate to help
you and be with you forever—the Spirit of truth. The

world cannot accept him because it neither sees him nor knows him. But you know him, for he lives with you and will be in you. I will not leave you as orphans; I will come to you. Before long, the world will not see me anymore, but you will see me. Because I live, you also will live. On that day you will realize that I am in my Father, and you are in me, and I am in you. Whoever has my commands and keeps them is the one who loves me. The one who loves me will be loved by my Father, and I too will love them and show myself to them."

Then Judas (not Judas Iscariot) said, "But, Lord, why do you intend to show yourself to us and not to the world?"

Jesus replied, "Anyone who loves me will obey my teaching. My Father will love them, and we will come to them and make our home with them. Anyone who does not love me will not obey my teaching. These words you hear are not my own; they belong to the Father who sent me."

John 14:15–24 (NIV)

Now that we understand the covenant, we can reflect on what God means when He says He will remember His covenant with us when we cry out to Him. In Numbers 10:9–10, it demonstrates how the sound of the trumpet is used to remind God of His people. In verse 9, it says if an enemy is oppressing you in your own land and battle is required to sound a blast of the trumpet, God will *remember you* and save you from your enemies during battle. In verse 10, it says during times of rejoicing to blow the trumpet over the burnt offerings and fellowship offerings, and these offerings will stand as a *memorial* for you before God. "Memorial" is a word that represents something set or established to serve as a reminder to someone. In this case, as they blow the trumpets over their offerings, it is representation of the one who offered it to God; in other words, God will remember you. He will also remember His covenant with us as we blow our trumpets. A few scriptures come to mind that can help emphasize God remembering His covenant with us:

"He remembers His covenant forever, the word which He commanded, for a thousand generations" (Psalm 105:8, NKJV).

"He provides food for those who fear him; he remembers his covenant forever" (Psalm 111:5, NIV).

"Know therefore that the LORD your God is God; he is the faithful God, keeping his covenant of love to a thousand generations of those who love him and keep his commandments" (Deuteronomy 7:9, NIV).

In summary, when we blow our horns, our trumpets, when we cry out, when we use our voice, when we shout, it is our sound to God. If we abide by His ways, follow Him, serve Him, obey Him, and love Him with all our heart and soul, He is bound by His word. He must fulfill His promises to us. He is a covenant keeper, and He will keep His covenant if we have remained faithful to follow His commands.

When we release our sound, He understands the meaning of our sound; He remembers His covenant with us and comes in whatever matter that we are in need of Him for. If we are crying out with repentance, He will hear from heaven, remember His covenant, and answer us with His unfailing love, grace, and mercy. If we are being oppressed by our enemies and we cry out, He will hear from heaven, remember His covenant, and will come as the God who delivers and rescues. If our land is dry and famine is prevalent, and we cry out, He will hear from heaven, remember His covenant, and come as the God who provides and send rain to the land. When we are rejoicing, and we praise Him and worship Him with our trumpets, horns, or voice, He will hear from heaven, remember His covenant, and come into our midst because we have prepared the way for His presence to enter in.

Preservation of God's Covenant through the Ark of the Covenant

Since we are speaking of the covenant God gave at Mount Sinai, it is appropriate to talk about ark of the covenant within the tabernacle. Let's first focus on the word "ark." The definition of the ark is "a boat or ship held to resemble that in which Noah and his family were preserved from the flood, something that affords protection and safety."[25] The word "preserved" found within the definition speaks heavily. Reason being, is that the ark of the covenant did just that: it preserved the contents of memories that were associated to God's covenant released at Mount Sinai. The words "protection and safety" are part of what God promised them if the people of Israel obeyed His commands and loved Him.

Not only that, did you know that the papyrus basket Jochebed, the mother of Moses, put Moses in as she placed Him on the waters of the Nile to protect Him from harm (Exodus 2:3) can be referred to as an ark in Hebrew? Just as the Noah's ark protected and preserved his family and the animals, the same went for this little basket that baby Moses was in. It served as a mini boat to protect and preserve Him from the harm that was issued to all Hebrew boy babies. The order was issued to kill them by throwing them in the Nile, but God protected and preserved baby Moses from harm through this mini ark and delivered him in the care of someone that could raise him in safety. This same child would be the same one that God would reveal Himself to at Mount Sinai. God would have a relationship with him, would consistently communicate with him, provide the Ten Commandments directly to him to give to His people, and would use him to guide His people to the

Promised Land. It was this same child God would give detailed instructions to build a tabernacle so that what is done in heaven can also be done on earth so that His presence could dwell with man. So, when we say ark of the covenant, we are also recognizing it as the "preservation" of the covenant because the ark of the covenant preserved the memories of what took place at Mount Sinai. We also see that the ark of the covenant served as solid proof that God is a keeper of His covenant because His presence resides over His promises.

As we know, the ark of the covenant contained the contents of all items connected to what took place at Mount Sinai. The Ten Commandments that were given to Moses, which is the law that God gave to His people to abide by to remain connected to Him, contained the budding staff of Aaron. This was when God said to call the leaders at staffs to place in front of the ark of the covenant, the one that buds will be His choice to lead the priesthood. God, in His infinite mercy, knew that it was necessary to have someone to pray and go before God on their behalf. God made it happen by selecting Aaron as part of the requirements necessary to prepare to have God live among His people, as God promised through the construction of the tabernacle. This also serves as a reminder of God's wonders and miracle-working power among the Israelites and how He delivered. It also contained the manna that serves as a reminder of His provision. The contents within the ark of the covenant were a representation of His covenant that was released on Mount Sinai. That may be why it is called the ark of the covenant.

These items were then placed within the ark of the covenant and covered with the mercy seat, also known as the atonement cover. This shows that these promises are sealed with His mercy and where His presence canopied over them. His presence was also protected by the cherubim. This shows that His presence, His protection, His provision, and His promises are preserved. Man had the access to get to God, just as God promised, at this point through the means of the tabernacle. God also instructed for ark of the covenant to be placed in the smallest room, which is the holy of holies within the tabernacle, a place that only one man could go into…only once a year. This demonstrates how set apart this room was; this is where God dwelled, where His presence gave light, and this was room that stands to be the chambers of the King. This was a place of intimacy that reflected the intimacy that took place on Mount Sinai. He bared all to His people at Mount Sinai, and the room in which the ark of the covenant stood in the tabernacle is where the people of God did the same.

With intimacy, there can also be pregnancy, meaning something is inseminated, incubated, and then birthed after being one with the other person. In the holy of holies, atonement by the blood of the Lamb was granted, and so was God's mercy and grace. There is "At one"-ment. Within the King's chambers, which is the holy of holies, we become one with God; He speaks, we receive, and then we become pregnant with purpose. That is why every time someone enters into His presence and comes out of His presence, they are a new creature; there is an empowerment and a change because they have been filled with His presence.

This is the place set apart for the highest level of communication, and that is being at one with Him, breath to breath, nose to nose, lips to lips. It is a place of complete submission, a private time, where no distractions are around. We worship, meaning we are giving Him worth and giving Him our complete attention. It is a one-on-one moment of an exchange of love. The ark of the covenant symbolizes the covenant between Israel and Himself and helps us to even remember the example of what a relationship is like with Him through the life of Moses.

The Covenant at Mount Sinai Symbolizes Relationship with God

Moses had an intimate relationship with God through His life of submission, obedience, reverence, and love He had for God. God was able to speak to Moses directly and what occurred at Mount Sinai highlights the one-on-one relationship between God and Moses. God was able to tell Moses through a conversation what He desires from His people. At this time, the Israelites became impatient after not seeing Moses for so long because he was still in the mountain with God. Moses was so in-tuned to what God was saying...but their conversation suddenly came to a halt. Just as human-to-human conversation can get interrupted due to distractions, so too did his and God's conversation get interrupted due to the corruption of the Israelites. Remember, distractions are considered as noise, which is listed as the fourth concept found within the seven concepts of communication. In God's omnipresence, God saw what the Israelites turned from Him by making a golden calf that they began to worship. God had to stop giving Moses instructions about His expectations for Israel to address the corruption He was witnessing from the Israelites worshiping the golden calf (Exodus 32:7–8). This corruption caused God to get angry because they were stiff-necked, and He was preparing to destroy the people and make Moses into a great nation (Exodus 32:9–10). Moses began to conversate with God more by seeking His favor by reminding God of the promises He made to Abraham, Isaac, and Jacob. He also made a great case before God in regards Him delivering them from Egypt. Moses was interceding on behalf of the people so that God would not destroy them. This caused God to hear him, remember His promises, and relent from destroying the Israelites.

Even after this, Moses headed down the mountain with the tablets, and Moses witnessed for himself how the Israelites were dancing before the calf. Moses reacted and smashed the Ten Commandments out of anger due to the Israelites' actions and reprimanded them. Moses went back to God to seek atonement for their sin, and God had mercy by restraining from destroying them; however, He did punish them with a plague for what they did. But as you can see, God loved Moses so much that He heard and honored his prayers, had mercy, and even remade the Ten commandments. This is relationship.

It later goes on to say that whenever Moses went to the tent speak with God, the cloud would come down and remain at the entrance of the tent while God spoke with Moses causing the Israelites to worship. In Exodus 33:11a (NIV), it says, "The LORD would speak to Moses face to face, as one speaks to a friend." It demonstrates what a relationship looks like with God and can be like. As we know, friends talk with one another, confide in one another, and are there for one another. This is a part of relationship that God is seeking from us. There came a time that Moses even sought the Lord to show him His glory. God answered his request but reminded him that he could not see his face, only his back. He said, "You cannot see my face, for no one may see me and live" (Exodus 33:20, NIV). God wants us to be able to desire Him as Moses did. Moses wanted to see God beyond their conversation; he wanted to see God in His fullness. God knew Moses could not handle seeing Him in all His splendor because no man can and live. However, God still found a way to grant His request by at least letting Moses see His back, which was still an amazing and glorious sight. That is how awesome our God is. He wants us to seek Him and see Him in a way that goes beyond talking with Him in a casual conversation; He wants us to know Him.

The relationship between God and Moses was so strong and healthy that even after smashing the Ten Commandments, God came down in a cloud before Moses and began to instruct him as He did before. He gave Moses His expectations for the Israelites again by continuing the conversation that they had before. Both God and Moses spoke with one another. God started the conversation again by proclaiming His name and speaking of His compassion, forgiveness, grace, love, and faithfulness. Moses responded by acknowledging the Israelites to be stiff-necked but to forgive them (including himself) and take them as an inheritance. God responded by saying He was making a covenant with Moses and the Israelites (Exodus 34:10) and restated His covenant at the conclusion of their conversation (Exodus 34:27). This conversation lasted long between God and Moses.

Moses was there before the Lord at Mount Sinai for forty days and forty nights without eating bread or drinking water. We see in Exodus chapter 34 that God was Moses' bread and water because God sustained Him and made it evident. By the time Moses and God finished that conversation and the new set of Ten Commandments were written by God, Moses came down from Mount Sinai, not realizing the radiance that came from his face! When we are connected to Him and are in communion with Him, we begin to look like Him, sound like Him, and walk like Him. Moses came out looking like God after talking with God. Moses' face was shining with the brilliance from the glory that came from being in God's presence; the rays of light from his face were likened to actual horns. So much so that the radiance was too much for man to even look at him. It says in the Word of God that the people were afraid to approach Moses.

> When Moses came down from Mount Sinai with the two tablets of the covenant law in his hands, he was not aware that his face was radiant because he had spoken with the LORD. When Aaron and all the Israelites saw Moses, his face was radiant, and they were afraid to come near him. But Moses called to them; so Aaron and all the leaders of the community came back to him, and he spoke to them. Afterward all the

Israelites came near him, and he gave them all the commands the LORD had given him on Mount Sinai. When Moses finished speaking to them, he put a veil over his face. But whenever he entered the LORD's presence to speak with him, he removed the veil until he came out. And when he came out and told the Israelites what he had been commanded, they saw that his face was radiant. Then Moses would put the veil back over his face until he went in to speak with the LORD.

Exodus 34:29–35 (NIV)

The fear that man had for God began to happen with Moses. Man feared to go near Moses after Moses came from the mountain after speaking with God. This was reverential fear. Just like man fears for their life if they were to look upon the face of God, they were fearful of making their way to Moses. Moses was in God's presence and radiated with God's presence. Just like the veil separated the inner courts from the holy of holies where the ark of the covenant was and God's presence resided, Moses had to cover His face with a veil when he was before the people. God's countenance was that strong upon Moses' face, and it was clear to the people that He was in the presence of God. Like the scripture of the priestly blessing, "The LORD bless you and keep you; the LORD make his face shine on you..." (Numbers 6:24–25a, NIV) This scripture is blessing that comes from God through relationship with Him. When we maintain our connectivity to Him, we shine like Him. This blessing is a part of His covenant through the maintenance of relationship. Think about it, the light that was shining from Moses' face was residue from the actual source, which is God. Just imagine if Moses only had the residue and the light was so brilliant and brought the fear of man, how much more brilliant and radiant is the light of God, who is the direct source of this light? It is uncontainable beyond our highest thoughts, but this is God, and this demonstrates His awesomeness, His power, and His might. And even though He has so much power, He desires to have a relationship with us and dwell with us, and in so doing, He will keep and maintain His covenant with us.

When God sounded His trumpet at Mount Sinai, He was making a call to come and commune with Him. In all, as God sounds His trumpet…He is telling us who He is, what He can do for us, and asking us if we are willing to take a chance with Him. If our answer is yes, He just requests a few things from us. If we follow Him, He promises to take care of the rest. He will remember all of His promises, and not one promise will fall to the ground. He is the covenant-keeping God, which is established through relationship.

"For the LORD you God is a merciful God; he will not abandon or destroy you or forget the covenant with your ancestors, which he confirmed to them by oath" (Deuteronomy 4:31, NIV).

CHAPTER 15

MOUNT SINAI (THE MOUNTAIN OF COMMUNICATION)—A DEPICTION OF THE TABERNACLE

The covenant that was released at Mount Sinai is a very important part of biblical history. Mount Sinai is the mountain where the trumpet of the Lord was blown for the first time as He revealed Himself as God of heaven and earth through the sound of His voice. Mount Sinai symbolizes the first place of communication between God and His chosen people...Israel. Not only was this mountain a representation of communication but also a depiction of the tabernacle. This is where God communicated His love and His desire to be loved. The tabernacle is likened to the church being the Bride and God being the Bridegroom. The Bride must go through all steps and all protocols as agreed per the commands of God, which consists of the outer courts, inner courts, and holy of holies.

Outer Courts

At Mount Sinai, God, through Moses, told the Israelites to get ready for His coming. He told them to consecrate themselves, wash their clothes, and abstain from sexual relations. By the third day, He would present Himself at the mountain. Since they were not yet consecrated, we can assume they were in the outer courts.

"And the LORD said to Moses, 'Go to the people and consecrate them today and tomorrow. Have them wash their clothes and be ready by the third day, because on that day the LORD will come down on Mount Sinai in the sight of all the people'" (Exodus 19:10–11, NIV).

The *brazen altar* was evident because they were also told to abstain from sexual relations (Exodus 19:14), which means they had to sacrifice the pleasures of their own flesh. It also represents the place of sacrifice because Jesus died on the altar for the sins of man so they could be cleansed. Consecration and cleansing are symbolic of the *brazen laver*, the place where the hands and feet should be cleansed by the water before performing any holy activities. Being holy, consecrated, and without the presence of flesh is necessary and a part of protocol to be before the Lord, who is Holy.

"Put limits for the people around the mountain. They may not approach or come near it, or they would die" (paraphrased) (Exodus 19:12, NIV).

The limits that were placed around the mountain are a representation of the *outer courts* to those who were standing outside of the limits, symbolizing the gates set up around the tabernacle. We must come with joy through the gates of praise; we must sacrifice and get rid of any flesh and sin that keeps us from Him because He is a sinless God and cannot look upon sin. Because of this, we must accept Jesus into our hearts and believe that He is the Son of God. Through this acceptance, we have been washed by the blood of the Lamb sacrificed at the *brazen altar* and cleansed by the water found at the *brazen laver*.

"Only when the ram's horn sounds a long blast may they approach the mountain" (Exodus 19:13b, NIV).

The ram's horn is symbolic of the ram in the bush when Abraham was about to sacrifice his son. It is also symbolic of Jesus being the perfect substitute and perfect sacrifice, which grants us with forgiveness and mercy so that we may have access to the Father. That is why God said when the rams' horn sounds—they may approach the mountain. This means they have gained access after the sound. This access represents the Door, who is Jesus Christ, the Horn of Salvation. Jesus died on the altar of the cross for our sins giving us access to God. Nothing can come to the Father accept through Him. By the sound of His horn, they were able to approach God at the mountain.

Inner Courts

"And the LORD said to him, 'Go down and warn the people so they do not force their way through to see the LORD and many of them perish. Even the priests, who approach the Lord, must consecrate themselves, or the LORD will break out against them" (Exodus 19:21–22, NIV).

This scripture demonstrates the inner courts; we can see the limitations placed upon the people at a certain point, or they would die. Which is symbolic of the *inner courts*; the Israelites could not enter this place; only the priests could. The people were limited to the outer courts because they could only go to the foot of the mountain, which was symbolic of the brazen altar. The people (Israelites) could go no further than the foot of the mountain. In this scripture, however, we see the priests were able to approach the Lord, but they had to be consecrated. In the tabernacle, only the priests could enter the inner courts, but they had to be consecrated and washed at the brazen laver before entering in or they would die. We also see that Moses was able to intercede at a later point on this mountain for the Israelites, which represents the altar of incense, which is a place of prayer and intercession. The fire that was on the mountain is also a representation of the Holy Spirit and God's jealousy for us (Exodus 34:14, Deuteronomy 4:24, Hebrews 12:29).

Holy of Holies

The Lord descended to the top of Mount Sinai and called Moses to the top of the mountain.

Exodus 19:20 (NIV)

Moses said to the LORD, "The people cannot come up Mount Sinai, because you yourself warned us, 'Put limits around the mountain and set it apart as holy.'"

The LORD replied, "Go down and bring Aaron up with you. But the priests and people must not force their way through to come up to the LORD, or he will break out against them."

Exodus 19:23–24 (NIV)

The top of Mount Sinai is likened to the *holy of holies* because it was a place set apart for the presence of God. The top of Mount Sinai, which is the highest point, but at the same time, the smallest point, is where God presented Himself as a cloud, fire, and smoke. This is where God spoke and revealed Himself. This was a place of intimacy. Not even the priests or the people could come up there, or He would break out against them. Just like the holy of holies in the tabernacle, only the high priest could enter. As we see here, only Moses could be there, and he allowed Aaron to come up with him. Aaron was later going to be God's choice as the first high priest.

The top of the mountain where the cloud of God's glory resided is like the holy of holies because the holy of holies contained God's glory cloud, which was His Shekinah Glory. Mount Sinai also is the place where the Ten Commandments were written and the place where the law of the covenant was established. It is from this place where God extended His mercy to the people. The holy of holies within the tabernacle contained the very same things, and the top of Mount Sinai was the birthing place of it all. Remember, the ark of the covenant contained the budding staff (Aaron, God's choice as high priest), the Ten Commandments (God's covenant), and the manna (God's provision—Moses did not have to eat or drink while on the mountain because God was his provision).

Just as God extended His mercy from Mount Sinai by not destroying the people when they created the golden calf to worship after Moses interceded for them, so too does the holy of holies have a place where God's mercy is released. This is the mercy seat, which is the lid to the ark of the covenant. Just as Moses stood on behalf of the people interceding for their sins, so too does the high priest do within the holy of holies by sprinkling the sacrificial blood upon the mercy seat to obtain the mercies of God for himself and the people.

This clearly shows that the tabernacle, although it was not yet created, was foreshadowed through this occurrence at Mount Sinai. Mount Sinai was a place of communication between man and God, depicting what was to come, which was the tabernacle, a dwelling place for God on earth that created way for communication between heaven and earth. At Mount Sinai, God sounded His horn of communication, initiating a conversation with man, and man responded to the sound.

CHAPTER 16

THE EARTHLY HORN—
THE SOUND OF SPIRITUAL
COMMUNICATION FROM
MAN TO GOD

Speaking of sound, have you ever wondered why a dog whistle makes no sound for us to hear, but the dog can hear it? That is because sound can come in ways that cannot be heard by the human ear. Just because we cannot hear it does not mean that it does not make a sound. Sound also comes in ways that we as a people have become so familiar with that we overlook the magnificence of how it may be heard and interpreted in the heavenlies. In general, we must know that there is more to know about sound that goes beyond our earthly wisdom. God, in His brilliant, splendiferous, and magnanimous power, has an interpretation of sound that is completely different from what we understand or perceive it to be.

Let me ask you this question: the sound of our voice can only be released by means of our mouth, right? Wrong.

As mentioned before, our voice is connected to our mind, thoughts, emotions, and body. So, if our mind, thoughts, and emotions are connected to the sound that we release, then we can also come to understand that our voice can come in this format as well.

In heaven, God hears and accepts our sound in various forms, which you will come to understand later in this book.

Throughout the Bible, we can see a plethora of examples of individuals who were able to come before the Lord and communicate with Him. These individuals received a response from God, yet at the same time, these individuals had their own personal experience when it came to sending a message to God. We can see that sound was not limited to the voice only but by other means. To precisely put it, these methods came by means of blood, sacrifice, prayer, cries, groans, thoughts, tears, worship, obedience, and more.

We must also realize that what God commanded in the beginning of time began first with a thought. This helps us to see that the voice is tied to the mind. The voice and breath are tied together. As mentioned before, the eyes, ears, breath, and mind are tied together. Breath is what gives way for the voice to be released, so this shows that all the listed parts of the body work together as one. Just as we learned previously about the Trinity.

I am reminded of the dream the Lord gave me about the heavenly choir worshiping God with the mouths made of a horn. The horn on their faces is what the Lord wanted me to focus on in the dream. Based on our findings about the horn, it is not just about the audible sound that comes from our mouth during worship that connects us to God. Instead, God is emphasizing what the horn instrument represents in the realm of the spirit; as we found before, it is our tool for communication. The horn represents our communication to God, and that is what God wanted me to see.

Since the dream had a setting that dealt with making sounds of adoration through the choir of heaven in worship, He was showing that the horn is our tool of worship. Worship is our song to God; it is giving worth unto God in various ways. Worship is giving Him the glory; worship is what connects us to God. Worship is our source of communication—it is our horn that connects us from the place we are to the place where God is. Our horn is our method of communication to God. This leads me to discuss one of the main points of this book…and that is the earthly horn.

The Earthly Horn—The Horn for Mankind

The earthly horn is the horn for humanity. It is the wind instrument created by the hands of God (not by the hands of man) that God gifted to mankind from the time they were created within the womb of their mother. The earthly horn is the tool God gave to mankind to make their sound to Him and communicate with Him while here on earth. This horn is like no other horn on earth because it was birthed from God's heart in the heavenlies and placed within the ownership of humanity as the first instrument as they were being formed. This instrument is what connects us with the eternity. The pure sound from the earthly horn comes only by the wind of the Spirit of the Living God. This horn is not only an instrument but also a weapon for mankind to utilize and exercise the power and authority God has given them within the earthly realm.

We can look at it as God creating us first in His heart within the heavens, sending us off to the destination He has for us (the earthly realm), and putting a spiritual phone in our hands to stay connected to Him. During our send-off, we can imagine Him to say these words as He gives us the horn, "Keep this with you…so we can stay in touch." In this chapter, when I speak of trumpets, horns, worship, and the communication from humanity to God, I am speaking of the earthly horn.

To be in a relationship with God, we must stay in communion with Him. Meaning we must continue to communicate with Him through our life of worship. Our horn is our unique sound and voiceprint in the heavens. Our horn is our personal identification and unique identifier in heaven. God desires our worship; in other words, desires us to have a relationship with Him. To have a relationship, we must communicate with Him continuously by maintaining the loop of communication. When we do this, we will have healthy communication with God. That is why God wants to utilize our horn to stay connected with Him. God created us to worship Him and to put no other gods before Him. If we are in a relationship with Him, we will worship Him only, and we would not want to do anything to displease Him if our relationship is true.

True worship requires relationship. Relationship is all about healthy communication. Healthy communication is a two-way stream, meaning there is a message being sent from the sender to the recipient and a response being sent from the recipient back to the sender. It is also a seven-step flow that requires participation from both ends to make it be healthy. Healthy communication contains the loop of communication, which is the response. We originally learned the seven concepts of communication, and we also learned that communication could come in different forms in addition to verbal communication. Since we know this, we can see that God is saying that our communication with Him does not rely on our voice only but on other forms as well.

I believe God is placing a high emphasis on the horn because He wants us to know that our horn keeps us connected. Our horn gets His attention. Our horn reminds Him of the covenant He made with us. He is a God that cannot lie and one who keeps His promises. When we utilize our horn, meaning as we stay connected to Him through relationship, which is our worship, we are connecting ourselves to all that He has promised us...meaning He will remember you and remember His covenant. What I am trying to say is when we release the sound of our horn, which is our means of communication with Him, whether it be verbally, nonverbally, written, visual, or even by how we feel, it is translated into the heavens as our personalized voiceprint—identifying who we are.

All methods of communication are attached to our personal

sound in heaven. Think about our horn being our social security number in heaven. On earth, we use our social security number as our personal identification to get things done. Although a person may use their social security number for various things, such as obtaining their birth certificate, driver's license, getting a bank account, buying a home, getting an education, obtaining a student loan, getting a car, getting insurance, opening accounts such as utilities, just to name of a few…it is still tied to the owner of the social security number. The different sounds you release from your horn are like the different things you do with your social.

You may worship with a message of joy and thanksgiving to God, which communicates to God through your horn as your personal sound and personal voiceprint in heaven, and God responds based on this sound. You may play a physical instrument to worship God, which can come from a physical shofar, a piano, a tambourine, or even that of a drum. This sound goes beyond the sound we hear and is transmitted into the heavenlies as a particular sound from your earthly horn, which translates into your voiceprint in the heavens. No matter what physical instrument you are playing, if you are using it to worship God, it communicates to God through your earthly horn. You may give to a homeless person in need; this is communication to God, making a sound through your horn, causing God to respond to you. You may later communicate to God through body language by laying prostrate before Him at the altar of your church. Believe it or not, this is still communication, which is nonverbal communication. This action turns into a sound released from your horn and is translated into a particular sound in the heavenlies, which catches the attention of God. He then responds based on this message that was sent through your horn, your tool of communication. You may communicate to God by calling out His name, "Jesus," when you need help. This cry is released and turns into a sound released from your personal horn in the heavens, which, again, is your voiceprint. God responds to the sound of your horn by coming to your rescue. No matter what type of message we communicate through our horn, it still transmits as a sound, which is your voiceprint, in the heavens. The power behind the horn is our communication, our oneness, and our connection to God. He wants you to understand this concept. He wants you to utilize the tool that He has given you to stay connected to Him.

That is why God places such an importance on the horn being the main instrument in heaven. All sounds from each horn will invoke a specific response attached and assigned to the sound released from the horn. Each horn has an owner. Although different sounds may come from a horn, these different sounds have different messages, but these sounds are tied to the owner of the horn. Therefore, when you sound your horn, God will know it is you. Each sound from your horn may be different because you may have a different message each time, but there is still one horn tied to you. So, when you sound your horn through healthy communication, He will respond in accordance with the sound you have released. His responses will be different based on the specific sound you have released. But His response to the sound of your horn will always be in response specifically to you or for you.

Our sound is our horn and our God-given instrument here on earth. God places a high priority on the horn, which is the wind instrument of heaven. If we are made in the image of God, then what we do here on earth should be patterned with that which is in heaven. Our horn, also known as our sound from earth, is a high-priority instrument to God and for mankind. Mainly because our horn is our means of communication from us to God. Our communication to God is our earthly horn and our sound. It ascends from the earth and is released into the heavens as our voiceprint. Our earthly horn is what God gave to us to stay in touch with Him by means of communication. The horn for humanity is the God-given earthly horn.

Again, I just want to reiterate that there is something special about the sound of the horn and/or wind instrument in heaven. Wind instruments seem to take priority over any other instrument in heaven when it comes to sound. As we previously learned, the ram's horn, also known as the trumpet, is the father of all other instruments. In the heavenly vision the Lord gave to me, the horn that was in the place of where the mouth should be in the choirs of heaven shows that God is emphasizing that the horn is the mechanism used to release our sound. But keep in mind that our voiceprint in heaven is not limited to our literal voice on earth. Our voiceprint in heaven is our horn and is tied to all methods of communication here on earth, which goes beyond our audible voice. Meaning, our feelings, thoughts, and emotions, our verbal, nonverbal, written, and visual communication to God, are all translated into one method in heaven...which is our heavenly voiceprint.

300 Trumpets of the Army of Gideon

We just talked about the ram's horn, also known as the trumpet, being the father instrument of all instruments. We also talked about the horn being the instrument of communication between humanity and God. We also learned previously horns signify power, dominion, and authority. With this knowledge, we are going to see how the word of God backs up what we now know about trumpets and communication. Let's see how people within the Bible utilized their earthly horn while communicating to God. The first story that comes to mind where trumpets and communication are amazingly used is in the story of Gideon.

In the story of Gideon found in Judges chapters 7 and 8, God used an army of three hundred warriors with three hundred trumpets in hand to defeat the Midianites. God clearly tells Gideon, "With the three hundred men that lapped I will save you and give the Midianites into your hands. Let all the others go home" (Judges 7:7, NIV). As we read on, we can see that emphasis is being placed on the trumpets throughout these two chapters in separate instances. It begins first when the scripture specifically singles out the trumpets when God downsized the warriors from 22,000 to 300. Judges 7:8 (NIV) says, "So Gideon sent the rest of the Israelites home but kept the three hundred, who took over the provisions and trumpets of the others." Why would it not say "provisions" only, without singling out the trumpet? The reason why is that the God wants us to pay close attention to the trumpet in this passage.

Here's why. God told Gideon that He would use the three hundred to give the Midianites into the hands of Gideon. We know that God's statement of giving the Midianites "into his hands" means giving him victory naturally. But God also wants us to see symbolically what Gideon placed into the hands of these men, which is a trumpet (horn), representing power, dominion, and authority. Meaning God gave Gideon and the three hundred men the power, dominion, and authority to defeat the Midianites. The Lord allowed Gideon to hear a dream from one of the men in the camp of Midian as well as the interpretation, which confirmed what God had already told him. In turn, Gideon bowed and worshiped God in reverence. After Gideon did this, he provided the three hundred men with trumpets as he obeyed the voice of the Lord. He realized the importance of the trumpet.

> When Gideon heard the dream and its interpretation, *he bowed down and worshiped.* He returned to the camp of Israel and called out, "Get up! The LORD has given the Midianite camp into your hands." Dividing the three hundred men into three companies, *he placed trumpets* and empty jars *in the hands of all of them*, with torches inside.
>
> **Judges 7:15–16 (NIV)**

In this scripture, we can see that once God gave Gideon instruction, Gideon immediately obeyed. God did not literally tell Gideon directly to get a trumpet to blow, but Gideon understood the symbolism of the trumpet and how it relates to the promises of God, which are everlasting. Gideon remembered the ordinance God gave to Moses long ago about the sounding of the trumpets, which we previously discussed in the chapter titled "Calls of the Horn and the Trumpet." But let's refresh our memory.

In Numbers 10:9 (NIV), God says, "When you go into battle in your own land against an enemy who is oppressing you, sound a blast on the trumpets. Then you will be remembered by the LORD your God and rescued from your enemies."

This ordinance was given to Moses, but God said that it should be a lasting ordinance for generations to come. Meaning that promise was for the Israelites during the time of Moses and for the Israelites that were to come. Gideon was an Israelite. Gideon understood that promise was for him and his people as well. With that in mind, Gideon followed the ordinance God gave to Moses and used it for his time too because he knew God's promise was still as true and effective as it was from back then. God's word never returns to Him void. Gideon was using the trumpet as a tool for communication to God as a symbolic demonstration for God to remember His promise. They were going into battle with the op-pressor (Midianites), and they were sounding the trumpet so God would remember His promise, remember them, and rescue them from their enemies. And that God surely did.

Gideon remembered God's promises and took action by uti-lizing the trumpet. Gideon obeyed God's instruction based on the ordinance that God gave long ago. He also obeyed God by using the three hundred men that God chose by sending the rest of the men home and by going to the Midian camp to attack. In addition to that, He obeyed God when God said to go to the Midian camp and listen to what they were saying to be encouraged. He was indeed encouraged after overhearing the men just as God promised. Upon this, Gideon bowed to God and worshiped him. All of this shows that Gideon was able to hear clearly from God because he was connected with God.

God's desire for us is to submit to Him, worship Him, and stay in communication with Him. This passage shows that Gideon was in right standing with God and maintained healthy communication with Him, as God desired. I say healthy communication because there was a message sent, a response given, and then the loop of communication continued. God initiated the conversation, and Gideon responded through obedience. After getting confirmation that God would give the Midianites into his hand, Gideon told the men that when he blew his trumpet, they were to do the same and shout, "For the Lord and for Gideon."

Since we are focusing on trumpets and communication in this section, let's see what happened when the trumpets of the three hundred men were sounded:

> *The three companies blew the trumpets and smashed the jars. Grasping the torches in their left hands and holding in their right hands the trumpets they were to blow, they shouted, "A sword for the LORD and for Gideon!" While each man held his position around the camp, all the Midianites ran, crying out as they fled.*
>
> *When the three hundred trumpets sounded, the LORD caused the men throughout the camp to turn on each other with their swords.*
>
> **Judges 7:20–22a (NIV)**

> *Thus Midian was subdued before the Israelites and did not raise its head again. During Gideon's lifetime, the land had peace forty years.*
>
> **Judges 8:28 (NIV)**

Victory was granted to Gideon and the Israelites because God delivered the Midianites into his hand, just as the Lord promised. God used the sound of three hundred trumpets to cause the Midianites to fight amongst themselves with their own swords. This sound caused Gideon and his men to win the battle bringing deliverance to the Israelites. Gideon realized the promises of God, understood what was required on his part for the promises to be fulfilled. He remembered what God commanded about the trumpet, and because of his knowledge and obedience, he was on the winning side. God said that He would give the Midianites into his hand and confirmed His word through the dream of someone in the Midianite camp to encourage Gideon. That's all that was needed. Upon this, Gideon made the next steps by banking on the promises God gave long ago about the trumpet while also taking action on his part to pursue the Midianites with the three hundred men that God gave him, knowing that God backed him and his men up.

The placement of the trumpet was not coincidental either; the mere fact that it was in the right hand of the men means empowerment. Empowerment means to give someone authority, control, and power over something, which goes back to the significance of a horn. Gideon knew they had been empowered by God and were granted with victory from God. Gideon and his men also used their shout, which also serves as a wind instrument and trumpet given by God to the human body. The Word also says, "... each man held his position around the camp" (Judges 7:21, NIV), meaning they took their God-given position of being conquerors and victorious. Gideon took the stance of victory because he was confident that God would deliver what He promised. Gideon and his men sounded their earthly horns, and God remembered them.

With this, we can remember that God does not necessarily have to tell us step-by-step what needs to be done for His promises to come to pass because He already did through His word, which still stands strong today. He wants us to come to the point of knowing from the tools He has given us. His word serves as a perfect manual that is always true. He wants us to take the position of authority and power; and know that because we serve Him, His promises are for us. If we are made in His image, we are victorious; we must take in hand His promises, be knowledgeable of His promises, obey, and utilize the tools He has given us to be victorious. The trumpet is our tool of communication with God that brings victory if we stay connected to God. If we blow our trumpets, meaning stay in communication with Him, He will remember us and remember His promises to us, which include His power, provision, protection, and presence.

Seven Trumpets, Seven Priests, Seven Days, and the Fall of Jericho

Again, the earthly horn is God's tool He has given to humanity for us to communicate with Him, and as we sound our horn, it is a reminder of God's covenant both to God and man. We see the power of God during the time of Gideon and how the sounding of trumpets caused confusion in the camp resulting in the victory of the Israelites. Keep in mind that we are still discussing trumpets and communication. Let's discuss another story that took place before the times of Gideon, where the trumpets were used as means of communication to God, which is Joshua and the Fall of Jericho, found in the book of chapters Joshua 5 to 6.

In the story of the fall of Jericho, God appeared first as a man with his sword drawn in hand to Joshua. Joshua then discovered that he was the commander of the Lord's army. The setting of this was near Jericho, a place that was highly secured by gates that prevented people from going in and out. During this encounter, Joshua worshiped by reverentially falling faced down to the ground. This reminds me of how Gideon gave reverence to God by worshiping Him after receiving confirmation of what God said He would do.

Joshua's actions of worship demonstrated that there was healthy communication between him and God. The Lord went on to tell Joshua that he delivered Jericho, the king, and fighting men into his hands. He then provided Joshua with a strategy that included the use of trumpets of rams' horns:

> *Then the LORD said to Joshua, "See, I have delivered Jericho into your hands, along with its king and its fighting men. March around the city once with all the armed men. Do this for six days. Have seven priests carry trumpets of rams' horns in front of the ark. On the seventh day, march around the city seven times, with the priests blowing the trumpets. When you hear them sound a long blast on the trumpets, have the whole army give a loud shout; then the wall of the city will collapse and the army will go up, everyone straight in."*
>
> **Joshua 6:2–5 (NIV)**

As we can see, this scenario is slightly different from Gideon's. In this story, God told His servant Joshua that He was giving the enemy Jericho into his hand and gave him specifics of how to conquer it. With Gideon, however, God only told him that He had given the enemy to Gideon without providing any further direction of how to conquer the enemy. Many scholars may have their reasoning behind the difference, but I believe that God gave specifics to Joshua because he was operating under the mantle of Moses, whose life was used to demonstrate God's wonders and establishment of God's Mosaic covenant.

Moses and Joshua were during the same dispensation. God was still making it known in the sight of man that He, the God of Israel, is the only true God. History was still being written during the timeframe the Mosaic covenant was released about how the God of Moses was faithful and delivered them, directed them, and provided for them as a demonstration of God's might and power so that future generations could hold fast to this. The establishment of God and His law was still fresh during the times of Moses and Joshua; they were still learning. During the time of Moses and Joshua, everything was taught directly by God and documented step-by-step in real-time so that those coming after would know the right way based on the recorded teachings of God. Joshua was operating during the same dispensation as Moses. He was maintaining all that was established and all that was still being established by God, so it required God's specific direction because it was still being established with man on earth.

However, Gideon's walk was during a different dispensation; he was a part of the "future generations" that relied on the teaching of God that Moses already laid out. During the times of Moses, God was revealing presently, and the people learned and followed what He was revealing at the moment. During the times of Gideon, God had already revealed these things and already moved in wonders during the times of Moses and made His power and might known before the Israelites and to the enemies of Israel. God's fame became prevalent by the wonders He continuously performed. So, Gideon went by what was revealed to his ancestors. The laws of Moses provided a reference to follow, and Gideon simply followed it. God did not need to do it repeatedly because it was already written and taught to generations thereafter. God still maintained that covenant. That is why Gideon referred to God's wonders in Egypt when the angel told him that he would save Israel out of Midian's hand. Gideon was aware of God and His might, based on the law and what took place with His ancestors.

I know we detoured slightly, but it is relevant to discuss so that we can understand why God gave specifics to Joshua and not to Gideon. To Moses, God gave the ordinance of the trumpets and promises that come with the trumpets (Numbers chapter 10). To Joshua, God demonstrated the promise that God taught Moses about the trumpets (Joshua chapter 6) so that future generations could be confident of its truth and use it as remembrance and memorial for what God has done. To Gideon, God maintained the promise of the trumpets (Judges chapter 7). Meaning, God gave the directions to Moses. God orchestrated for the ordinance of the trumpets to be applied in the fall of Jericho during Joshua's time and demonstrated the promise of the trumpets through His wonders again when Joshua followed God's direction. Gideon believed the promise given to Moses was ensured by how that promise was applied during the times of Joshua and automatically obeyed the promise by applying it to his time because he knew how God moved powerfully with the trumpets in the lives of his ancestors.

So how exactly did God move during the times of Joshua with the trumpet? Let's go back to the story. Joshua obeyed and had seven priests blow the trumpets of rams' horns, which means there were seven trumpets that were blown. We know rams' horns are not created by man but by God and represent bending to the will of God. Man was bending to the will of God because they could not do anything by their own strength—it had to be by the strength of God. God specified "seven" because He was completing the promise of delivering Jericho into His hands. He did this by using those set apart for His service to lead in the blowing of trumpet, and He also saw that it was necessary for the ark (meaning God's presence) to be among them. The priests were blowing the trumpets, making way, and making an announcement of the King who has complete power to do the impossible and is true to His promises.

The presence of the ark means that His presence, containing His manna, His law, and the staff, is represented as a remembrance of the covenant He has with Israel. This means that all God says shall come to pass with completion, and it will be by His wonders, which came through the sound of the horns. The armed guard marched in front of the priests, and the rear guard followed behind the ark. The heavenly protectors, the cherubim, were in position, enthroning God's holy presence within the ark. The earthly protectors, which were the armed guard and rear guard, were in position enclosing the holy things (the priests and the ark) within. They marched around for seven days, with seven priests and the blowing of seven trumpets; on the seventh day, they marched around the city seven times. Everything is seven because God was about to complete a mighty work. Here's what happened when the trumpets sounded as the Lord directed...

> *When the trumpets sounded, the army shouted, and at the sound of the trumpet, when the men gave a loud shout, the wall collapsed; so everyone charged straight in, and they took the city. They devoted the city to the LORD and destroyed with the sword every living thing in it—men and women, young and old, cattle, sheep, and donkeys.*

> **Joshua 6:20–21 (NIV)**

God did it! God caused the walls of the city of Jericho to collapse just as He promised by the sound of the earthly horn. A fortified wall came tumbling down supernaturally, all by sound. The sound of the earthly horn in the story of Joshua consists of both the trumpet from the horns of rams and from the trumpet from the shout of their mouths. God gave Joshua and the Israelites the power to conquer what seemed to be a stronghold. God made the impossible possible by demonstrating His wonders! God made it clear to the Israelites and the people of Jericho that He was with the Israelites when they obeyed by blowing their earthly horns. This sound was more than the physical sound of the trumpet; this sound was their earthly horn because this was the sound of communication from man to God. God heard, remembered them, and remembered His covenant with them. When they sounded their horns, God responded to their sound with action by causing the walls of Jericho to come down. This reminds me of when the veil was torn in the temple from top to bottom once Jesus finished His work as a man on earth. Only God could do such a thing.

It is also important to discuss when God directed Joshua to have the priests sound a long blast and shout. As we reflect on what we learned about the calls of the trumpet, we can see that sounding a long blast of the trumpet is Tekiah Gadolah. Tekiah Gadolah is the sound of atonement, being one with God, and a place of connection and wholeness with God. "Wholeness" meaning completion, which goes back to the number seven. This is where man has cried out, and God hears and answers. The shout that Joshua and his men released was also significant; our shout is our cry of joy; this is a sound of victory and triumph. Joshua and his men were empowered to get victory over the enemy. The sons of Korah wrote Psalm 47, which can also be applied to what took place at the fall of Jericho; it says, "Shout to God with cries of joy. For the LORD Most High is awesome, the great King over all the earth. He subdued nations under us, peoples under our feet" (Psalm 47:1b–2, NIV).

"God has ascended amid shouts of joy, the Lord amid the sounding of trumpets" (Psalm 47:5, NIV).

"For God is King of all the earth; sing to him a psalm of praise. God reigns over the nations; *God is seated on his holy throne.* The nobles of the nations assemble as the people of the God of Abraham, *for the kings of the earth belong to God*; for He is greatly exalted" (Psalm 47:7–9, NIV).

Although this scripture was possibly written at a different time, it accurately explains what happened during the times of Joshua. "God has ascended amid shouts of joy…and the sounding of trumpets" in the above scripture is likened to God being exalted through the shouts of Joshua's army and the sounding of trumpets from the priests in Joshua chapter 6. In the above scripture, where it says, "God is seated on his holy throne," it can be likened to

God's presence hovering over the mercy seat of the ark that was carried while they marched around the wall. Where it says, "for the kings of the earth belong to God," it is likened to the king within Jericho being handed over to Joshua. Amazing!

So here are two stories of two leaders (Gideon and Joshua) that guided their men to blow their trumpets and shout. These were two men who experienced the promises of God come to pass as they followed the ordinance of the trumpets. God empowered both to do His mighty exploits, all by their obedience and by their use of the trumpet. They were connected to God, and God came in His completeness by defeating the enemy and giving them victory. God gave man authority to have power, dominion, and authority, and He expects us to know who we are and exercise the authority by using our God-given wind instrument, our earthly horn, which is our sound and our cry and our tool of communication to God. When we blow it, God hears from heaven, remembers us and His covenant with us, and responds to the call of the one who releases the sound.

We have just journeyed into the lives of two men who used their earthly horns to communicate with God. Even though they used physical trumpets to communicate with God, it still represented an earthly horn based on its symbolism because they were connected to God, and it was what they used to communicate with God. They held on to the ordinance God gave to Moses; they were confident of God's power and His faithfulness to back up what He said He would do, and they applied it to their lives and situations. Now let's take this ordinance of the trumpets, be confident that He will remember us and that He will be faithful to His covenant with us, and then let's apply it to our lives and our situation. This will be discussed in the next chapter which is about sounding your earthly horn.

CHAPTER 17

THE EARTHLY HORN IS THE SOUND OF MAN'S HEART

"As she kept on praying to the LORD, Eli observed her mouth. Hannah was praying in her heart, and her lips were moving but her voice was not heard..." (1 Samuel 1:12–13, NIV)

This is the prayer of Hannah as she was asking the Lord to bless her with a son. Eli, the priest, saw what happened but did not understand, but it was not for man to understand. Although her voice could not be heard from her lips, God understood because her prayer was from her heart. Her sound came from her heart.

As we know, sound is more than what we audibly hear. We previously talked about how our sound from earth to heaven is not always dependent upon a literal sound. Our sound on earth is not limited to our voice, but it is more about our various ways of communicating with Him, which can be inwardly and outwardly verbal, nonverbal, written, and visual. All these methods of communication are sent to the heavens and translated into our heavenly voiceprint. These methods of communication from man to God are our earthly horn. When we sound our horn, God hears us from heaven and remembers us. God wants to understand the power that He has given us on earth by way of our horns. I must reiterate that we were made in the image of God, one who has all power, all authority, and all dominion both on heaven and on earth. Since we were made in His image, we must also know that God has given us the same power, authority, and dominion here on earth. However, some of us don't know who we are yet in God. God desires us to come to a place of knowing.

In this chapter, we are going to discuss the earthly horn beyond what we would expect it to be. Before, we talked about horns based on the presence of the literal words "horn," "trumpet," "shout," "voice," "sound," and "cry" being made known in the scripture. Our discussion of horns was also based on the actual man making a sound that can be heard amongst other individuals or what can be seen by other individuals. But what about when those actual words are not present? What about when sounds are made that cannot be heard by another individual or seen by another individual? Does it mean that the horn is not depicted? By all means, no. So, if we know that the earthly horn is our method of communication from man to God, and if we are aware that it is not limited to one method and one form, then that means there is more to this than what our ears can hear and what our eyes can see.

Think about it, when we say something with our voice or blow the trumpet, there is more to it than the result, which is the audible sound. There is a process that took place that cannot be seen or heard before the actual sound was released. Sound is the result of something that already was. There is something that happened inwardly within an individual for the sound to be released outwardly. With that in mind, we are going to not only talk about the horn that can be heard naturally. We are also going to talk about the horn based on an individual inwardly, which eventually results of the horn being expressed outwardly.

First Peter 3:3–4 (NIV) says, "Your beauty should not come

from outward adornment, such as elaborate hairstyles and the wearing of gold jewelry or fine clothes. Rather, it should be that of your inner self, the unfading beauty of a gentle and quiet spirit, which is of great worth in God's sight."

The above scripture refers to beauty from within a person rather than what is seen outwardly. The same concept is used when referring to sounds that come from our earthly horn. Sound begins internally and is expressed outwardly in multiple ways. Even though there are multiple ways to communicate with God using our earthly horn, there is one important detail that I saved for this part of the book, which is what our heavenly voiceprint is tied to. Here it goes…

Our earthly horn and our heavenly voiceprint are one in the same, but the foundation and seed of it all is our heart and the voice that comes from it. Since our earthly horn is our heart, it is proven to be the wind instrument of eternity because God has set eternity in our hearts.

Our earthly horn is the sound of our heart. Our heavenly voiceprint is the sound of our heart. When we sound our earthly horn, our heart is speaking. Ecclesiastes 3:11 says that God has set eternity in our hearts, which means we have access to be connected to the Eternal God if our heart is connected to Him. God only looks and understands the heart. The various methods of communication from man to God by way of the earthly horn are simply the different expressions of the sound of our heart from man to God. Our thoughts start from our heart, our cries start from our heart, and our actions start from our heart. The communication from man to God must involve the heart. That is why God says, "And now, Israel, what does the LORD your God ask of you but to fear the LORD your God, to walk in obedience to him, *to love him*, to serve the LORD your God *with all your heart* and with all your soul" (Deuteronomy 10:12, NIV). If the heart is not involved, we are not effectively communicating with God. Which further means our earthly horn is not being utilized and our heavenly voiceprint is not being utilized. If our hearts are not there, then what we believe to be communication from us to God is in vain. Our heart is the key to everything.

If we say we worship God, but our hearts are not there…God does not accept this, and our communication is all for naught. If we pray, but our hearts are not there, it is useless. If we are doing the works of God, but our hearts are not there, then we are only empty shells. If we say we love Him, but our hearts are not there, it is meaningless. Our hearts are tied to love.

First Corinthians 13:1–3 (NIV) speaks of this clearly,

> *If I speak in the tongues of men or angels, but do not have love, I am only a resounding gong or a clanging cymbal. If I have the gift of prophecy and can fathom all mysteries and all knowledge, and if I have a faith that can move mountains, but do not have love, I am nothing. If I give all I possess to the poor and give over my body to hardship that I may boast, but do not have love, I gain nothing.*

When our hearts are missing from the puzzle, that means we are not utilizing our earthly horn in the way it was purposed to be used. That means our heavenly voiceprint is not being used in the heavens. The earthly horn and heavenly voiceprint are only activated if the heart is connected to them. Healthy communication with God means our hearts are connected with God, which also means our earthly horn is in use and our heavenly voiceprint is in use. When our horn is connected to God by means of the heart, that means our earthly horn is activated, making our voiceprint actively heard in the heavens. When this happens, God hears our horn, our voice, and our heart and remembers us and His promises to us and makes His response. That is why God said in 2 Chronicles 7:14 (NIV), "If my people, who are called by my name, will humble themselves and pray [...] and turn from their wicked ways, then I will hear from heaven, [...] and heal their land." This scripture contains a condition: they must be God's people, they must be called, they must be humble, they must pray, they must repent... when this happens, God hears and will heal whatever circumstance or situation that His people may be in. The scripture starts with "If my people..." Well, who are His people? The answer is Israel. We may think that God is referring to Israel, the nation alone, but He is also referring to the spiritual Israel. Romans 9:6b (NIV) says, "For not all who are descended from Israel are Israel." Romans 2:28–29 (NIV) also says,

> *A person who is not a Jew who is one only outwardly, nor is circumcision merely outward and physical. No, a person is a Jew who is one inwardly; and circumcision is circumcision of the heart, by the Spirit, not by the written code. Such a person's praise is not from other people, but from God.*

This scripture also solidifies and supports what we discussed earlier about how God looks at the inward, which is where the heart is found...not the outward appearance that is usually judged by people. The next part of 2 Chronicles chapter 7 that I want us to focus on is when God says, "Called by my name," meaning they belong to Him. Those who are called are those who have heard His call to come to Him, love Him, and live for Him by accepting Him into their hearts. The scripture says, "You did not choose me, but I chose you and appointed you so that you might go and bear fruit—fruit that will last—and so whatever you ask in my name the Father will give you. This is my command: Love each other" (John 15:16–17, NIV). He called us and appointed us to multiply His kingdom on earth, which is the domain that He has given us as authority over. So that when we pray, whatever we ask through communication with Him, He will hear from heaven, and it will be granted by Him. But He requires that we do this in the name of Jesus and from our heart. That is why God continued this word by saying, "This is my command: Love each other" because for us to receive the promises, we must have love...which requires our heart.

God looks inward and communicates with mankind inwardly through the heart. That is why during the time God rejected Saul as king and had David anointed as the next king, God said to Samuel, "Do not consider his [Saul's] appearance or his height, for I have rejected him [Saul]. The LORD does not look at the things people look at. People look at the outward appearance, but the LORD looks at the heart" (1 Samuel 16:7, NIV). God can only understand our ways by way of our heart, which is why when we communicate with God, it must be inwardly. Our communication to God must be from our heart. This all comes through healthy communication from man's heart to God's heart, which is our earthly horn.

Physically, the heart keeps blood flowing and pumping throughout the body. It is the supplier of nutrients and oxygen to our tissues and rids us of carbon dioxide. The heart is the sustainer and maintainer of our life. If the heart dies, so does the body; we need our heart to maintain our life. If the body dies, there is no breath. We need to breathe to survive. We need our heart to breathe. The heart is the most important organ. That is why God created this organ first and gave it a sound when He created us because it is the core of our survival naturally and is symbolic as the core of survival spiritually—everything we do is dependent on the heart.

Proverbs 4:23 (NIV) says, "Above all else, guard your heart, for everything you do flows from it."

The pumping of the heart keeps us alive and gives us the oxygen we need to breathe so we can survive naturally. The pumping shows that the heart is active. As long as our heart pumps... our sound is heard. God gave our heart a sound as He created us; this sound serves a purpose in the heavens and on earth—it is the sound of our life in heaven and on earth. Of the two, the sound of our spiritual heart supersedes that of the natural heart because the spiritual heart survives forever more. At the same time, the spiritual heart must be set to the correct frequency while we are here on earth, which is to God. Because this dictates where our heart and spirit will be when our natural heart is no longer active. The Holy Spirit helps us to maintain the correct frequency with God in heaven. The Spirit of God is the breath of life that is in our heart and provides the oxygen we need to survive spiritually. Everything that has to do with spiritual communication is dependent upon the heart and Spirit. The Holy Spirit breathes life to our spiritual communication with God, therefore, pumping the heart of our communication to God and keeping our connection with God active. The Holy Spirit is the sustainer and maintainer of our spiritual life. The heart and the Spirit of God move together. The Holy Spirit is the breath of our earthly horns. We, as men, cannot communicate to God without His help.

We know that our earthly horn is connected to our heart, but that is not all I want us to be aware of. We must also consider who dwells within our hearts. The one who dwells within our heart is the maintainer of communication, who is the Spirit of God. The Holy Spirit is the activator and translator of our heart and our horn from the earth to the heavens. He also does the same from the heavens back to earth. That is why our earthly horn is dependent upon the heart to successfully communicate with God because the life of the message of our heart is dependent on the Spirit. Galatians 4:6 (NIV) says, "Because you are his sons, God sent the Spirit of his Son into our hearts, the Spirit who calls out, 'Abba, Father.'" It is the Spirit of God who blows the breath of life upon the message of our heart and translates it from flesh to Spirit. Our earthly horn is powered by the Holy Spirit and given way only by and through Jesus so that God, the Father, may hear us from heaven, remember us, and respond.

CHAPTER 18

VARIOUS SOUNDS OF THE EARTHLY HORN ARE VARIOUS EXPRESSIONS OF THE HEART

Now that we have that understanding, let's go more into healthy communication from man to God by discussing the various expressions of the heart, which also means our various sounds of our earthly horn. These expressions will be referred to as sounds from our earthly horn, which begin from the inner man that can later be expressed through the outer man.

We are going to switch the order up a little bit during this explanation because God works from the inward out. Because of this, we will discuss the communication we have with God from within, known as inward expressions of the earthly horn. We will then discuss the communication we have with God that can be outwardly, known as outward expressions of the earthly horn. Inward and outward expressions of the earthly horn are both dictated by the heart and tied to the spirit. The heart expresses our communication with God in different ways and multiple methods, which in turn produces various sounds, but we must first understand the heart and the spirit are one and serve as the core of all expressions.

We must also understand that the earthly horn is the sound of our heart and can only be activated by the Spirit.

The inward and outward expressions of the earthly horn make a sound from the make-up of a man, which comes from the spirit, soul, and body. These expressions work from the inside out, beginning with the spirit, which is the core of a man, the soul, the next level within a man, and then the body, which is the outer part of a man.

Inward Expressions of the Earthly Horn

Inward expressions of the earthly horn are sounds released to communicate from the heart of man to God that cannot be seen or heard by other people. These inward expressions consist of the spirit and the soul (the mind, will, and emotions). Inward expressions are formed from the nonphysical part of a person and do not include the use of one's body. For the earthly horn to make a sound through inward expressions, the soul must line up with the heart and spirit of man to the heart and spirit of God.

The Sound of Our Spirit

What is the spirit of man? It is the core of a man and the breath-giving force within a person that gives life to man. It is what God gives us so we can have life and what goes back to God at the end of life. It is the deepest and innermost part of a person that is unseen. We connect with God, worship God, and express our love and devotion to God through our spirit because God is a spirit. Our experiences with God by way of the spirit are limitless.

To understand this better, we are going to speak about the spirit of Jesus during His prayer at Gethsemane. We will look at how Jesus experienced a fight between His spirit and flesh. We will also see how He managed to get His spirit to be victorious by looking at what took place during the crucifixion.

Let's look at this from Matthew chapter 26. This was when Jesus went to the disciples to keep watch with Him and pray. Jesus was cautioning them about the battle between the spirit and the flesh. Jesus said, "Watch and pray so that you will not fall into temptation. The spirit is willing, but the flesh is weak" (Matthew 26:41, NIV). He knew that they could fall into temptation, which are the traps set up by the evil one, if they were not on guard by staying connected to God through prayer. Jesus knew they were willing to pray, but their flesh was weak because it later says they were sleeping "because their eyes were heavy." The eyes are a part of the flesh, and the flesh is bound to things of the world, causing limitations with our communication to our ultimate source of strength, God. The flesh brings a separation between man and God. That is why the enemy always tries to entice the flesh to keep us disconnected from God and our God-given mandate. Jesus was aware of this weakness and made it known to the disciples so they could be aware as well. He wanted the disciples to allow their spirits to conquer the flesh, which is not an easy task and takes an action on our part. Jesus cautioned His disciples with authority about this matter because He was encountering it at that moment as well. While He was there praying at Gethsemane, He was struggling with His flesh because He was asking God to take this cup from Him.

What was this cup? This cup was His God-given mandate to save mankind by dying an agonizing and excruciatingly painful death upon the cross to redeem the world from their sins. As Jesus asked God to take this cup from Him—this was His flesh speaking. However, He went on to pray, "Yet not as I will, but as you will" (Matthew 26:39, NIV). When Jesus said, "yet not as I will," He was referring to the will of His flesh. His flesh wanted to avoid the crucifixion, but His spirit was willing to be the one to be crucified for the sins of man. He knew that His flesh was weak, and He did not want to give in to His flesh. That is why He spoke it into being that He will not allow His flesh to have its way. He was speaking it into existence that He will not give into His flesh. But instead, He was giving way for His spirit, which was willing, when He said, "...but as you will." His heart and spirit were lined up with the will of God. He had to put His flesh of weakness into submission to line up with His heart by giving way to His spirit that was willing. Jesus understood how the spirit and flesh are always at war and what it takes to conquer the flesh. He was experiencing the battle of the spirit and flesh heavily at the Garden of Gethsemane and knew the strategy necessary to allow the spirit to win.

That is why He was able to identify what was happening with His disciples as they slept when they should be praying. Although their flesh was experiencing a different battle than His, it was still a flesh versus spirit battle. Sleep is something the flesh does; praying is what the spirit does. Jesus gave them the antidote to overcome the flesh, which was to watch and pray.

Jesus knew to watch and pray on His own behalf, and He overcame the flesh. He accepted the cup that was given to Him, which was to be crucified. The very last thing Jesus spoke about was His spirit as He completed His purpose of being the ultimate sacrifice as He was crucified for the sins of mankind. He willingly gave His spirit to God, the Father. Luke 23:46 (NIV) says, "Jesus called out with a loud voice, 'Father, into your hands I commit my spirit.' When he had said this, he breathed his last." As we know, the spirit we have is what gives our mortal body life. It is the wind and Ruach within us. We need air to not only breathe but to survive. Jesus' spirit spoke clearly to God and connected with God from the humble beginnings of His life and maintained the connection to the very ending of it on earth. God is Spirit, and the Spirit of Jesus reached and communicated with the Spirit of God, therefore, activating His earthly horn while He walked the earth.

Throughout His lifetime, His earthly horn remained active because His communication with God remained healthy to the very end of His earthly life. He was always speaking what the Father was speaking because He made sure that His spirit and heart were one with God.

As His mortal body began to lose life upon the cross, He completely surrendered His wind, also known as His breath, and His spirit to the God of all gods. As He breathed His last breath, Jesus released a sound from His spirit, which was His very last blow of the earthly horn before His spirit exited His mortal body. His spirit was willing to do what God desired, and He allowed His spirit to triumph over His flesh rather than the other way around. God heard the sound of His spirit through Jesus' earthly horn because His heart was connected. As a result, God heard from heaven, remembered Him and the promise He made to His people, and responded.

God responded by tearing the curtain of the temple in two from the top to the bottom, breaking the barrier that was between man and God. Jesus finished the task and brought liberty, redemption, salvation, and made a way for mankind to be reconnected back to God once and for all. God gave Him authority to sit at the right hand of the throne where He now lives, rules, and reigns in heaven, giving Him the power to be the Heavenly Horn in His now glorified body, where He releases His sound as the Heavenly Trumpet in heaven.

As He ascended to the heavens to rule and reign, He sent a helper to us, who is the Holy Spirit. When He died and rose again, He gave us access to the throne of God and gave us His Spirit to communicate through us. It is different from the days of old when man depended on themselves and the law to help them walk in the ways of God. We now have the Holy Spirit to guide us and help us communicate to God. He empowers us to stay in communication with God from our heart and spirit to God's heart which is spirit. If we allow Him to help us, He translates all we have inside of us that sometimes is expressed outwardly to communicate with God. It is the Spirit of God who helps us to overcome the flesh. He is now living within our heart, and His law is written upon our heart. Remember, the heart is tied to the spirit. The Holy Spirit helps our spirit to make a sound through our earthly horn, thus allowing our heavenly voice to be heard and activated in the heavenly realm.

> *In the same way, the Spirit helps us in our weakness. We do not know what we ought to pray for, but the Spirit himself intercedes for us through wordless groans. And he who searches our hearts and know the mind of the Spirit, because the Spirit intercedes for God's people in accordance with the will of God.*

Romans 8:26–27 (NIV)

The Sound of Our Soul

What exactly is the soul of a man? The soul of a man is the next layer outside of the spirit but at the same time, embodied within a person. It is the human nature of a person that contains morals that deal with the mind, will, and emotions. The soul is the essence and innermost part of a person. It is the entirety of a person that is nonphysical that makes up who they are as a person. The soul of a person is what gives expressions to God through feelings that derive from our humanity. Our expressions to God by way of the soul have limitations and are dependent upon the spirit for help. The soul is the eternal part of a person because it continues on after the body dies. Since the soul is eternal, it travels to the spiritual realm and spends eternity in heaven or hell based on the choices made by the person while they were allotted time here on earth. It cannot be seen by others.

During the prayer at Gethsemane, we see the soul of Jesus depicted. At this point, He was troubled. So, He told one set of disciples to sit while He prayed but took a select few (Peter, James, and John) to go along with Him as He prayed. In Mark 14:34a (NIV), Jesus said to them, "My soul is overwhelmed with sorrow to the point of death." He showed His vulnerability to the few disciples He called to come with Him as He prayed. He was able to identify that the sorrow He felt was from His soul. Sorrow exists in the soulish realm, which is bound to our humanity. That is why He had to push past the soulish feelings by praying to God so that He would not allow His feelings to keep Him from fulfilling His purpose. He wanted His soul to line up with what His spirit wanted to do, which was to do the will of His Father in heaven. When He identified what the soul was doing, He was exposing the real matter so it could be dealt with specifically through prayer. He used the authority granted unto Him to take control over this soulish feeling bound to the nature of man by maintaining His connection and communication with God.

God wants us to understand that when our flesh is at work, we can take authority over it by allowing our spirit and heart to line up with the Spirit of God. Our soul must give way to the Spirit of God to be heard in the heavens and stay connected with God. When our soul submits successfully to the Spirit of God, our soul makes a particular sound through our earthly horn to the heavens. In turn, causing God to hear, remember, and respond, thus maintaining our relationship with God. We briefly discussed that the soul is made up of the mind, will, and emotions. With this knowledge, let's take some time to discuss all three.

The Sound of Our Mind

Let's start by talking about the horn of our mind. Within our mind, we have thoughts. Thoughts are the production of ideas and opinions within our mind. Matthew 9:4 (NASB) can help us bring light to this subject; it says, "And Jesus knowing their thoughts said, 'Why are you thinking evil in your hearts?'" This scripture proves that Jesus was responding to a voice that was unheard to the natural ear of man. He was responding to the thoughts of man.

The words that we release from our mouth with the sound of our voice begin first with a thought. God created us in such a way that our very thoughts have a voice. Think about it, when you think internally or when you read silently, there is a voice that you still hear, right? No one else around you can hear the voice inside, but you and I know it is very real. If we try to communicate with another person and don't make a sound, gesture, or write it out, there is no way for them to understand what we are trying to communicate. Communicating with someone requires more than just thinking about what we want to say. We must take additional steps for them to understand the message we are trying to relay—by speaking it, writing it, or using some other means of communication to get our point across. However, the situation is completely different with God. Even before those words touch our lips, God has heard and understood it already. Why? He is the All-knowing God. God does not depend on the natural means of sound to be able to understand and hear what we have to say. Our thoughts can be an instrument of communication as well.

According to Psalm 139:2, God "knows our thoughts." If He knows our thoughts, that means our thoughts have a sound. As I was saying before, producing an audible sound for the natural ear to hear is not necessary when it comes to communication with the God our Father. Let's look at the woman with the issue of blood, which will help bring clarification.

"For she *thought* to herself, 'If I can just touch his robe, I will be healed'" (Mark 5:28, NLT).

According to this scripture, it says she "thought to herself." This means she did not speak what she was thinking aloud for anyone to hear. This woman had a need; she made the first step by having faith in her thoughts that she would be healed. This woman's thought demonstrated faith. She believed in Jesus and His power so much so that she knew that she didn't need for Him to lay hands on her. All she needed was to touch His garment. This was her level of faith. She challenged herself to do the unimaginable by acting on what she spoke in her thoughts and did just that. She touched His robe, and she was immediately healed.

"Immediately the bleeding stopped, and she could feel in her body that she had been healed of her terrible condition" (Mark 5:29, NLT).

Now keep in mind, she did not yet have a conversation with Jesus. Yet, the issue that no one knew about was dealt with. The Bible said her bleeding stopped. Her issue was no more because of what she thought and believed...which can also be referred to as faith.

Did you know that faith is something that you must train the mind to do? Our mind is the playground for the enemy; it is the first place that is tested to prove our faith. Which goes to show that faith is tied to our thoughts. Faith is something found within the heart, but the mind must line up with our heart. Think about the man who said, "I believe, Lord, but help me not to doubt." This is the heart battling with the mind. So, it is something that we must conquer.

Jesus stopped what He was doing among the busyness around Him and responded to those around Him to show that although they had important duties to attend to, this person who touched Him was just as important...so important that He was driven to put His important tasks on pause until He attended to the woman who needed His help. He felt her need based on her thoughts of faith and steps of action and immediately released His power to meet her need. God responds to faith. The faith of the woman with the issue of blood caused a transaction to take place immediately before her earthly words were even uttered from her mouth. This demonstrates that it is not only the audible voice that the Lord responds to…it goes way deeper than that; He hears our thoughts as well. Her thoughts were lined up with the faith of her heart and, therefore, activated her earthly horn, and the Son of God heard, remembered her and His promises, and responded by healing her.

Now, I must clarify that when the woman with the issue of blood made the additional step to touch Jesus' robe falls under the category of outward expressions of the heart because her body was used to make an action that was seen by others. But for the purpose of this section, we are focusing on her thoughts that could only be heard by God, and her thought caused God to respond. Her thoughts were inward expressions of her earthly horn. Her mind and thoughts successfully sounded her earthly horn because they lined up with her heart and spirit.

This an example of how God can hear your thoughts of Him, and if your thoughts are lined up with your heart, it has now become your tool of healthy communication to God. In this case, your thoughts become your earthly horn, and your voiceprint becomes activated by making a sound in the heavenlies that reaches God. Your heart is therefore making an expression to God. When this takes place, God hears from heaven, understands your thoughts, remembers you and remembers His covenant with you, and responds in the capacity that you need.

The Sound of Our Will

We know that God has given us all a will. Our will can also be viewed as our own desires. This is something that God gifted us with as He created humanity. God gave us the ability to have free will by allowing us to make decisions on our own. We have free will to worship God or not. We have free will to obey Him or not. We have the free will to choose life in Him or not. Free will is all about choice, and God placed that within our power to do. Our will is not something that can be seen, but it is something that lies within us. We may later act out what our will is, but remember, the will first starts from within. The "within" part is what we are focusing on in this section. Even though our will is within us, this is a sound that communicates to God because our heart is involved, thus causing our earthly horn to make a sound. With this knowledge, let's go into the lives of a few people in the Bible who demonstrated the horn of our will.

Since we talked a great deal about Mt. Sinai within this book, we can start from there. Remember when God gave instructions on the mountain, which included the Ten Commandments, His laws, and the covenant He made with Israel? We can find an example of the will of the people as they answered with one voice. In Exodus 24:3 (NIV), "When Moses went and told the people all the LORD's words and laws, they responded with one voice, 'Everything the LORD has said we will do.'" They did not have to obey the commands of the Lord, nor did they have to accept. God gave them the ability to choose. And although for some of them, their obedience lasted but a moment, they still obeyed at this time.

We can also see during the time that God commanded that those who have abilities and skills to construct a sanctuary for him should do the work of building it. Exodus 36:2 (NIV), "Then Moses summoned Bezalel and Oholiab and every skilled person to whom the LORD had given ability and who was *willing to come and do the work*." Bezalel and Oholiab were commanded by name and made the action to come, which showed they had the willingness to obey. But what stands out even more are the workers who were not mentioned by name but still took heed to God's command by taking actions to use their ability and do the work. This is a demonstration of people using their free will to obey the commands of God. In this same passage, we can see free will demonstrated by the people bringing freewill offerings to assist with the construction of the sanctuary. Exodus 36:3–5 (NIV) goes on to say:

> *They [the workers] received from Moses all offerings the Israelites had brought to carry out the work of constructing the sanctuary. And the people continued to bring freewill offerings morning after morning. So all the skilled workers...said to Moses, "The people are bringing more than enough for doing the work the Lord commanded to be done."*

Not only does this passage mention "freewill offerings" to demonstrate that the offerings were given out of free will, but we can also see that they were going above and beyond the expectations of God. They gave more than what the construction of the sanctuary required to get the job done. This shows that they had a willingness to give for the work of God to be accomplished. This is free will.

Another example is when David wanted to build a house for God. This you can find in 2 Samuel chapter 7. David saw that he had his own palace, but the ark of God was in a tent. It was in David's will to build the house, but God did not want him to build it. God responded by saying David's offspring would be the one to get that accomplished. The fact that David wanted to build this for God without God requesting for it to be done shows that David willed it. He meant well because of his love for God. His desire to build was a demonstration of free will.

The Virgin Mary, the mother of Jesus, can serve as an example of someone who had free will to obey the Lord. When the angel Gabriel spoke to her, saying that she would conceive and give birth to son, who would be called Jesus, she agreed to be used. This was a choice that was given to her. God does not force Himself on anyone. He waited for her consent before He placed the Son of God within her womb. By her free will, she responded by saying, "I am the Lord's servant…May your word to me be fulfilled" (Luke 1:38, NIV). God knew ahead of time that she was a willing vessel. He knew that she would allow His will to come forth because of her love for Him. Her response was a manifestation of what was already formed from within. She willed for God to bring His Son to earth through her, regardless of what would come next. She followed through by being the mother of Jesus and made sure to stand strong in the purpose of God's will for her life, so His will could be done through her.

In John chapter 6, we can see the power of free will in two different ways. Meaning, we can see those who chose to follow Jesus and those who chose not to follow Him. This happened after Jesus was revealing that He was the Bread of Life when He was teaching in the synagogue in Capernaum. He said, "Whoever eats my flesh and drinks my blood has eternal life, and I will raise them up at the last day" (John 6:54, NIV).

At this time, many disciples were grumbling, and some could not accept it. They chose not to believe. Believing requires the will of man, which happens from within. Jesus already knew what would happen; He knew some would not believe.

"'Yet there are some of you who do not believe.' For Jesus had known from the beginning which of them did not believe and who would betray him" (John 6:64, NIV).

All of the disciples heard the teachings of Jesus and were given the opportunity to choose to believe and choose to follow Him. They were not forced by Jesus to believe, which is a choice that still stands for us today. After this, some stayed, and some left.

John 6:66 (NIV) says, "From this time many of his disciples turned back and no longer followed him."

But both choices were by free will. The will of all the disciples happened first from within and demonstrated after by their actions.

Jesus did not need to see the actions of those who literally walked away after His teaching. Nor did He need to see the actions of those who decided to stay with him. He already knew their choices ahead of time, based on their will that resided within them. The action of many of the disciples walking away was merely a manifestation of what could not be seen by man and only seen by God, which was their free will.

This same concept applied to those who stayed with them as well; Jesus already knew what they would do. After the "many disciples left" part, Jesus revealed that He knew who had the free will to stay with Him, which were His twelve disciples. That's why He chose them because He knew they loved Him.

The Word goes on to say, "'You do not want to leave too, do you?' Jesus asked the Twelve" (John 6:67, NIV).

Even though Jesus asked the question, He already knew the answer. He already knew what the will of each disciple was. Simon Peter answered the question of Jesus by declaring that they have come to believe and know that He is God. Simon Peter's answer was only a manifestation of what God already knew their will to be. Jesus also knew that of the twelve, there would be one who would not choose Him but would instead betray Him. That is why He said, "Have I not chosen you, the Twelve? Yet one of you is a devil!" (He meant Judas, the son of Simon Iscariot, who, though one of the Twelve, was later to betray him.)" (John 6:70–71, NIV).

As you can see, the betrayal that would come from Judas had not yet come to pass, yet Jesus knew the heart of Judas was not with Him. That is why He said one of the twelve was a devil. Jesus did not need to see the manifested actions of the will of Judas because it was already revealed from what was within, which was his will. Jesus knew that it was in the will of Judas to betray Him. Jesus knew the will of the hearts of all the disciples. He knew who willed to stay with Him, and He knew who willed to leave Him way before they demonstrated it by action. This is free will.

The last example that will be used for this section is none other than the Son of God, Jesus Christ. Amazingly, we will be able to find examples of the earthly horn's sound of the will, emotions, spirit, and soul in one place. These all occurred during Jesus' prayer on the Mount of Olives at the Garden of Gethsemane. We can see the different points of view in Matthew chapter 26, Mark chapter 14, and Luke chapter 22. Jesus knew what awaited Him because the time was drawing near for Him to be betrayed by Judas and given over to the chief priests, officers, and temple guard. The Word of God states that He fell to the ground to pray "for this cup to be taken" from Him. Meaning, the human side of Him wanted to not go through with it due to the excruciating death that He knew He was going to have to suffer for the sins of mankind. But He continued to pursue what He was called to do because His will was whatever the will of God is. We can see that when He said, "Father, if you are willing, take this cup from me; yet not my will, but yours be done" (Luke 22:42, NIV).

Jesus was God in the flesh, meaning He was God but also man. Jesus originally willed to not have to go through with the cross. It was overwhelming for Him to have the knowledge of the pain that He would endure so He could make right what Adam made wrong. It was a hard task that was ahead of Him, which is why He prayed so intensely for God to help Him so that His will could line up with God's will. Jesus had a choice to give up and forget about His call to be the ultimate sacrifice for the sins of mankind. However, He did not give up but instead was strengthened and finished the task. His will was not something that a man could see with the natural eye, but God the Father knew the will of Jesus and what was in His heart. Through prayer, the will of Jesus was connected to the will of the Father, which made a unique sound in the heavenlies, activating His earthly horn, which produced a sound of His will.

God heard from heaven, remembered His Son, and responded by sending an angel (Luke 22:43) to strengthen Him during this time.

The Sound of Our Emotions

In this same passage, we can see the emotions of Jesus being revealed. His emotions became utterly intensified as this time came. In different translations of the Bible, Luke 22:44 uses different words to describe how Jesus felt, knowing that His hour has come to take on the sins of the world. Various versions of this scripture use descriptive words of His emotion at this time, words that say Jesus was in "anguish," "agony," "deeply troubled," "distressed," etc., so much so that He began to sweat blood as He prayed. If we look at just one of these descriptive words, we can see that the man part of Jesus was experiencing emotion to an extreme level. The word "anguish" can be described as "extreme unhappiness caused by physical or mental suffering."[26] We know Jesus was not experiencing physical suffering at this time because He had not been beaten, flogged, pierced, or hanged just yet. So physical suffering is not applicable for this moment. The anguish Jesus was feeling during His time of prayer at Gethsemane was mental suffering. He was in anguish of what was about to happen to Him. He is God in flesh and knows all things. His mind knew what He was about to suffer for the sake of man to save man.

It was hard for His flesh to prepare and endure what was to come to the point of sweating blood. Sweating blood is a rare medical condition known as hematidrosis. Hematidrosis takes place "when a person feels intense fear or stress...like someone who is about to face death."[27] During highly stressful life-threatening situations, the body goes into survival mode, known as fight-or-flight, which releases chemicals such as adrenaline to alert and prepare us for the approaching danger. Although it rarely happens, when the body goes into survival mode due to high levels of fear or stress, the blood vessels near the sweat glands can rupture, causing the body to sweat blood. The Man, Christ Jesus, was experiencing hematidrosis during this moment. He feared like mankind fears; He was stressed due to His situation like mankind gets stressed. That is why He asked God in prayer if He could "take this cup from me." Now, we can see why He kept asking the disciples to stay up and pray and why He could not be lax with His prayer. He was afraid and felt alone, that He saw that not even His close disciples could stay up with Him and pray.

Inwardly, His emotions were intensified to the point where His body expressed them outwardly by sweating blood. Jesus was experiencing the bodily response of fight-or-flight due to His high level of stress and fear at this moment. His body began to release these chemicals to alert and prepare Him to run from the approaching danger (the crucifixion) or fight through it. As we know, Jesus chose not to flee but instead to fight through it. His emotions did not get the best of Him. Instead of running, He stayed put and prayed to God. He overcame His fear and conquered His stress. He was able to channel His anguish, agony, trouble, and distress to God through prayer by connecting His heart to God's heart. He knew that He was not alone, that although man may abandon Him, God never will. God, the Father, was right there and understood what was happening.

His emotions released a sound into the heavens because God heard, remembered Him, and responded by equipping His Son, Jesus, to stay strong to endure to the end. This caused Him to be the Lamb of God, the One who was slain for our sins. The Son of God utilized His earthly horn while praying at Gethsemane by staying connected to the Father through His emotions…which first began in His heart.

Outward Expressions of the Earthly Horn

Outward expressions of the earthly horn are sounds that are released to communicate from the heart of man as a heavenly sound to God that can be seen by other people but not in all cases understood or heard by other people. This is when man communicates to God inwardly from the heart, that later manifests outwardly. These outward expressions are broken into four different methods of communication: verbal, nonverbal, written, and visual. Outward expressions take place from the physical part of a person and include the use of one's body.

(Nonverbal Expressions of the Earthly Horn) The Sound of Our Body

The nonverbal expressions of the earthly horn are sounds that are released from the heart of man on earth and communicate as a heavenly sound to God in heaven without the use of words. These expressions of communication begin inwardly and are expressed outwardly using the body, which includes postures, facial expressions, physical movements, and body language. The body is the physical part of a human made up of flesh, bones, and organs that operates through the five sense organs: eyes, ears, tongue, nose, and skin. Our experiences with God through the body are limited to the earth, therefore, temporal because the body eventually passes away.

With this knowledge, let's see how the five sense organs of the body communicate with God.

SHARLENE SHANTALLE HYLTON

The Horn of Our Eyes—The Heavenly Sound of Sight

The eye is the sense organ that allows a human to see. The eye receives visual images and transmits them to the brain. The eyes and brain are in constant communication. The eye provides vision.

So, what does God say about the eyes, and how do the eyes apply to communication from man to God?

We can get some answers in Matthew 6:22–24 (NIV), which says:

> *The eye is the lamp of the body. If your eyes are healthy, your whole body will be full of light. But if your eyes are unhealthy your whole body will be full of darkness. If then the light within you I darkness, how great is that darkness!*

If the eye is the lamp to our body and determines if our body is healthy or unhealthy, full of light or full of darkness, that means we must guard what we see. The eyes of a man can be devoted to good or evil. Meaning whatever we allow our eyes to focus on, it tells us if we are devoted to God or devoted to Satan. So, we should avoid using our eyes to do evil, such as coveting what is not ours, viewing perverted things, and looking upon anything that is not of God. Our eyes can cause us to sin.

A good example of this can be found in the story of David and Bathsheba. Although King David was a man after God's own heart, he allowed his eyes to make him sin. The story of this took place in 2 Samuel chapter 11 when he saw Bathsheba bathing, the wife of Uriah the Hittite. His eyes caused him to sin by intentionally taking the wife of another and by setting Uriah up to die by the sword. The sin of David's eyes communicated to God negatively and caused God to respond with punishment, David's eyes sinned, and God's eyes witnessed it. God used prophet Nathan to ask David, "Why did you despise the word of the Lord by doing *what is evil in his eyes?*" (2 Samuel 12:9a, NIV) Since David's eyes sinned, God sent punishment for David's eyes to behold.

> *This is what the LORD says: "Out of your own household I am going to bring calamity on you. Before your very eyes I will take your wives and give them to one who is close to you, and he will sleep with your wives in broad daylight. You did it in secret, but I will do this thing in broad daylight before all Israel."*
>
> **2 Samuel 12:11–12 (NIV)**

David's sin made an unhealthy sound to God through nonverbal communication. Even though it was unhealthy communication, it still communicated to God because David's heart was with God. David's heart, for this brief moment, gave way to sin due to the lust of his eyes and flesh, causing his sound to be out of tune. David's nonverbal communication of darkness through the eyes made a sound from his earthly horn, and God heard the sound, remembered His covenant based on this sound of sin, which was curse for disobedience, and God responded from heaven to David with punishment.

If we serve God, we must direct our eyes to things that are like God. In the same scripture we were discussing in Matthew 6:22–24 about the eyes, the word mentions something very important in the meticulously placed scripture right before it, which is, "For where your treasure is, there your heart will be also" (Matthew 6:21, NIV). The placement of this scripture before the scripture about the eyes was not coincidental. God is letting us know that however we entertain our eyes, that means that is what is within our hearts. If our heart is connected with God, it will guide our eyes to see the right things, the things that are good, pure, and lovely, the things pertaining to God. When our eyes are tuned in with our heart, and if our heart is connected with God, then we will be drawn to see things from a heavenly perspective, causing our lights to shine and our sound from our earthly horn to be heard and be healthy. We will also want to see things that are good and avoid seeing evil things. If we use our eyes to focus on things pertaining to God, our earthly horn makes a particular sound in the heavenlies and communicates to God.

David understood that he had to guide his eyes to line up with his heart, which was to be one who was after God's own heart. So, what did he do next? How could he turn his negative communication positive again? What did he do to get his earthly horn tuned up again to release a healthy and good sound? Well, he repented in Psalm 51 and accepted the consequences of his iniquitous sin. David's weakness was with his eyes, but he loved the Lord. He was human and was vulnerable to the weakness of his flesh. He was aware that he had to pray over his eyes to stay in the ways of the Lord. If we look into the life of David, we can see all the good that he did for God. David was found to be highly favored of God, so much so that God blessed him abundantly. David was so blessed and so favored that God chose his son Solomon to build a temple for the Lord and made an everlasting covenant with him that his house/throne would be established forever.

Although David was a man after God's own heart, he fell short by succumbing to his flesh like any other human, which was through his eyes. Since one of his weaknesses was his eyes, he made a declaration to God regarding his eyes to keep them guarded. David said, "*I will not look* with approval on anything that is vile. I hate what faithless people do; I will have no part in it" (Psalm 101:3, NIV). This was a good step to overcoming his weakness. It can be believed that he guarded his eyes for the remainder of his life because there is nothing more recorded in the word of God that discussed his eyes, causing him to sin again. First Kings 15:5 (NIV) says, "For David had done what was right in the eyes of the LORD and had not failed to keep any of the LORD's commands all the days of his life—except in the case of Uriah the Hittite." This testifies that the horn of his eyes was tuned back to the correct frequency of God. He learned from his sins of the past and guarded his future, specifically in reference to his eyes to maintain his relationship with God. He maintained healthy communication with God through his earthly horn, and his eyes began to make a healthy sound to God again. God remembered him and His covenant and responded by allowing the dynasty of David to remain forevermore through his descendent, the Messiah, who now sits at the right hand of God forevermore.

We just discussed how our eyes make a sound that communicates to God through our earthly horn in a negative and unhealthy way through David, which eventually turned positive. We will now focus on the positive and healthy communication of the earthly horn through the life of one woman that I believe can apply to all sense organs for nonverbal communication. The woman we are going to study about communicated with the Son of God without words but spoke very loudly through body language and her alabaster jar.

The story of this woman can be found in Luke chapter 7. She was known to be a sinner. While Jesus was in the home of a Pharisee reclining at a table after being invited for dinner, the woman came with her alabaster jar. She then anointed Him in the most peculiar way in preparation for His crucifixion. While this was happening, the teachers of law were devising a plan to have Jesus killed. We will not go into the whole story in this section but instead break the story down in a way that is applicable to each sense organ. Since this section is dedicated to the eyes, let's see how her eyes communicated to God. We can find it in Luke 7:38a (NIV), "As she stood behind him [Jesus] at his feet weeping, she began to wet his feet with her tears." We know that weeping, crying, and tears are associated with the eyes, an outward expression of our emotions. Naturally, crying is good for us. It helps us to release stress and helps relieve burdens. It is helpful to our health and is tied to our emotions. Crying helps bring stabilization to our emotions. Spiritually, these tears represented her sorrow and need for forgiveness due to her sins. She did not say anything with words, but her tears said everything.

The fact that her tears wet the feet of Jesus represents her acknowledgment of who He was, what His destination was, and what His God-given purpose was all about. This was also a prophetic act of where these feet would go and what they would do for mankind. There would be weeping at those same feet that would soon be pierced for her sins to bring forth forgiveness to not only her but for the sins of mankind. She knew she was not worthy. Her weeping was an outward expression of what was in her heart…a sinner who loved Him, was sorry, and needed His forgiveness. The tears from her eyes were connected with her heart and communicated clearly in a healthy manner to God. The horn of her eyes, through tears, successfully made a particular sound through her earthly horn to the heavenlies; God heard, remembered her and His covenant, and responded. He responded by granting her the forgiveness she needed of the sins that she had committed.

The Horn of Our Ears—
The Heavenly Sound of Hearing

The ear is the sense organ that allows a human to hear and perceive sounds.

So, what does God say about the ears, and how do the ears apply to communication from man to God?

Our answer can be found in the invitation to those who are thirsty. It says, "Give ear and come to Me, listen that you may live. I will make an everlasting covenant with you, my faithful love promised to David" (Isaiah 55:3, NIV).

I believe that this scripture is inviting mankind to come to Him firstly to hear what God has to say. To hear, we must use our ears to listen. If we take the next step to not only hear but listen to Him and accept Him by obeying His commands, then we will receive life. This life will come from the everlasting covenant that He made to David and will automatically be the covenant He makes with us as well. Because when we accept Him and obey Him, we become joint heirs with Christ.

In Romans 10:17 (NIV), it says, "Consequently, faith comes from hearing the message, and the message is heard through the word about Christ."

Faith comes from hearing the message of Christ. The message of Christ is an invitation to all to come to Him, give ear to Him, accept Him into their hearts, and obey His commands.

So how does this apply to the woman with the alabaster jar? Pretty much everything. As we jump back into her story, we can see that she used her ears because she accepted the invitation to listen to the message, which is the good news of Christ, so that she may be saved. When Jesus sat at the table after being invited for dinner, it was really an invitation to all who have heard His message, believed it, accepted Him into their heart, and chose to obey. The woman with the alabaster jar obviously heard His message and believed. That is why it was incumbent upon her to be where He was so she could be forgiven and saved.

Luke 7:37 (NIV) says, "A woman in that town who lived a sinful life learned that Jesus was eating at the Pharisee's house, so she came there with an alabaster jar of perfume."

We can see that this woman knew that Jesus was God and had come to bring salvation to the sinners, or she would not have made the effort to go see Him and bring a sacrificial gift to Him. She knew He was more than an ordinary man and obviously knew about Him. Jesus said her *faith* had saved her (Luke 7:50). The only way she could have faith, according to the Word, is from hearing the message about Christ. Although the Bible does not tell us the details of her going to hear the teachings of Jesus, we know she heard because the Bible tells us that faith comes from hearing the message of Christ. She believed and received salvation.

The woman with the alabaster jar produced a particular sound from the horn of her ears by hearing. Those around her did not understand that she heard the message and accepted His invitation into her heart, but God understood. Because of this, God heard the sound from her earthly horn, remembered her and His covenant, and responded by providing her with not only forgiveness but, more importantly, salvation. The sound released from the horn of our ears is silent to man but communicates powerfully to God.

The Horn of Our Nose—The Heavenly Sound of Smelling and Breathing

The nose is the sense organ that allows a human to smell, perceive various smells, and breathe.

So, what does God say about the nose, and how does the nose apply to communication from man to God?

Based on my research, I found that the nose can symbolize three things in the Bible, but also may not be limited to these three things:

1. The nose can represent the breath that gives life to a man.
   - "Then the LORD formed man of dust from the ground and *breathed into his nostrils* the breath of life and man became a living being" (Genesis 2:7, NIV).
   - "For as long as life is in me, And the *breath of God is in my nostrils...*" (Job 27:3, NASB).

2. It can be associated with the aroma of sacrificial worship from mankind (the Bride of Christ) that is acceptable to God.

- "And when the Lord *smelled the pleasing aroma*, the Lord said in his heart, 'I will never again curse the ground because of man, for the intention of man's heart is evil from his youth…'" (Genesis 8:21, ESV)

- "For we are to God the *pleasing aroma* of Christ to God among those who are being saved and among those who are perishing" (2 Corinthians 2:15, NIV).

- "How delightful is your love, my sister, my bride! How much more pleasing is your love than wine, and the *fragrance of your perfume* more than any spice!" (Song of Songs 4:10, NIV)

- "The priest is to take a handful of the finest flour and some olive oil, together with all the incense on the grain offering, and burn the memorial portion on the altar as an *aroma pleasing to the Lord*" (Leviticus 6:15, NIV).

3. It can be associated with the anger, wrath, and judgment of God that comes from the stench of sin from His people or when He comes as a defense for His people when they are being pursued by the enemy.

- "Such people are *smoke in my nostrils*, a fire that keeps burning all day" (Isaiah 65:5b, NIV).

- "In the greatness of your majesty you threw down those who opposed you. You unleashed your burning anger; and consumed them like stubble. By the *blast of your nostrils* the waters piled up. The surging waters stood up like a wall; the deep waters congealed in the heart of the sea" (Exodus 15:7–8, NIV).

- "The earth trembled and quaked, and the foundations of the mountains shook; they trembled because he was angry. *Smoke rose from his nostrils*; consuming fire came from his mouth, burning coals blazed out of it" (Psalm 18:7–8, NIV).

Now that we have a background of what God's Word says about the nose, we will see which of the three meanings apply to the life of the woman and her alabaster jar. Some translations of the Bible say "alabaster box" as an "alabaster jar" instead. I think this is important because a box represents something ordinary that requires little to no thought based on its design. It has limitations of how it contains a substance or object due to its generic shape, commonality, lack of uniqueness, and structure. A jar, on the other hand, represents something that is unique and requires the skill of a designer; it requires thought to create a different shape, usually varying in size, form, and structure. The substance that a jar contains must be considered before putting it in. Jars are also used as a vessel to contain and preserve something of importance.

The woman with the alabaster jar in Luke chapter 7 was referred to as a sinner. It says that she went to the Pharisee's house with her alabaster jar that contained perfume. Alabaster is made of a precious stone that can be likened to marble, which is known for its strength, worth, and beauty. The jar alone was expensive, so we can just imagine how much more worth with the perfume included in it. She used this perfume to pour over the feet of Jesus. "As she stood behind him at his feet weeping, she began to wet his feet with her tears. Then she wiped them with her hair, kissed them and poured perfume on them" (Luke 7:38, NIV). Since we know this perfume was expensive, we know that it was a high sacrifice for her to give it up. We also need to take into the matter who she chose to give that perfume to as a sacrifice, which was Jesus. This demonstrates that she believed anointing the feet of Jesus was far more valuable than the earthly value of her expensive perfume. Perfume, as we know, is liquid fragrance for a person's body that is made from the oils of flowers and spices to release an aroma pleasing to the noses of those around.

The act of this woman pouring this expensive perfume shows that she was making a sacrifice to Jesus. This is reverence. Naturally, she was releasing a fragrance that belonged to her, which represented her, and placed it upon the feet of Jesus. Jesus was able to smell the aroma through His nose, a physical sensor organ, and so was others. But the natural smell was way more than what we would think it to be. Her actions of giving her best and most expensive perfume were a representation of what she was doing spiritually. She was giving the sacrifice of worship through her actions, therefore, sending a pleasant aroma that was acceptable to God, the Son, and God, the Father.

If we go back to the three symbols we previously discussed about the nose in the Bible, we can now see that the woman with the alabaster jar applies to reason number two, which is that the nose can be associated with the aroma of sacrificial worship from mankind (the Bride of Christ) that is acceptable to God. This woman was giving sacrificial worship to God, which therefore released a fragrance into the nostrils of God. Her worship spoke of the love she had for Jesus.

Jesus said, "You did not put oil on my head, but she poured perfume on my feet. Therefore, I tell you, her many sins have been forgiven—as her great love has shown..." (Luke 7:46–47a, NIV)

When we connect that to the scripture in Song of Songs 4:10, previously mentioned under reason number two, we can see that the man refers to the beauty of the love of His bride being better than wine and the oil of her fragrance being better than spice. When Jesus referred to her love, He was referring to her unique fragrance of worship. When we love Him, we worship Him. When we worship Him, we smell like Him, thus becoming one with Him, because we are the aroma of Christ to God (1 Corinthians 2:15). Love belongs to the heart, and her heart was connected to God's heart. Her earthly horn was activated through communication of the nose, which released a heavenly sound from her earthly horn clearly to God.

Those who were in the room the day she anointed Jesus' feet may have physically smelled with their nose the natural fragrance from her expensive perfume. But the natural fragrance was not what was communicating to God. The fragrance emitted from her that God smelled was the aroma of her sacrificial worship. Man could not smell the aroma of her worship. Man could not hear the heavenly sound from her earthly horn by way of the nose. Furthermore, man could not understand her worship.

It was not for man to smell, hear, or see. This was spiritual communication reserved for her and God only. Her worship was a pleasing aroma to the Lord. Her worship communicated loud and clear to Him because she had a heart of worship that sounded her earthly horn by way of the nose, thus releasing a sound in the heavens, which activated her voiceprint in the heavens. A kingdom exchange was made from earth to heaven and then from heaven to earth. God heard her worship, inhaled it through His nostrils, and accepted it. He then remembered her and His covenant and responded by granting her with forgiveness.

The Horn of Our Skin—The Heavenly Sound of Our Touch/Actions

The skin is the sense organ that is the largest on the body and allows a human to touch and perceive pain, temperature, textures, and pressure.

So, what does God say about the skin, and how does the skin apply to communication from man to God?

Well, there are various scriptures that use the actual word "skin." As I did the research for the subject matter of skin, the scriptures that linked to the word were not applicable to this subject matter. I thought to myself, *Surely there must be something about skin that relates to this discussion.* This caused me to selah for a moment, and I began to pray for the Lord to help.

After a brief prayer, the Lord directed me in a different way that required His revelation. He began to reveal to me that the subject matter of skin is all over the Bible, even from the beginning of time, just not in the way I expected. He began to remind me that the way we see things is not how He sees things because, as He says, His thoughts are higher than our thoughts and His ways are higher than our ways.

In God's sight, skin is more than what mankind perceives it to be. He wanted me to come up higher and see it from His perspective, which I didn't see until this very moment of writing. God removed the veil from my eyes and began to speak to me by saying...

> *"When mankind says 'skin,' I say 'flesh.' Flesh is what I use to create mankind; it is what houses the spirit of a man and what differentiates the angels from man; it is what testifies that man is of the earth. Flesh is what I clothe My creation with for the environment I created for man to dwell and thrive in, called earth. Flesh is bound to the earth and is limited to the earth. When man departs from the earth, the flesh goes back from where it was first created, which is the dust of the earth. Flesh cannot depart from the earth because flesh and the dust of the earth are one. The outer part of a man is the garment of flesh that I have given to them for their allotted time on earth; it is earthbound.*
>
> *When I created Adam and Eve, I clothed them...they were not naked in my eyes because they lived in My presence. They were made in my likeness, and all that I make is good. Flesh was meant to be their earthly robe of light, life, power, and righteous authority,*

but sin caused them to lose their robe and turn what was beautiful into darkness and death. The sin they committed while in their robe of flesh caused their robe to be defiled, causing the symbolism of flesh to turn from good to evil. The garment of flesh became sin, tainted, weak, disgraced, unholy, unrighteous, impure, and doomed to death and darkness in My sight. When they sinned by disobeying Me, they were separated from My ways and My presence and lost the authority I had given them. They began to see themselves from a lower perspective by being influenced by the serpent, causing them to see from the perspective of the serpent, which is the one who I made low. They saw through the eyes of sin and rebellion, which is from the enemy.

Because of this, they no longer could see their flesh from a heavenly perspective, which was the garment of power for mankind and the robe of authority for mankind, but instead from the lower perspective, which was the garment of lost power for mankind with a lost robe of authority. When anyone loses something, that means they have been stripped of something. When you have been stripped of something...you have become naked from that thing that once was. They were stripped of the light, life, power, and righteous authority from their robe and became naked. That is why they saw themselves as being naked because the enemy robbed them of their robe of authority for mankind to have rule and have dominion over the earth. They were bamboozled into legally handing their rule and authority over to the serpent.

But My Son came to earth as a man and sacrificed His flesh to win the authority back for mankind and is now robed in majesty, authority, dominion, and power of heaven and earth. Although the enemy may rule the earth for a while, his time is allotted; the time is coming for mankind to rule and reign with Me once again, as I empower them to do so, for the battle is already won," so sayeth the Lord of heaven and earth.

Wow! As I am writing this, the Lord came in to reveal this mighty word. Thank You, Lord, for Your word! I believe this is beneficial for the Body of Christ. That although He spoke this to me, I am sharing this word He spoke to me for the masses through this book. Now that we have this awesome revelation between skin versus flesh, let us refer to skin from God's higher vocabulary by using the word "flesh." With that in mind, let's review a few out of a multitude of scriptures that describe what else God says about flesh (skin) in the Bible.

"Those who are in the realm of the flesh cannot please God" (Romans 8:8, NIV).

"For if you live according to the flesh, you will die; but if by the Spirit you put to death the misdeeds of the body, you will live" (Romans 8:13, NIV).

Now the works of the flesh are evident: sexual immorality, impurity, sensuality, idolatry, sorcery, enmity, strife, jealousy, fits of anger, rivalries, dissensions, divisions, envy, drunkenness, orgies, and things like these. I warn you, as I warned you before, that those who do such things will not inherit the kingdom of God.

Galatians 5:19–21 (ESV)

"For everything in the world—the lust of the flesh, the lust of the eyes, and the pride of life—comes not from the Father but from the world" (1 John 2:16, NIV).

Based on the scriptures above, we can see that the flesh is tied to things associated with sin, death, pride, and earthly desires, such as sexual immorality, impurity, sensuality, idolatry, etc. Everything that opposes God is likened to the flesh. The flesh desires to do wrong from the time of birth. Therefore, to God, the flesh stinks and is not pleasing to Him. That is why God emphasized to prophet Samuel that He does not look at the outer. Why? Because the outer layer of any living being on earth is flesh, which reminds Him of the sin that was brought on to mankind through Adam. In the Old Testament, He directed the Israelites to sacrifice the flesh of animals through burnt offerings and sin offerings to rid them of their sins and to stay in communion with Him, which is symbolic of flesh being sacrificed and burnt on the altar. In the New Testament, He is still wanting the same, but this time He wants our flesh to be sacrificed by giving way to the Spirit of God through submission and living a life with Christ, the one who crucified His flesh so that we may be like Him. Meaning, just as Jesus crucified His flesh, so are we to do the same. If we do so, we will live. Here are some scriptures that talk about the solution to the limitations of the flesh.

"And those who belong to Christ Jesus have crucified the flesh with its passions and desires" (Galatians 5:24, NIV).

"I have been crucified with Christ and I no longer live, but Christ lives in me. The life I now live in the body, I live by faith in the Son of God, who loved me and gave himself for me" (Galatians 2:20, NIV).

Based on these scriptures, we can see that when we live a life for Christ, we have crucified our flesh. Even though we are here in the earth, if we live a life through faith in Jesus, who is the Son of God, we will have everlasting life. Jesus gave us the ability to do so by conquering the penalty of death through His crucifixion, which could only be done by coming here in flesh and overcoming the temptation that comes with it.

"The Word became flesh and made his dwelling among us. We have seen his glory, the glory of the one and only Son, who came from the Father, full of grace and truth" (John 1:14, NIV).

Jesus not only came as the Word in the form of flesh, but He also conquered the flesh by crucifying it, thus gaining victory for mankind. The victory was granted when He completed His purpose and got the keys of death back from the enemy, giving us life forevermore. We received proof of Him conquering death and gaining back the authority that was once lost when He was raised from the dead and walked among mankind. As a man on earth, He wore the robe of flesh on the earth as God originally intended it to be, restoring this garment of flesh for mankind that was once stripped away back to the power, life, light, and authority. Jesus appeared to man as flesh, and blood triumphing over death, hell, and the grave and was among them. The Word said He stood among men (the disciples), and this is what He said: "Look at my hands and my feet. It is I myself! *Touch* me and see; a ghost does not have flesh and bones, as you see I have" (Luke 24:39, NIV).

He rose from the dead and appeared to the disciples in the flesh. He told the disciples to "touch him" so that they could feel Him and know that He was really among them in the flesh, just as they were flesh and not a ghost. That is why He said the spirit does not have flesh and bones as He had at the time. Touch is something that the flesh does. Jesus knew that He had to relate to mankind in a way they understood when He appeared to them which was in the flesh and through touch. Touch is the physical way for us to communicate with God. Our touch makes a sound. If our touch is lined up with our heart as unto God, then this can be another example of an expression of our heart, which shows we are actively using our earthly horn. Touch is as an action. Before the serpent was successful with swaying Eve to sin, she made reference back to the words of God regarding touch, which says, "The woman said to the serpent, 'We may eat fruit from the trees in the garden, but God did say, 'You must not eat fruit from the tree that is in the middle of the garden, and you must *not touch it*, or you will die'" (Genesis 3:2–3, NIV).

The actions of our physical body fall under the category of the horn of our flesh. When Adam and Eve touched and ate of the fruit, these were actions that spoke what their heart was saying; it made a negative sound of disobedience to God. God remembered His covenant and responded by bringing death to mankind. Their actions made a sound, and so did our actions until this very day. These actions can include what our hands do, where our feet tread, and what our skin feels. When we see the word "hands" in the Bible, it represents our works. When we see the word "feet" in the Bible, it represents our destination. We also see that skin is also a representation of flesh that indeed connects to touch, but more importantly, connects to the workings of the flesh. The workings of flesh are the sinful nature of mankind. If we apply our actions back to the four methods of communication, the horn of our flesh (skin) would be nonverbal communication.

Let's apply this knowledge to the woman with the alabaster jar quickly by first focusing on touch, which is an action of the flesh (skin) that deals with the physical part of man. We see in Luke chapter 7 the woman anoints Jesus by washing His feet with her tears, wiping them with her hair, and pouring perfume on them. All of the above are actions she made through the use of her flesh because they involved touch. To anoint someone involves, it involves touch. To wash something involves touch. To wipe something involves touch. To pour something involves touch. She was using her hands, a part of her flesh, to touch Christ. This is one way to view it, but let's look deeper by referring to the severity of the fleshly ways in the sight of God. We'll do this by first pointing out the title of Luke chapter 7 (NIV): "Jesus Anointed by a Sinful Woman"; the word "sinful" immediately shows us that there was an emphasis placed on the fleshly ways of this woman. Flesh, as we just discussed, is the sinful nature of mankind. We see the flesh is represented in both ways that we discussed through actions made by the physical touch of mankind and through the sinful nature of mankind in the scripture below, "When the Pharisee who had invited him saw this, he said to himself, 'If this man were a prophet, he would know who is *touching him* and what kind of woman she is—that *she is a sinner*'" (Luke 7:39, NIV).

The Pharisee talked about the woman with the alabaster jar touching Jesus; this is the physical horn of the flesh. He also talked about her being a sinner, which is the sinful nature of the flesh. In this passage, we see that this woman had a sinful nature by using her flesh to do things that fell under the works of the flesh, such as sexual immorality found in Galatians 5:19; we also see that she used her flesh to bring glory to Jesus by anointing Him.

She was using her earthly horn of the flesh to nonverbally communicate with God through her actions because her heart was connected. The Pharisees saw what she was doing but could not understand; they were looking through the eyes of the flesh, which is a lower perspective…not God's perspective. The Pharisee saw a sinner that did not have a right to be near Jesus nor have the right to be touching Him. But in the sight of Jesus, He saw a sinner that has decided to lay her sinful nature down by crucifying her flesh to follow Him. She tuned the sound of her earthly horn from sin to holiness. She sounded her earthly horn of her flesh by touch and her human nature to communicate in a healthy manner to God. God heard the sound of her heart through her touch, remembered her and His covenant, and responded. Luke 7:48 (NIV) says, "Then Jesus said to her, 'Your sins are forgiven.'" When man thought one thing, God thought another. The sound from our earthly horn speaks only to God—not man.

This shows us that whatever we do here on earth, we must allow our flesh to submit to the Spirit. Our hearts must not let the sinful nature take control. Instead, we should stay in healthy communication with God through our actions that first start with our hearts. We communicate in a nonverbal manner through our flesh to God. When we crucify our flesh daily, we are making a sound through our earthly horn of our skin to God that allows our voiceprint to be heard in heaven. We then stay in relationship with Christ and are giving way to be guided by the Spirit. When we die to flesh, we are alive to the Spirit, causing our sound to be clearly heard in heaven resulting in a maintained relationship with God through spiritual communication.

(Verbal Expressions of the Earthly Horn) The Sound of Our Body

The verbal earthly horn is communication from man on earth to God in heaven by releasing a sound from our lips that can be heard by the natural ear. It is when man expresses themselves in an audible manner to God, but the heart must be connected.

The Horn of Our Tongue— The Sound of Our Voice (Authority)

The tongue is the sense organ that allows a human to taste and perceive various flavors.

In the previous section, we discussed nonverbal expressions that were outward from the earthly horn by focusing on the woman with the alabaster jar because she did not speak any words. In this section, her story is not applicable because we are discussing outward expressions that are verbal. With that in mind, we will focus on communication by way of the tongue through other people in the word of God.

So, what does God say about the tongue, and how does the tongue apply to communication from man to God?

Let's start by acknowledging what the tongue is used for as unto God. First of all, we can see that the tongue can be used for the following: to speak, shout/cry out, pray, intercede, petition, command, make supplication, give thanks, encourage, teach, preach, declare, prophecy, sing, etc.

From the list above (with the exception of a few), we can see the benefit of the Body of Christ. This means it is communication that we make horizontally with those around us. What we do for others is a gift God has given through us to others. This shows that God is the sender of the message, meaning He is giving out. This section is more so talking about the direct communication we make to God by way of the tongue. Of the list that I provided previously, we will focus on vertical communication from the tongue from man directly to God without the use of horizontal communication. That would leave us with prayer, intercession, crying/shouting out to God, making petitions to God, singing to God, giving thanks and praise to God.

"Do not be anxious about anything, but in every situation, by prayer and petition, with thanksgiving, present your requests to God" (Philippians 4:6, NIV).

"I urge, then, first of all, that petitions, prayers, intercession and thanksgiving be made for all people" (1 Timothy 2:1, NIV).

"During the days of Jesus' life on earth, he offered up prayers and petitions with fervent cries and tears to the one who could save him from death, and he was heard because of his reverent submission" (Hebrews 5:7, NIV).

We can see that Abraham, Moses, Samuel, Jeremiah, and Job, to name a few, continually prayed and interceded to God. We see that the Israelites cried out to God when they were held in captivity. Miriam, the sister of Moses, Deborah, the judge, and Mary, the mother of Jesus, have songs of praise and thanks. These are just a few of many people who used their tongues to communicate with God. Let's now focus specifically on what the word says specifically about the tongue (mouth) and what it can do.

"The tongue has the power of life and death, and those who love it will eat its fruit" (Proverbs 18:21, NIV).

"The soothing tongue is a tree of life, but a perverse tongue crushes the spirit" (Proverbs 15:4, NIV).

"Those who consider themselves religious and yet do not keep a tight rein on their tongues deceive themselves, and their religion is worthless" (James 1:26, NIV).

"What goes into someone's mouth does not defile them, but what comes out of their mouth, that is what defiles them" (Matthew 15:11, NIV).

"But the things that come out of a person's mouth come from the heart, and these defile them" (Matthew 15:18, NIV).

Based on the scriptures provided, we can see that the tongue of a person can bring life or death. This tells us that our tongue has the authority to create and also to destroy. That is why we have to keep it bridled so that all that comes from it is good. If we are righteous and remain connected to God, then we will sound like Him. The Word says, "The mouths of the righteous utter wisdom, and their tongues speak what is just" (Psalm 37:30, NIV). Righteousness, wisdom, and justice are all found in God. Since we were made in the likeness of God, we know that the words that come from our mouths with our voices were meant to create. I say this because when God spoke in Genesis chapter 1…creation was formed. When it was formed, we can see that God saw that it was good. God is the Creator. If we are made in His image, then that makes us little gods with the ability to create through the God-given instrument of our tongue. Just as when He spoke, He was able to create, and His creation was good; we have the authority to do the same. However, since we are human, we have a sinful nature, meaning that sinful nature has the tendency to cause our tongues to do harm instead of good. Rather than creating good, we sometimes use our words to create evil, which can be defiling, deceitful, destructive, and perverse. These are characteristics of the enemy that we should clearly avoid.

The men and women of God in the Bible were aware of the tendencies of the human tongue, so they had to make a stance to protect it. Throughout the Bible, we can see how the psalmists and writers had to guide their tongue and guard it to do right. But there is one psalmist that I would like to focus on in this section because he was one after God's own heart, and we know the heart is connected to the tongue. That psalmist goes by the name of David. Let's review a few scriptures that he wrote to tame his tongue because of his relationship with God.

"May these words of my mouth and this meditation of my heart be pleasing in your sight, LORD, my Rock and my Redeemer" (Psalm 19:14, NIV).

"I said, 'I will watch my ways and keep my tongue from sin; I will put a muzzle on my mouth while in the presence of the wicked'" (Psalm 39:1, NIV).

Our tongue is an instrument that is used for prayer, but it has to be cleansed daily to be effective. As we can see, David consistently had to pray and make declarations over his tongue to abstain from sin. He prayed for his mouth and word to be guarded with a muzzle. In addition to praying over the words of his mouth, he prayed that his heart would always be acceptable to God. He knew that the words from his tongue were connected to his heart. To tame his tongue, he had to get to the root of his words, which was his heart. He knew that his words could only be righteous and acceptable in the sight of God if his heart was first. David knew that what came from his tongue had to be clean to reach heaven; he had to pass the barrier of uncleanliness first before it could be effective for anything else. He understood that to connect and communicate with God effectively through prayer, he must first be in right standing with God. Due to this, David prayed over his tongue, so he could then pray about everything else. He knew what his tongue was created for, which was to communicate with God, but it had to be cleansed to do the work it was created to do. David stayed in communion with God by continuously staying connected to God by depending on God to bridle his tongue. So that through intimacy and a clean tongue, he could remain in communion with God by the power of prayer through the horn of his tongue.

Our mouth and tongue were created as instruments of praise and worship. Praise and worship are the highest forms of warfare and what we use as an outward testimony of giving worth to our maker. In Psalm 35, David was being pursued by the enemy. The enemy was plotting against him and wanted to seek his life without cause. He began to ask the Lord to fight on his behalf and disgrace those who were coming against him. As he made these requests to the Lord, believing that God would move on his behalf, he began to declare what he would do in return for God, which was to give praise with his tongue.

"My tongue will proclaim your righteousness, your praises all day long" (Psalm 35:28, NIV).

David clearly understood the power of the tongue. He knew that what came from his mouth and tongue should always be good. That is why he declared it shall give God praise "all day long." With this saying, he is decreeing that his tongue should represent good and righteousness not some of the time—but all the time. During David's time, the Holy Spirit did not yet live within people but only came upon people, so it took the effort of the man to keep his tongue bridled. He had to make an effort to keep his tongue under control. But thank God during our time, we have the Holy Spirit living within us to convict us and guide us, so our effort no longer comes from our own strength but instead from the strength of the Spirit of God who is within us.

The next thing I would like to focus on is the power of our voice. As we already know, God gave us authority to create things as we speak, which shows us the power we hold. Our tongue gives way for our voice, which is the audible horn that can be heard for all, both on heaven and on earth. Our voice is the sound that comes from the horn of our tongue. Remember, a horn represents power and authority...especially the ram's horn, which is the shofar, which brings me to this scripture below...

"Raise your voice like a shofar" (Isaiah 58:1a, TLV).

It came from God's own mouth by likening our voice to a shofar. In this scripture, the Lord was speaking from His very own mouth, which is the heavenly horn, to His people to use the horn He has given them. He did this so they could do a true fast due to their rebellion. He said they could not fast and pray as they were used to and expect for their voice to be heard because they were living in strife and contention and did what was wrong in the sight of the Lord while they fasted. God was placing an urgency on them to do a *true* fast, which required their true hearts to be involved. He said to raise their voice like a shofar. Throughout Isaiah chapter 58, God uses words like "cry" and "call" when referring to the people reaching out to Him during this fast, specifically in verse 9. These are all identifying words that are tied to the sound of the shofar. He wanted them to use their God-given earthly horn of their voice. He mentions that if they do so with true sincerity and humility, then they will experience triumph and joy from Him. That goes to show that God would hear from heaven, remember them and His covenant to them, and respond.

We can apply what God said to these people in Isaiah chapter 58 for David as well because he lived a life of repentance by continuously calling out and crying out to God. His voice was like a shofar; when he did wrong, he made the necessary steps to make things right through fasting and prayer. We see from the life of David how he made it a priority to guide his tongue to do good and give praise to God.

David knew how to keep his earthly horn in tune with God. While he did this, God continuously responded by delivering him and keeping him safe. We see that David was pursued by the enemy but was not harmed. He lived a long life and ruled over God's people as king and died of natural causes, not from the hands of the enemy, and was able to have a long-lasting dynasty.

We also see that David sang songs unto the Lord. Singing unto God is a form of communication from man to God in heaven by use of the earthly horn of the tongue ensuring a life of relationship and intimacy with God. He continuously raised his voice like a shofar; God heard from heaven, remembered him and His covenant, and responded because David's heart was connected. He walked in triumph, joy, and oneness with God because God responded to the sound of the earthly horn of David's voice, which was his shofar. The horn of the tongue includes the mouth and voice; this is an example of the outward expression of our heart that releases a sound through verbal communication from man to God.

The Written Expression of the Earthly Horn

Written expressions of the earthly horn are sounds that are released from the heart of man as a heavenly sound communicating to God through writing that can be visible and read by other people but not in all cases completely understood by other people. Written expressions of the earthly horn start from the inward part of a person manifested outwardly using written words.

So, what does God say about writing, and how does writing apply to communication from man to God?

"And the LORD answered me and said, "Write the vision and make it plain on the tablets, that he may run who reads it'" (Habakkuk 2:2, ESV).

In this scripture, God is telling Habakkuk to make sure to write out his vision on tablets so it can be documented in stone and made clear to those who come across it. These words will come to life and speak to those who read them. During those times, composing words on tablets of stone was the normal way to write (which later evolved into scrolls). God Himself wrote with His finger the Ten Commandments on stone tablets so that all could look upon His words of law and remember them. In general, when we think about the Law of Moses and the law of anything, it is a collection of words that have been written as a documentation for those who read it in the present time and for those who read it in the future. At this day and age, we no longer compose our words by writing on tablets of stone (at least on a regular basis). Instead, we compose our words in various forms, such as writing on paper, on boards, through our electronic devices such as our phones, computers, iPads, electronic tablets, etc. Even though the various methods of writing have evolved throughout the centuries, the actual art of writing through expressing thoughts by composing visible words, symbols, marks, and/or signs reflecting a language to convey a message for others to read and understand has not changed.

As we reflect back on Habakkuk 2:2 and apply it to our daily living, we can see that God is not literally saying to write on tablets to us in modern times; He is simply saying to make our thoughts concrete (permanent) by capturing the thoughts in words on something to make it visible. As this happens, the words become more than thoughts that are within a person but instead brought out of the person to communicate to others. That is why God said to "make it plain." Meaning, make your thoughts plain for others to see so that the one who reads the message may run with it. If someone "runs" with it, that means they have read it, understood it, and made actions based upon the message. Which furthermore means they have received what they read, showing that the message was successfully communicated to the reader.

In addition to what God is saying about tablets in the Old Testament, as He is speaking to Habakkuk, it is necessary to see what God shows us in the New Testament, that the law is no longer written on tablets of stone but on our hearts instead (Hebrews 8:10). That means in the sight of God our heart has become a tablet that holds a collection of writings that testify what is within our heart. When we read anything, we are taking in a message that has been sent by the one who conveyed the message. The words that have been written reflect the heart of the author who wrote them. The Bible contains a collection of words that God wrote and of words that He inspired others to write to make plain for those who read it back then, those who read it now, and those who will read it in the future. The Bible is the word of God communicated to us from the heavens; it represents life; the Word of God is Him and reflects who He is. When we write, it reflects our thoughts, perceptions, ideas, and feelings in the form of a composed text that is made plain and communicates to the readers—which is derived from the heart.

Notice how I just mentioned the Bible contains the words of God and the words of people that He inspired to write. With that being said, we will discuss a man who wrote words inspired by God that were recorded in the Bible for us to read to this very day. The man we are about to discuss was a songwriter, musician, shepherd, king, warrior, and after God's own heart (Acts 13:22) who goes by the name of David. Since we have been on the subject matter of David and psalms in the previous section, we will continue to stay in the same flow while discussing the written expression

317

of the earthly horn.

The book of Psalms is a collection of songs and hymns that were sung with music to give worth to God. To simply put it, the book of Psalms is a book of worship songs. We previously talked about David maintaining his relationship with God through continuous prayer over his heart and tongue, which was found in the book of Psalms. But now, we are going to view his psalms from a different angle in the manner he delivered the psalms, which was through writing. It is found that David wrote close to half of what was written in the book of Psalms, 73 to 75 out of the 150, to be exact. There is no doubt that David had a passion for writing to God; therefore, he is the perfect person to discuss the written expression of the earthly horn. For this section, we will focus on how writing can communicate to God.

We see that David had a life that demonstrated his times of ups and downs, celebration, trials, victories, reflections, adoration, desires, pain, fears, prayer, and more. He was a real person, just like you and me, in a real world with real situations. Throughout his lifetime, he would document his thoughts and feelings by writing them that were recorded in the book of Psalms. As he did this, God heard his sound through the written expression of his heart.

In Psalm 2, David was asking questions about those who are plotting against the Lord and His anointed one. He then speaks of how it is in vain because the Lord laughs in the heavens. He then begins to write words that are quoted by the Lord, discussing the triumph of the Son of God and His Kingdom, and then concludes this psalm by saying to serve the Lord with fear, and those who trust in God will be blessed.

This psalm shows that David sees how the enemy devises plans against the Lord and His anointed ones, but they will not succeed. It also shows that he understands how powerful God is, and it is better to serve and trust God. These words were not empty words from David; these were his thoughts and beliefs. We also see these words demonstrated in his life. He consistently saw how the enemy tried to defeat the plans of God through the sins of man, which came from those who opposed God, but in the end, God always received the victory. We also see how David feared God and did not come against God's anointed, which was King Saul. Even though Saul was filled with rage and jealousy, He would not lay a finger to harm Saul because he understood God's power and the power of serving. He put his trust in God to keep him safe from harm, and he knew that God gave him the victory. We also see that he had a relationship with God because he was able to quote words that God spoke (Psalm 2:7–9). This demonstrates that he was able to hear the voice of God; hearing comes from communication. This psalm shows that he actively communicated with God.

In Psalm 23, we can see that David was at a place of fear, but he put his trust in God by reflecting on the provisions of God, particularly in Psalm 23:4b (KJV), "I will fear no evil, [...]; thy rod and thy staff they comfort me." In this psalm, we can see that David needed comfort due to the fear that was trying to present itself to him. He began to make declarations that he would not fear because of what God had given him. He realizes that death may have presented itself to him, but it is just a shadow. This was a psalm that David wrote, showing his humanity that he at times feared but knew that God would take him through.

In Psalm 51, we can see that David was at a place of sorrow and repentance because of the sin he committed against the Lord. This psalm shows how he was feeling; it was a cry of desperation that he was communicating directly to God.

In Psalm 138, David was giving thanks unto the Lord. In Psalm 139, David was reflecting on the omnipotence, omnipresence, and omniscience of God. He realized how he was created by God, and there is nothing that God does not know and nowhere that a man can go to hide from God. In this Psalm, he was asking God to search him and his heart so that he may be led in the ways of God.

The list of psalms goes on and on; each written psalm of David demonstrated his humanity at different periods of his life. Through it all, David used writing to communicate what he felt to God, which we can still access to this day and relate to in various ways. The writing of David reflected his heart to God. Since the heart of David was communicating to God through writing, it made a heavenly sound from earth to God's heart in heaven, thus activating his earthly horn. God heard from heaven, remembered him, and it can be found that God responded continuously through the study of the life of David. He was one who always inquired of the Lord, and the Lord would talk back to David through his servants, prophets, the presence of God's angels, and through priests. All of these are demonstrations that God responded to David's psalms and, more so, David's heart. If God responds, the seventh concept of communication has been reached, completing and activating the loop of communication. Since the seventh concept was reached, that means there was healthy communication between David and God.

The Visual Expression of the Earthly Horn

Visual expressions of the earthly horn are sounds that are released from the heart of man as a heavenly sound communicating to God through visuals that can be visible by people but not in all cases completely understood by other people. Visual expressions of the earthly horn are first developed in thought from the inward part of a person and manifested outwardly by expressing the thought through the creation of an object(s) by use of his/her hands, which can include expressions in artwork, drawings, illustrations, pictures, paintings, images, carvings, inventions, crafts, designs, etc. Visual expressions are basically the expression of a man's heart that communicates to God through creativity, skills, and workmanship.

So, what does God say about visuals, and how do visuals apply to communication from man to God?

In the word of God, we can find the mention of visuals through creativity and workmanship. As we know, we were made in the image of God, who is the Creator. He designed us, molded us, and formed us in His image. Basically, God created us because He is the Creator, demonstrating His gift of creativity and workmanship.

"So God created mankind in his own image, in the image of God he created them; male and female he created them" (Genesis 1:27, NIV).

"For in him all things were created: things in heaven and on earth, visible and invisible, whether thrones or powers or rulers or authorities; all things have been created through him and for him" (Colossians 1:16, NIV).

We are the visible expression of the heart of God through the work of His hands, and so is every other living thing on this earth. If we are made in the Creator's image, that means that we are mini-creators. Based on this, let's review some scriptures that give light to this subject.

"For we are his workmanship, created in Christ Jesus unto good works, which God hath before ordained that we should walk in them" (Ephesians 2:10, KJV).

This scripture means that we are the workmanship of Christ and created in Christ to do good work. Because of this, He has purposed for us to walk in these good works by utilizing our hands as unto Him. If we are to use our hands for His purpose, that means He has already equipped us to do so. God is Spirit, and He needs our physical hands to allow His will to be done here on earth, so He does His part by equipping us to make things happen. We can see a sample of how God equips His people to use their hands so that His will may be done here on earth.

"And he has filled him with the Spirit of God, with skill, with intelligence, with knowledge, and with all craftsmanship" (Exodus 35:31, ESV).

"He has filled them with skill to do all kinds of works as engravers, designers, embroiderers in blue, purple and scarlet yarn and fine linen, and weavers—all of them skilled workers and designers" (Exodus 35:35, NIV).

The above scriptures were in reference to the building of the tabernacle of Moses. It was God who gave all of the workers the skill, intelligence, and knowledge to do the work of building the tabernacle. The fact that they used their hands and utilized the skill, intelligence, and knowledge that God gave them to help build the tabernacle, God's dwelling place on earth, testifies and communicates to God that their hearts were willing and driven to do what gives God pleasure. Remember, God gave man free will. They could have used their God-given abilities and talents for selfish purposes and selfish ambitions to do what pleased themselves, but they chose to use their gift of creativity and workmanship to honor God. Our workmanship and creativity testify that God has given us the ability to communicate through the use of our hands. Our hands were made to give glory to God, and what we create with them serves as a visual expression of our earthly horn. When referring to what the hands create, I am also referring to the visual expressions of our earthly horn.

The objects we create with our hands express and communicate that which is in our heart, so our heart must be lined up with the heart of God. Our hands can speak in a positive manner to God when our hands create that which is good. It is also important to note that our hands can communicate in a negative manner when our heart is not lined up with His. For instance, when the Israelites created an object with their hands known as the golden calf to worship when Moses was at Mount Sinai talking to God. The golden calf was an object of the Israelites' creativity and workmanship and a visual expression of their earthly horn. This object communicated negatively to God, demonstrating that their hearts wanted to worship another god that could not see or speak. This, in turn, ultimately communicated to God that their hearts had turned away from Him. Their creativity and workmanship of the golden calf released a negative sound from their earthly horn to God because their heart was out of sync with God in heaven. As we can see, our creativity and workmanship are a visual expression of our heart, and it makes a sound from our earthly horn to God in heaven. However, we must make sure that our heart is in tune with the heart of God by making a pure and heavenly sound from our earthly horn so that what we express communicates in a positive and healthy manner to God in heaven.

With that in mind, let's apply the visual expression of the earthly horn to King David. Again, I can't reiterate enough that David was a man after God's own heart. Everything David did demonstrated what his heart was speaking. In this section, we can see how David used visuals through the work of his hands to express what was within his heart to communicate to God. We can start first by taking note of the instruments David made. David, as we know, was a musician, and he heard sounds to give praise to God that did not even exist yet. Due to this, he invented and created instruments to make the sounds he was hearing from within to make them become a reality. Let's look at it in the word of God.

> David said, "Of these, twenty-four thousand are to be in charge of the work of the temple of the LORD and six thousand are to be officials and judges. Four thousand are to be gatekeepers and four thousand are to praise the LORD with the musical instruments I have provided for that purpose."
>
> **1 Chronicles 23:4–5 (NIV)**

"The priests took their positions, as did the Levites with the

LORD'S musical instruments, which King David had made for praising the LORD and which were used when he gave thanks, saying, 'His love endures forever'" (2 Chronicles 7:6, NIV).

"So, the Levites stood ready with David's instruments, and the priests with their trumpets" (2 Chronicles 29:26, NIV).

The scriptures mentioned above show that David created musical instruments for the purpose of praising the Lord. The actual object of musical instruments that David created is a visual expression of David's heart, which communicated positively to God because the instruments were made for God's good pleasure. David provided these instruments for God's work to be used by the Levites to give God praise.

David appointed musicians by the name of Asaph, Heman, Jeduthun, and their families to be musicians and leaders of worship in the temple of God. It is interesting to point out that Jeduthun means lauder and praising. A lauder is a person who gives high praise through communication. These three men and their families were "trained and skilled in music for the LORD" (1 Chronicles 25:7, NIV). These men and their families were set apart to play music in the house of God, and God gave them the skill to do so. They had the free will to make a creative sound unto God by utilizing the musical instruments that God inspired David to create, and it was for them to willfully play the musical instruments as unto God. The sound that is released from those who play the musical instruments also communicates to God. Any music released from a musician is also a demonstration of visual expressions to God. Music is a form of our creativity and expressions of our hearts using musical instruments that exist physically. Although we cannot visibly see the sound with our naked eye, it is existent through sound waves. Every musical note released are all visible expressions that communicate to God. It is important to add that although David created these musical instruments to praise God, sometimes the player of the musical instrument can pervert what was intended for good. If a sound is released, the player of the musical instrument must be in tune with the frequency of the Spirit of God so that the sound released is pure and holy. The sounds we release from musical instruments are sounds that reflect what is within our hearts. As we play these instruments, it must be from the standpoint of a heart that wants to give glory unto God. The word sheds light on this matter by explaining what it is to sing songs and make music from the heart and Spirit.

"Instead, be filled with the Spirit, speaking to one another with psalms, hymns, and songs from the Spirit. Sing and make music from your heart to the LORD" (Ephesians 5:18b–19, NIV).

David made it clear that he had a heart to give praise to God through creating musical instruments to make music to accompany singing to give praise to God. The book of Psalms concludes with praising God with instruments, which is found in Psalm 150. Anytime a book ends, that ending is to be memorable for the reader. The book of Psalms ended with the following psalm:

> *Praise God in his sanctuary...his mighty heavens... for his acts of power...for his surpassing greatness... Praise God with...the trumpet...harp and lyre...timbrel and dancing...strings and pipe...clash of cymbals...with resounding cymbals...everything that has breath praise the LORD.*

Psalm 150:1–6 (NIV)

The last psalm shows us that God wants to drive a lasting point to us. That driving point is for us to remember that all His creation should praise Him in His environment and dwelling place (which is our heart, our earthly temple, and in the heavens), praise Him for who He is, and then *praise Him with instruments* and dancing. All living creatures have breath; therefore, it is incumbent that we praise Him. This is the visual expression of communication which is through praising Him with instruments and dancing. If God concludes the book of Psalms by describing the visual expression of communication, that means He is emphasizing this means of communication with Him is not only important to Him but also powerful! On top of that, let's take note of the first instrument that was listed in this psalm for praising Him, which is none other than the trumpet, proving again that this instrument is the father of all instruments.

Other creations of David that visually expressed his heart and communicated to God can be found through his desire to please God. David communicated through a visual expression of his earthly horn in various ways. For example, David built an altar on the threshing floor at Araunah to stop the plague on the people that came due to his wrongful actions of taking a census of Israel and Judah against God's will. The altar he built stood as a visual expression of his repentance, sacrifice, and need for God to answer his prayer on behalf of the people. Building an altar shows creativity and workmanship by the work of our hands, which creates a sound from the heart of man to the heart of God. God saw the altar and accepted the sacrifices and offerings of David that were made at that altar. It says in 2 Samuel 24:25 that the Lord answered David's prayer and stopped the plague that was upon the people of the land.

Another example can be found in 1 Chronicles chapter 22 when David made preparation to build a temple for God. He designed it, and his son Solomon gave the orders to have it built. The design and preparations that David made are visual expressions of his heart to God. David told Solomon that it was in his heart to build it, but God told him that due to his life of war and his hands that have shed extensive blood, David was not qualified to build it, but God allowed his son to do so. The fact that God responded to David by having a temple built through his son Solomon by honoring the preparations David made shows that God was responding to the visual expression of his heart.

The examples of David clearly show us how effective communication can be to God through our earthly horn of visual expressions. When we create objects through the works of our hands as unto God, it makes a heavenly sound and causes God to respond as long as our heart is in right standing with God. This goes to show that our creativity and workmanship are a form of communication. Our creativity and workmanship are a visual expression of our horn, and if our heart is connected to God, it communicates to God, causing God's response. When God responds, we see that the loop of healthy communication is in effect from the heart of man to the heart of God.

All forms of expressions of our earthly horn make various sounds and communicate to God through inward and outward expressions from our heart to God's heart, which consists of non-verbal, verbal, written, and visual expressions that we should now understand after the reading of this chapter. We saw examples of how the earthly horn can be utilized in these various expressions by studying the woman with the alabaster jar, the woman with the issue of blood, through the life of King David, and, most importantly, through the life of Jesus.

Our earthly horn is our instrument of communication to God. Our earthly horn is our musical instrument that supernaturally speaks from our heart to God through worship. Why? Because our earthly horn is our horn of worship that speaks to God through the Son of God, Jesus Christ, and is filled with the wind of the Holy Spirit. Making sounds unto God is worship. After all, our earthly horn is our trumpet and our God-given instrument that expresses everything that we do and translates those doings into a particular sound in heaven uniquely set apart as our communication tool and voiceprint in the heavens. Our life is a song of worship. Our worship is the sound that comes from our earthly horn. The sounds released from our earthly horn come from various expressions of our heart, all these expressions are various acts of worship to God. Our earthly horn is the horn of worship.

CHAPTER 19

THE HORN OF WORSHIP— GETS GOD'S ATTENTION AND INVOKES GOD'S RESPONSE

Now that we have taken the time to understand the importance of sound, we can now dive deeper into the various aspects of sound and how it relates to worship. We will be able to see what sounds are necessary for certain levels of worship. The sound that a person releases through worship can also help determine the type of response one receives from God in worship. That response to sound can come in various ways depending on the type of sound released from a vessel and by the level of faith. Keep in mind that all of this must be done by the leading of the Holy Spirit of God.

What is worship? Worship is the act of giving worth, adoration, homage, honor, reverence, and glory to our God. We, meaning humanity, were created to worship God. He created us with the inclination and void within our hearts to worship Him that only He can fill. We must also take into consideration that because of the free will He has given us to choose to worship Him or not worship Him, that void in our hearts can be filled with other things. No matter what, man will find a way to worship something, even if it is not God, because we (mankind) were created for the purpose of worship. Whatever we give our utmost attention to is what we worship. It is for us to make the choice of worshiping God Almighty.

Worship is the most important thing we could ever do in our lifetime here on earth and will be all we ever do once we are in heaven...that is, if we choose to worship Him. God made us in His image, so He can have someone in His likeness that He can relate with to give Him worth. Our worship is our relationship with God—it is our very purpose. Our worship is how we communicate with God and how we relate with God. Worship is our connection with God that takes place in such a deep way that no man can truly understand but God; because it comes from the secret place, our intimate place, and innermost being place. That place is the throne room of our hearts. Our heart is the holy of holies within our bodily temple.

Think about it, we did a study earlier on the tabernacle, which is separated into three parts. The tabernacle was a place set apart for God to dwell here on earth. The tabernacle was a place of continuous worship to God by following strict protocols of worship due to the law of the covenant that God gave to Moses for the people. When Jesus died and rose again, He fulfilled the law causing us to no longer need to worship God through a man-made tabernacle/temple. We now have access to worship God by way of Jesus through our bodily temple as we are here on earth.

That means our bodily temple is also separated into three parts and three levels of worship, the outer court, inner court, and holy of holies. The *outer court* is our flesh which must be sacrificed and cleansed daily by the blood of Jesus to get to the next level of worship. The *inner court* is our ministry and service before God, our works, and maintenance of relationship through prayer, fellowship, worship, and communing with God by the help of the Holy

Spirit. The *holy of holies* is our heart, the place where God dwells and speaks to us. Instead of laws written upon tablets of stone, it is now written upon our hearts, enclosed within and protected by the ark of God's new covenant that was spoken even before it came into being.

"I will give you a new heart and put a new spirit in you; I will remove from you your heart of stone and give you a heart of flesh. And I will put my Spirit in you and move you to follow my decrees and be careful to keep my laws" (Ezekiel 36:26–27, NIV).

The holy of holies within our bodily temple is not only the place of God's awesome presence but also the place of God's response to us. In the holy of holies, the heavenly horn meets with the earthly horn of the man. The Horn of Salvation is present here in His highest and truest form. This is also where our earthly horn is present without inhibitions, meaning this is where our heart communicates to God in its deepest and truest form. The holy of holies in our hearts is where we are completely surrendered and set apart for Him. This is the place where flesh is no longer present but where our spirit becomes one with God. This is where we are no longer busy doing the things of God but instead at a place of stillness where we are hearing from God and getting His direction. This is also the place of exposure of our true selves and the place of empowerment where God allows us to see His glory, where we begin to look like Him, sound like Him, and walk like Him. The holy of holies is the place of intimacy between man and God, behind the veil, where the crowd is no more; it is just one on one. The holy of holies in our bodily temple is the place of the kingdom exchange, where all that we have communicated to God has been heard and is now being answered by His response. This is where God reveals Himself to us. As it relates to the seven concepts of communication, this is the place of the seventh concept, where the receiver (God) has heard the message and is now sending a message back to us. This is the place of response!

The response that is released from God represents life itself, which can be viewed as the heavenly response. His response to an earthly vessel can come forth without notice, but His response always comes after something leaves earth first. You may ask the question, "What is that something?" That something is worship. Worship tugs on God; it catches His attention and draws Him nigh to the person worshiping Him. The moment we make a sound of worship to Him is the moment He responds.

The woman with the issue of blood was one who demonstrated this in Mark 5:24–34 (NLT) when she received a heavenly response from God in the flesh, Jesus Christ:

> *Jesus went with him, and all the people followed, crowding around him. A woman in the crowd had suffered for twelve years with constant bleeding. She had suffered a great deal from many doctors, and over the years she had spent everything she had to pay them, but she had gotten no better. In fact, she had gotten worse. She had heard about Jesus, so she came up behind him through the crowd and touched his robe. For she thought to herself, "If I can touch his robe, I will be healed." Immediately the bleeding stopped, and she could feel in her body that she had been healed of her terrible condition.*
>
> *Jesus realized at once that healing power had gone out from him, so he turned around in the crowd and asked, "Who touched my robe?"*
>
> *His disciples said to him, "Look at this crowd pressing around you. How can you ask, 'Who touched me?'"*
>
> *But he kept on looking around to see who had done it. Then the frightened woman, trembling at the real-*

*ization of what had happened to her, came and fell to
her knees in front of him and told him what she had
done. And he said to her, "Daughter, your faith has
made you well. Go in peace. Your suffering is over."*

The woman pulled on Jesus' garment in complete belief that
the Lord would heal her. Since there was a crowd of people around
Jesus, one can only imagine the tugging and commotion of all the
people surrounding Him. However, during all that, Jesus still felt
virtue leaving His body due to the actions of one individual. In the
Word of God, the moment she pulled on His garment, it says that
"immediately" Jesus felt virtue leave His body. This is the heavenly
response being demonstrated in the Word. There was an exchange
that came due to the action made from a vessel here on earth. In
this example, the vessel was the woman with the issue of blood.
She caused Jesus to stop what He was doing at that moment. Virtue
left from Him that moment, and that virtue entered the woman that
moment. That virtue was His presence, which came with healing
to make her whole. The heavenly response that followed her proactive step of action came not only with healing but also with the
sound of His voice when He asked, "Who touched my clothes?"
We can look at it as God saying to her, "[...] you've got my full
attention." This is also another demonstration that His mind was
not preoccupied with anything else but her at that moment.

Jesus responded to her after she made the first step. Why? Because of the degree of worship and belief that came from the woman that needed Jesus and His healing power. This is also applicable to us when we worship. The measure of what we give to God
through our sacrifice of praise and worship is the measure of what
we receive back from the Father. A response always comes after a
sound is released. The heavenly response takes place after we take
a proactive step of action when it comes to worshiping the Lord.
Meaning an act on our part is required first before that heavenly
response can come into play.

Once she received the attention of Jesus, she not only received her healing but was able to get the confirming word from Jesus Himself, which came with direction. He said to her, "Daughter, your faith has healed you. Go in peace and be freed from your suffering" (Mark 5:34, NIV). Jesus' words to her reassured her that her healing was not a temporary thing, but He responded by speaking directly to her, saying that she was completely healed, and He brought her peace by speaking His shalom over her to worry no more.

The healing she received was only a part of what He had to offer her. He also gave her His time and attention. Meaning, when we have God's time and complete attention, we can then share with Him our concerns, our requests, and our supplications. It says in the Word of God that once He stopped, she began to tell Him all that she had been through. He listened to all she had to say. Once she laid out everything before Jesus, He responded to her directly by giving her direct guidance by His word of what to do moving forward.

Let's break what the woman with the issue of blood did when she crossed path with Jesus down into simple steps so we can take note of this and apply it to our lives:

1. believe;
2. act by reaching out to God;
3. make your supplications;
4. have faith and expect Him to move;
5. wait;
6. listen for His voice and prepare your spirit, heart, and body;
7. receive His response of empowerment and direction;
8. act by obeying and following His commands.

The woman with the issue of blood is an example of an earthly vessel using her earthly horn, which is the horn of worship unto God. Her faith and belief in Jesus Christ demonstrated that she was utilizing her horn of worship. Worship is all about relationship from the worshiper to the deity being worshiped. Relationship is an exchange of communication between two parties. When we worship God, we are communicating our love and devotion for Him from our heart, and He, in turn, is responding from His heart. When we worship God, we are relating to Him, which causes Him to give us His full attention and respond.

The woman with the issue of blood demonstrates what relationship and communication with God are all about. She believed in Him, and the worship within her heart connected with Jesus demonstrating healthy communication from the first concept of communication all the way to the seventh concept; there was a sender of the message, a recipient of the message, and a response from the recipient completing the loop of communication.

Jesus listened to all she had to say, and she, in turn, listened to what Jesus had to say as a response. This was an exchange of communication from earth to heaven and heaven to earth. Through her actions, she was able to be a recipient of His benefits because her heart was in tune with Jesus. She had a heart of worship, causing the response of Jesus to be invoked, which means her earthly horn made a powerful sound that got Jesus's attention because it was filled with worship. She knew the power of giving worth through her horn of worship; Jesus understood this and responded, demonstrating relationship between God and man.

There is power and authority granted to us when we understand that the sound of our earthly horn is our horn of worship. God wants us to understand and use the God-given instrument of the earthly horn He has given us in the way that He intended and purposed for it. The sound of our earthly horn, which is our worship, is our instrument of authority and power that God originally gave us from the time He created us, and we must grab a hold of it. Adam and Eve once held the power to rule and have dominion over the earth, but they were tricked into giving that authority to the enemy because they were not in complete awareness of the God-given power they held on earth. Positively, Jesus paid the price as the second Adam and gave us the opportunity to gain access to our God-given authority again that was once lost by the first Adam. Remember, the horn is a representation of power and authority. Your earthly horn is your God-given means to have authority and power within the earth. But to utilize this authority, we must first understand the power and authority of our sound.

CHAPTER 20

UNDERSTANDING OUR GOD-GIVEN AUTHORITY BY MEANS OF SOUND

To understand our God-given authority, let's revisit the woman with the issue of blood. Keep in mind that this woman had the issue of blood for twelve years, and she dealt with various physicians spending everything she had, only to return to her sickness. Not only that, but with all her visits with various physicians... she only grew worse. One could only imagine the constant defeat and struggles that she may have had before, where she had high hopes of being healed but was constantly let down and constantly disappointed because of her illness remaining. Jesus knew that she not only needed the physical healing but also needed the mental and spiritual healing as well. The encouraging words from Jesus, stating that she was made whole, caused her to be uplifted and confident in the healing that she had just received from Jesus.

God speaks in numbers, so it is important to take note of the timeframe of the plague that she was dealing with before it came to an end. That number is twelve, which is God's perfect number; it also means authority and government and Israel in completeness as a nation. God wants us to know the authority that He has given us here on earth. This woman had the power and the authority to make a change to her situation. All He wanted her to do was make use of that authority, and on the twelfth year of her issue, she finally stood in her God-ordained position by utilizing the authority He gave to us here on this earth. It is important to add that our authority does not come by our own strength but by the strength of God. She was empowered with authority to change her circumstance by worshiping God and believing that He could and would heal her. It all came by her taking the initiative and by using her authority by thinking, "If I just touch his clothes, I will be healed" (Mark 5:28, NIV).

If we look in the Word of God, we can see that God takes special pride in the number twelve. He created twelve tribes from the twelve sons of Jacob. These twelve men became the foundation of Israel and the vessels used for His promises to come through. These twelve men became a mighty nation. God also commanded Joshua in Joshua 4:1–4 to have twelve men, one representing each tribe, to take a stone on his shoulder from the Jordan. Shoulder also represents "government"; anything connected to government represents authority, rulership, control, and leadership over a people, community, organization, state, and/or nations.

The twelve men chosen by Joshua were directed to take the stones from the middle of the Jordan, carry them over to the place they were to lodge, and then lay them down at that place. These twelve stones from the Jordan River stood as a memorial for future generations. Jordan signifies deliverance. Understand that God will deliver us from what seems to be the impossible and carry us to a place of authority. What seems to be a stone, stumbling block, or blockage in our lives, we must rest assured that God has us covered and will deliver us as long as we know who we are and take authority. We must use our God-given authority to make decrees; God will most assuredly meet with us and deliver us from all adversities. Not only should we use our God-given authority, but we shall make it as a monument and a testimony for others to be brought into faith as well.

In the tabernacle, God specified that there must be twelve loaves of unleavened bread on the table in Leviticus 24:5. In Revelation chapter 7, it speaks that 12,000 from each tribe of Israel receive the seal. In Revelation chapter 21, it shows us that there are twelve pearly gates in the new Jerusalem, and to each gate, there is an angel totaling the amount of twelve. The city measured 12,000 stadia, and its breadth and height were the same. The foundation of the city's wall was covered with twelve precious stones. In Luke 2:42–52, we see that at the age of twelve, Jesus stayed at the temple among teachers to learn by questioning them and listening to their responses. It was at this point that the Bible records the words of Jesus acknowledging God as His Father to His earthly parents. Another example of twelve can be found in the New Testament when God sought for disciples. These twelve men turned out to be those who continued the work of Jesus by spreading faith and the Gospel of Jesus. There are other recordings of twelve in the Word of God, but for the sake of this reading, we can see the importance of the number twelve within the Bible. The constant references of the number twelve show us how important it is to understand authority and government. That way, we can see the number twelve as a memorial of His power and the power and governmental authority He has given to us as vessels here on earth.

Now, I know that we are focusing on sound at the moment. In the case of the woman with the issue of blood, she didn't make an audible sound when she reached for the hem of Jesus' garment. But I want to say to you that she did make a sound, a sound that began first with a thought (which we discussed in a previous chapter), which lined up with her heart and caused that heart's desires to turn into an action. She used her God-given authority by speaking from within, "I will be healed" (Mark 5:28, NIV) if she could touch the garment of Jesus. The words "I will" are words of declaration that come from the unseen but real dimension of faith. Declaratory words are commands; commands can only come from someone that holds authority. She grabbed hold of this authority by allowing her earthly horn of authority to be utilized under the operation of her faith.

Faith and belief are the sound of the heart emitting a powerful blast from our earthly horn that gives us the power and authority. The sound that comes from our faith and belief is what communicates from our vessel on earth. This sound causes us to gain access to the spiritual existence of the thing we are believing for in the heavenly realm and bring it back down to the earth realm causing it to become reality.

"Now faith is *the substance* of things hoped for, *the evidence of things not seen*" (Hebrews 11:1, KJV).

This scripture shows us that faith is something tangible because it says it is "the substance" and "the evidence" of something that is not yet seen. These are two descriptive words that prove it is something that is real. Although it is not yet seen in the natural, it exists and carries a heavy weight in the spiritual. Faith is clearly seen and heard in the supernatural. Faith pulls what is in the spiritual into the natural. Having the ability to bring what was not into something that is shows that power and authority are in operation. Think about faith as a boomerang. Once a boomerang is thrown, it comes right back to the sender. When faith is in operation within us, it is released from our heart, pierces into the heavens, and legally brings back to us what we are believing to receive from heaven. That's why Jesus said,

> *"Have faith in God...Truly I tell you, if anyone says to this mountain, 'Go throw yourself into the sea,' and does not doubt in their heart but believes that what they say will happen, it will be done for them. Therefore I tell you, whatever you ask for in prayer, believe*

that you have received it, and it will be yours."

Mark 11:22–24 (NIV)

What we believe for is ours if we have faith in God to do it. Whatever is in heaven, we have the authority and power to gain access to it because Jesus gave us the access to do so by His blood and through His name. He came to this earth as a man and gave us an example of how we can operate with power and authority as God originally ordained us to. As we can see, Jesus was able to perform signs, miracles, and wonders, which are all a part of the supernatural realm. He brought what was in heaven to earth because He knew who He was and understood His purpose and stayed connected to the Father in heaven. Jesus utilized and sounded His horn to the maximum potential while here on earth, which is why Jesus has the authority as "the Horn of Salvation."

That same power and authority have been granted to us as well. That is why Jesus told His disciples that they would do greater works than Him. But these greater works could only happen by using their earthly horn under the operation of faith and through the name of Jesus. What Jesus said to His disciples, He is also saying to us. We shall do greater works and walk in authority and power by sounding our earthly horn under the operation of faith. Our faith makes a sound, and it is what takes hold of the authority and power God granted us with.

Based on what we have learned about sound, we can understand that God's interpretation of sound is completely different from what a lot of us believe it to be here on earth. It is the norm to believe that sound can only come from a source that produces something that can be naturally heard and audible to our ears. However, as we previously discussed, sound does not have to necessarily be heard from the natural hearing; in God's perspective, sound is heard through the spirit. What we hear audibly is only that which is paired with the spirit. In other words, the sound that we hear and release naturally is a manifestation of what took place first in the spirit. The sound that God hears comes from our earthly horn, the God-given instrument of spiritual communication that derives from the heart.

Before moving on, I want you to understand there are different levels of authority. There is a language that belongs to each level. But God wants us to embrace and take hold of the full authority that comes in the highest level, which is the level of faith... the highest realm of authority that God has granted humans with. However, some of us are living below this realm or level. Here are some sample words that belong to the highest level of authority:

Faith—is paired only with the Spirit—*I will, I believe, I shall, I expect, assuredly, most certainly, confident, evidence, possible, approved, etc.*

Hope—is paired with a semblance of doubt, which includes flesh. This is the belief and an expectation that something might happen while also giving room to believing that it may not happen; it is a desire for a promise to come to pass; some samples of words that are used in this realm are: *If it be your will, my desire is that...; I wish, I long, I yearn, I anticipate, possibility, etc.*

Doubt—is paired with a large percentage of the flesh and a minimal to no amount of the Spirit of God. Doubt is being uncertain, having disbelief, and/or no conviction. This includes a lack of faith, mistrust, distrust, uncertainty, hesitation, questioning, suspicion, vacillating, insecurity, wavering, unease, disbelief, and the presence of fear. Some samples of words that are used in this realm are: *I don't know, not sure, if it is true, then, unless I see, maybe, who knows, I will not, I can't, etc.*

Faith is something that is necessary for our God-given authority to operate in its fullness. Doubt places limitations on the authority and leaves little room for God to move. If we don't believe in what God can do, that means we don't completely know God...which shows that our relationship and communication with Him are not where it clearly needs to be. Faith is a large part of our relationship with Christ because this shows our acceptance of Him as who He truly is. Our worship is all about giving worth to God, who we cannot see. Our spiritual communication is all about communicating with God, who we cannot see. Our belief in God, Jesus, and the Holy Spirit is all about believing in Him, who we cannot see, so our relationship with Him is all based on a foundation of faith. If faith is missing, we already have lost maximum access to the power and authority that God gave to us. Power and authority come from our connection to the one who holds all power and authority. If we don't have faith, we have automatically placed limitations on the God-given authority and power within ourselves. We also place limitations on what God can do through us and for us.

But when you ask, you must believe and not doubt, because the one who doubts is like a wave of the sea, blown and tossed by the wind. That person should not expect anything from the Lord. Such a person is double-minded and unstable in all they do.

James 1:6–8 (NIV)

To receive anything from the Lord, faith and belief are required for Him to respond and perform. His response comes from the sound we make from our earthly horn. But if we have doubt, that means we have no clarity of mind and become unable to walk with assurance leaving us with limited access to receive from God, walk with God, and move in the authority that God has given us. If we lack assurance and lack sure-footedness, we lack authority and power. True authority and power come from being one with the One who holds all authority and power. To walk in authority, it is important that doubt is not present; with doubt, it is impossible to move in power. Think about the story of doubting Thomas. He did not believe that Jesus appeared to the others unless he witnessed seeing Jesus for himself. "Unless I see the nail marks in his hands and put my finger where the nails were, and put my hand into his side, I will not believe" (John 20:25b, NIV).

This statement Thomas made of "unless I see..." reflected Thomas' doubtful heart and his lack of faith, which shows us that the relationship he had with Christ was not at the maximum level and potential that God had intended for him. It says in the Word that Jesus appeared to him so Thomas' natural eyes could see that He was really alive from the dead, and Jesus showed him His nail-pierced hands and feet to prove it. It was only after Thomas saw Jesus in the flesh with the nail marks that he believed. After seeing the marks on Jesus, Thomas proclaimed, "My Lord and my God!" (John 20:28, NIV) Upon this statement, Jesus responded by saying, "Because you have seen me, you have believed; blessed are those who have not seen and yet have believed" (John 20:29, NIV).

When Jesus used the words "not seen and yet believed," it is the evidence of faith, which is the key to the authority and power. Jesus' response spoke powerfully because He calls the ones who don't see Him but believe in Him blessed. Blessed are the ones who have faith and do not doubt; these are the ones who have a heart that is connected to God. A heart that is connected to God is a heart that worships God freely without limitations. When you are connected to God, all that comes from Him and all that belongs to Him also belongs to you...which includes walking in authority and power. That means when you pray for something, declare something, and believe for something, it will be granted. Going back to the number twelve, God gave us the governmental authority to rule within this earth, but we have to come into a knowing of the authority that we have. We have to grab hold of it. God has given us the horn of power, but we have to take the action to pick it up and use it—it is not forced upon us.

Thomas was given access to authority and power that God intended for him because he was one of the chosen twelve. Twelve, meaning he was given direct access to hear from God in the flesh, believe, and continue the purpose and responsibility of spreading the gospel with power and authority. He could have moved into a higher realm of authority; however, as we see, he didn't. He did not take the opportunity to pick up his earthly horn and utilize the authority and power granted and freely given to him. We don't see any stories of Thomas moving in authority when Jesus ascended to the Father. We see what Peter did, we see what John did, we see what James did, and many more of the twelve disciples because we see that they took actions and moved in authority and power after Jesus ascended into heaven. They moved in signs, miracles, and wonders, expanded the Gospel of Christ, and became history-makers and kingdom-shakers by the help of the Holy Spirit, who empowered them. Some of them have a book for themselves in the New Testament, making their mark on this earth. Why? Because they had a knowing of who they were in Christ. They were men of action. They had faith and belief in the one they served. They had a relationship and maintained communication with God and moved in power and authority because they were hooked to the source of power and authority. This shows their earthly horn, their God-given instrument of authority of power, was actively in use because of their heart of faith. They worshiped God, and their heart was connected, therefore, making a sound from their earthly horn to its maximum potential of power and authority.

However, Thomas did not utilize his earthly horn of authority and power to its maximum potential. He was living below His God-given authority due to his doubt and lack of belief in Jesus, who is the Horn, the power and authority holder of salvation. Thomas does not have a book for himself in the New Testament because he lacked a heartfelt connection and relationship with God because he was not a man of action and, furthermore, not a man

345

of faith. Instead of being remembered as one of Jesus' twelve disciples that carried on the mission of spreading the Gospel of Jesus Christ, he is forever marked as the one who doubted. So much so it is to the point where he has been named as a patriarch of doubt, known as "Doubting Thomas," a term used to depict a person's lack of belief even today.

We must put action to what God says and not only be listeners. Be doers of the word, men of action, like most of Jesus' disciples. Ancient Hebrew thought is based on action. The Hebrew language is based on function, purpose, and doing. Jesus chose to come through the race of the Jews as He dwelled with us on earth, which holds a language that is based on action. Jesus came to earth as a man of action and expects us to be men of action as well:

> But be doers of the word, and not hearers only, deceiving yourselves. For if anyone is a hearer of the word and not a doer, he is like a man who looks intently at his natural face in a mirror; for he observes himself, goes away, and immediately forgets what kind of man he was. But he who looks into the perfect law of liberty and continues in it, and is not a forgetful hearer but a doer of the work, this one will be blessed in what he does.
>
> **James 1:22–25 (NKJV)**

We are blessed when we believe in the one that we serve. It is our faith that allows us to be empowered and to walk in authority. Empowerment comes from the Holy Spirit. Our faith allows us to gain access to the spiritual and heavenly realm causing that natural to become supernatural. We have the power to cause what is in heaven to also be done on earth through the authority that God has given us. That authority comes from knowing who we are, having faith and belief in who we serve, understanding the full potential of our earthly horn that God has given us to use. Not only understanding the full potential but utilizing it and sounding it in the way it was originally ordained to be used through faith in Him and staying in communion with God. When we do this, we go from not only making a sound from earth and it being heard in heaven but also gaining access to bring what is in heaven to earth.

Understand your authority and walk in it by consistently sounding your earthly horn by faith. Understand the power you hold as a believer and walk in it. Sound your earthly horn and act through faith. Understand the power of your horn; it gives you access to what is rightfully yours since you are one with Christ. Leave no room for doubt and keep blowing it, symbolizing your healthy communication and relationship with God in heaven. Make your declarations, pray, and have expectation within your heart. What you believe shall come to pass, by the help of the Holy Spirit, and through the name of Jesus, because of your faith and because of your sound. God will hear, remember, respond, and grant you with that which you are believing for—you have the authority and power because God gave it to you, and with that comes the victory, so use it. Your earthly horn is not only your sound but also your weapon!

CHAPTER 21

THE EXALTED HORN EXPLAINED

Now that we have discussed the power and authority of our earthly horn, we see that it gives us victory if we use it to the maximum potential that God originally intended for it. Victory is accessible when we blow our earthly horn, hooking to the source of who holds all victory, and that is what brings us to the subject matter of the exalted horn. If you remember, we briefly touched on the exalted horn while discussing the significance of the horn in the earlier part of this book. However, I believe that it is worth breaking "the exalted horn" down further in a chapter for itself. Reason being, is that it has everything to do with strong communication with the Lord.

What Is an Exalted Horn?

This is when a righteous person has received victory and success by the power of God. This victory and success come by obtaining power, strength, honor, glory, and dominion from God in front of those who surround them, particularly in front of his/her enemies. Meaning God has come to the defense of the righteous. It also represents a righteous person being elevated from their current status.

Throughout the Word of God, there are various passages that refer to God exalting the horn of someone. On the other end, we can also see where people in the Bible prayed for God to exalt their horn, or they acknowledged that their horn had been exalted. The question is, what took place in these various scenarios of "the exalted horn" where this was spoken and what was prayed? Let's take a look at the scripture that make reference of the exalted horn.

The Prayer of Hannah:

"And Hannah prayed and said: 'My heart rejoices in the LORD; *My horn is exalted* in the LORD. I smile at my enemies because I rejoice in Your salvation'" (1 Samuel 2:1, NKJV).

Written by King David:

"All the horns of the wicked also will I cut off; but *the horns of the righteous shall be exalted*" (Psalm 75:10, KJV).

Written by Ethan the Ezrahite:

> *For thou art the glory of their strength: and in thy favor our horn shall be exalted. For the LORD is our defense; and the Holy One of Israel is our king. Then thou spakest in vision to thy holy one, and saidst, I have laid help upon one that is mighty; I have exalted one chosen out of the people. I have found David my servant; with my holy oil have I anointed him: With whom my hand shall be established: mine arm also shall strengthen him. The enemy shall not exact upon him; nor the son of wickedness afflict him. And I will beat down his foes before his face, and plague them that hate him. But my faithfulness and my mercy shall be with him: and in my name shall his horn be exalted.*

Psalm 89:17–24 (KJV)

Writer Unknown:

"But my horn shalt thou exalt like the horn of an unicorn: I shall be anointed with fresh oil" (Psalm 92:10, KJV).

"They have freely scattered their gifts to the poor, their righteousness endures forever; *their horn will be lifted high* in honor" (Psalm 112:9, NIV).

As we can see, there are plenty of people who experienced an exalted horn in their lifetime. Those whose horns were exalted included Hannah, King David, Ethan (who referred to David in this scripture), and even those who we are unaware of, yet their writings are captured in the Word of God. This shows that God was faithful to bring honor and strength to them by lifting them up in their time of need and before their enemies. For this chapter, we will go into the life of one of these people, who will be Hannah, a powerful intercessor in the Word of God, one who was found to be in a lowly state but brought high by God, based on what is recorded in the Word of God. Let's discuss the prayer of Hannah by reviewing her back story.

Hannah was married to Elkanah, son of Jeroham, and so was Peninnah. While Peninnah was able to have children for Elkanah, Hannah could not because she was barren, but Elkanah loved her very much. Peninnah would constantly provoke and taunt Hannah because she could not have children. This constant irritation from Peninnah caused Hannah to get to a place of deep anguish where she cried out to the Lord. Eli, the priest, misunderstood Hannah's cry for the behavior of a drunkard. So not only was she taunted by Peninnah, but also incorrectly judged by Eli. Even though she was highly loved by God and by her husband, she was recognized by others in a negative light.

In biblical times, the expectation of a woman in society was to be a mother through fruitfulness and multiplication by having children and caring for them. Bearing children was a gift that only

God Himself can give because He is the giver of birth and death. It is God who causes the womb of a woman to be opened or closed, fruitful or unfruitful, fertile or infertile, blessed or not blessed. When a woman had a child, it revealed that God's hand was upon her to continue the line of a generation. A woman who was able to have children was viewed as someone who was highly valued, highly favored, blessed, and adored.

Barrenness, on the other hand, was shameful to the woman whose womb was closed. It was understood that if a woman could not have a child, God was putting a halt of the continuation of a generation through that chosen woman, and His hand of blessing was withdrawn from her womb. A barren woman was viewed as someone who was scorned, a person of reproach, who had possible hidden sin or fault that was punishable by an infertile womb. Barrenness was often linked to a woman in distress. This goes to show that the status of Hannah in the sight of others, such as her rival Peninnah, seemed to be inferior. The fact that Eli thought she was a drunkard shows that he believed she was one who indulged in fleshly pleasures because it is associated to lust, gluttony, lack of wisdom, and being easily led astray. In general, we can see that she was a wrongfully judged woman because her dilemma incorrectly labeled her status and who she was as a person.

However, Hannah did not allow her dilemma to label her. She made a stance by utilizing her earthly horn because she prayed from the deepest depths of her heart. Hannah prayed for a son and made a promise that she would give him back to God. She also utilized her authority by speaking forth what will happen when her son does come, that he will be given to the Lord all his life, and no razor will touch his head. Not only that, but she was specific of what gender the child would be; by saying son, she was declaring that it would be a boy. This was the sign of faith and belief—she was using the power and authority God had given her to speak things into being. With that, God remembered her, responded, and gave her the desires of her heart by granting her with a son in the presence of those who wrongfully judged her. She used her horn, and God caused her dilemma to turn into victory.

God changed her lowly situation by giving her a son that was used mightily for the service of God. God elevated her status from being barren to being remembered by God. She was highly favored of God and blessed with a son who became a prophet to kings and was a priest to God's temple. All of this happened before her enemy Peninnah, in front of the priest Eli, who originally accused her of being drunk, and in front of the crowds (representing society). This is an example of someone whose horn was exalted, and Hannah realized it. That is why she acknowledged in her prayer that her horn was exalted in 1 Samuel 2:1; God gave her power, strength, honor, and victory in the presence of her foes and the judgments that come along with society. That was the story of Hannah and how her horn was exalted.

As we viewed the life of Hannah, we can see how God changed her situation and exalted her horn. We can also apply that to the lives of others within the Word of God and even to our lives and the lives of others in our present society. Anytime God comes to the rescue of someone after they cry out to Him and God exalts them changing their situation from defeat to victory, from sorrow to joy, from death to life, from lack to abundance, from low to high, and so forth, we see that their horn has been exalted. Although the actual words "exalted horn," "lifted horn," "raised horn," etc., may not always literally be said, they can always be represented. This happens when God has elevated someone's status who is in right standing with Him by giving them power, strength, honor, and victory over their negative circumstance while also bringing down the proud. To keep it simple, the exalted horn is when God exalts the lowly and makes low the proud.

Psalm 148:14 shows us that Israel, the godly ones who have

His heart, is a people who have been lifted up and have been given a Horn, who is the Horn of Salvation. This is not just Israel as a country, but the spiritual Israel, those who are one with Christ through their faith, love, and belief within their hearts for Him. We experience the exalted horn daily if we are in right standing with him. We have been lifted up from our lowly state of sin and death and are exalted with Christ because He has given us forgiveness of sin and life more abundantly. We have the victory!

Now that we have discussed the exalted horn in depth, let's look into the One who exalts the horn of His people, God the Father. When God blows His heavenly horn, it is referred to as the great trumpet, which is known to sound three times within the Bible. He blows this when He communicates with His bride in preparation to exalt the horn of His bride from her lowly state to being brought high with Him. The sound of His great trumpet comes as a warning for the church whom He loves to get ready so He can exalt us in the presence of the enemy and the ungodly within this world. He and His bride will get the victory through the defeat of Satan, so we must take heed to His call.

CHAPTER 22

THE THREE GREAT TRUMPETS

In the Word of God, there are three great trumpets, also known as three great blasts of the shofar. These blasts of the three great trumpets are extremely important and stand as a marker of three significant events of God. The names of these trumpets are the first trumpet, the last trumpet, and the great trumpet, which we will discuss in this chapter.

The First Trumpet

We previously discussed the first great trumpet sounded by God Himself at Mount Sinai. This is the first record within biblical history of the sound of a shofar being released and being heard. We see that this was a call to assemble and a time to usher in God as King. We also talked about "Tekiah" as one of the four sounds from a shofar, which can mean a call to assemble. As God sounded the trumpet, the sound increasingly gained volume. This brought fear and trembling to not only the people of Israel but to Moses and to the mountain itself. God came as the initiator of communication by blowing the trumpet at Mount Sinai to prepare them for what was about to come. It was at this place that the Ten Commandments were written by the very finger of God. This was the place where God revealed Himself through fire, smoke, flashes of lightning, and rumbles of thunder. The mountain trembled, and the place was dark with the cloud of God's presence that descended from heaven and rested upon the top of the mountain. His cloud hovered over the mountain like a canopy similar to the canopy used in a Jewish wedding, which, in most cases, is made of the prayer shawl of the Bridegroom. This demonstrated that this was a place where a memorial could be created to remember the union between God and Israel.

God revealed to the people that Moses was His trusted servant and that Moses was able to hear from Him as the Commander to give them His command and instructions. It was at this place where God emphasized that they should put no other God before Him and to love and obey Him. If they did, He would provide for them and protect them as their loving Bridegroom. As we discussed earlier, they accepted and became betrothed to God. This is where the Mosaic covenant was birthed. Mount Sinai is a place of remembrance of God's call to us. It was His proposal to us. He initiated the communication and the desire to be one with us, to be among us, and live with us if we loved Him and obeyed Him. He sounded the first trumpet with His shofar; this sound was His voice. He made the first step by reaching out to the Israelites. He made Himself known and bared all before them. He put Himself in a vulnerable state, making His offer to give them Himself, putting Himself in a place of possible rejection. Remember, He gave us the gift of free will, so we can either accept Him or reject Him. He showed us the power of communicating with the horn, showing us that we can and should do the same. The first trumpet marked the event of relationship and covenant between God and His people.

The Last Trumpet

The last trumpet will sound when the church, which is the Bride of Christ, will be taken up into heaven by the Bridegroom. This trumpet is the announcement of the coming of the Bridegroom. Those who have been preparing for the coming of Christ by giving their lives to Christ will be raptured. The dead in Christ will rise into the clouds first, and those who are alive in Christ will rise after to meet God in the air. This is where those in Christ will remain with Him forever. This will happen suddenly when we least expect it. The ones who remain on earth after the Rapture will quickly be changed. "Listen, I tell you a mystery: We will not all sleep, but we will all be changed—in a flash, in the twinkling of an eye, at the last trumpet. For the trumpet will sound, the dead will be raised imperishable, and we will be changed" (1 Corinthians 15:51–52, NIV).

> *According to the Lord's word, we tell you that we who are still alive, who are left until the coming of the Lord, will certainly not precede those who have fallen asleep. For the Lord himself will come down from heaven, with a loud command, with the voice of the archangel and with the trumpet call of God, and the dead in Christ will rise first. After that, we who are still alive and are left will be caught up together with them in the clouds to meet the Lord in the air. And so we will be with the Lord forever.*
>
> **1 Thessalonians 4:15–17 (NIV)**

So, it is best that believers in Christ be ready at all times, which is a depiction of the story of the ten virgins (Matthew 25:1–13). There were five foolish virgins and the five wise virgins who went to meet the bridegroom with the lamps. The five foolish virgins did not take oil with them, and the wise ones took oil in jars. It says that it took a long time for the bridegroom to come, and all of them fell asleep, but at midnight there was a cry that awakened them, announcing that the bridegroom had arrived to meet with them. They all were able to trim their lamps, but the five foolish could not light their lamps and depended on getting the oil from the wise virgins but were unsuccessful. The five foolish had to buy oil, and while doing so, the bridegroom came, took the five wise virgins, and left. The five foolish missed the opportunity to enter the wedding banquet due to lack of preparation because it says the doors closed, so they were not able to enter.

The cry at midnight is the sound of the last trumpet. It is the second coming of Jesus Christ. It will happen suddenly...because the Word of God says He will come like a thief in the night. This will separate those who give their lives to Christ and live a life completely set apart for Him, that maintain a relationship with Him by means of the Spirit from those who don't. The five wise that kept oil in jars show their maintenance of keeping the fire burning on the altar, which is being in consistent communication with God. The oil is a representation of His Holy Spirit, the One who leads us and guides us daily to help maintain the connection with Christ. If we are guided by the Spirit, we will know what to always do and will not miss the coming of our Lord. Five also represents grace. We are now in the season of grace, also known as the "Age of Grace," to make the right decisions before His coming.

In the earlier part of this book, we discussed *the Shannon-Weaver model of communication* and likened it to spiritual communication. I find it extremely profound that the Shannon-Weaver model of communication was developed in 1948. Reason being, is that 1948 is the same year the fig tree rebloomed, which signifies the rebirth of Israel and His second coming. The fig tree was originally cursed by Jesus to dry up because it was not producing fruit (Matthew 21:18–22). The fig tree is symbolic of Israel, and I believe it to be spiritual Israel as well, meaning those who believe in Him. Although the spiritual Israel is not born of Israel, they have been engrafted in the promises that belong to Israel due to their faith and allegiance to Jesus, the Messiah. Israel, both natural and spiritual, is God's chosen people who God loves. The fig tree blooming again is showing restoration to His chosen people. In Matthew chapter 24, Jesus began to discuss the end of the age and signs of His coming to the disciples. During this time, He discusses the fig tree:

> *Now learn this lesson from the fig tree: As soon as its twigs get tender and its leaves come out, you know that summer is near. Even so, when you see all these things, you know that it is near, right at the door. Truly I tell you, this generation will certainly not pass away until all these things have happened. Heaven and earth will pass away, but my words will never pass away.*

> Matthew 24:32–34 (NIV)

This scripture refers to His coming being near when we see the sign of the budding fig tree. The model of communication was birthed in 1948, and the fig tree rebloomed in 1948. I believe that God is connecting the two by emphasizing the importance of spiritual communication with Him so that we can prepare for His coming. We have been reborn with Christ, and it is time to stay awake, be alert, and be watchful like the wise virgins. God is wanting spiritual communication with us. He wants restoration, and He wants us to prepare for the trumpet call by maintaining healthy communication with Him. That way, when He sounds the trumpet, we are prepared and ready to go home with Him. His church will be raptured into the heavens.

This is the time that He has given us to prepare, but we must make sure that we utilize this time wisely by taking the posture of being a wise virgin and not take the route of a foolish virgin. The foolish virgins seemed to be doers of God, but their works were empty because they lacked the Spirit. If we are connected to His Spirit, we are connected to God. We will take the right actions if we are submissive to the leading of the Holy Spirit, which will help us to be always prepared, like the wise virgins. The last trumpet is the coming of the Bridegroom and the claiming of His prepared Bride. We will be ready at the midnight cry, which is the last trumpet, to meet God in the air. Afterwards, this will usher in the times of tribulation.

The last trumpet is also what the Jews celebrate as Yom Teruah, which is the Day of Trumpets, also known as Rosh Hashanah. Rosh Hashanah also represents the last trumpet because it is symbolic of the Day of Awakening, sleepers shall be awakened, and relationships with God shall be restored.

The Great Trumpet (The Final Blast)

The great trumpet will sound on the day of God's final judgment of humankind before the complete destruction of the old heaven and earth. The Jews recognize this on Yom Kippur, which is the Day of Atonement. In the Jewish calendar, it is considered as the holiest day of the year. The sound of the great trumpet will mark the event of God's return as judge over the earth, also known as the Day of the Lord. At this time, God will deal with the sin residing within the world and come against the enemies of Israel and spiritual Israel. The sound of the great trumpet will be preceded by a sound of an alarm. This alarm is the war cry when God's army will be released on the earth, which I believe to be the events of war that take place when the first six trumpets are blown by the angels in Revelation.

> Blow the trumpet in Zion; sound the alarm on my holy hill. Let all who live in the land tremble, for the day of the LORD is coming. It is close at hand—a day of darkness and gloom, a day of clouds and blackness. Like dawn spreading across the mountains a

*large and mighty army comes, such as never was in
ancient times nor ever will be in ages to come.*

Joel 2:1–2 (NIV)

We can find the great trumpet in the book of Matthew:

*For then there will be great distress unequaled from
the beginning of the world until now—and never to
be equaled again.*

*"Immediately after the distress of those days 'the sun
will be darkened, and the moon will not give its light;
the stars will fall from the sky, and the heavenly bodies will be shaken.'*

*"Then will appear the sign of the Son of Man in heav-
en. And then all the peoples of the earth will mourn
when they see the Son of Man coming on the clouds
of heaven, with power and great glory. And he will
send his angels with a loud trumpet call, and they
will gather his elect from the four winds, from one
end of the heaven to the other."*

Matthew 24:21, 29–31 (NIV)

As mentioned before, there will be those that remain on earth
after the last trumpet. The church will no longer be on earth because the Bride of Christ would have been raptured into heaven.
The Antichrist will reign, and there will be seven years of great
tribulation. It will be the "Age of the Gentiles," and wickedness
will be rampant on the earth. I also believe it to be the "Age of
Mercy." It will be a time of darkness, bitter waters, a meteor will
destroy part of the ocean, and another to destroy fresh water.
During this time, God will show His mercy by giving them another opportunity to believe in Him and accept Him as their Messiah
before the final blast of the trumpet. God's mercy will be shown
through the 144,000 who are sealed by God, 12,000 from each

tribe who will have a voice to proclaim the gospel. They will be evangelists in the end times.

He will also send two witnesses clothed in sackcloth (Revelation chapter 11), with the spirit of Elijah and Moses, to preach and appeal to them about the importance of accepting Jesus as their Savior. They will serve as a lifeline to those left behind to give the hearers a message that God is giving them a second chance through His divine mercy. The two witnesses will do this for three and a half years, and upon the completion of performing this task, they will be killed. Their bodies will lay in the streets for all to see. For a short time, their carcasses will be looked upon by all and mocked by the unbelievers. But on the third day, the Spirit of God will breathe life into the two witnesses, and they will stand to their feet. The two witnesses will then be raptured by being brought into the clouds before all men, and a great earthquake will follow, and a tenth of the city will collapse. This will bring great terror to all, and some will turn from their wicked ways and believe. All of this will happen before the seventh trumpet. Then, in God's perfect timing, the great trumpet will sound as the last blast marking the end of war, the final defeat of the enemy, the victory of God and the Lamb, and the final judgment. This is the seventh trumpet.

"The seventh angel sounded his trumpet and there were loud voices in heaven, which said, 'The kingdom of the world has become the kingdom of our Lord and of his Messiah, and he will reign for ever and ever'" (Revelation 11:15, NIV).

The seventh trumpet will be the time of final victory for His Kingdom! The Day of the Lord is a terrible day for those who do not believe in Him. This marks the day that He separates the sheep from the goats. The sheep will enter His Kingdom and have eternal life, and the goats will have eternal punishment (Matthew 25:46). There will be massive destruction upon the earth, and God's wrath will be poured out on those who are against Him—it will be final judgment and the complete destruction of Satan and his angels, the unrepentant, and the unbelievers. This can be found in Revelation 20:7–15. The dead will stand before the throne of God and be judged according to their deeds. It will be the final call for the believers in Christ and will also mark the grand finale of God's judgment on the sins of the world. Those whose names are not written in the book of life will be judged harshly for all eternity.

"'Surely the day is coming; it will burn like a furnace. All the arrogant and every evildoer will be stubble, and the day that is coming will set them on fire,' says the LORD Almighty. 'Not a root or a branch will be left to them'" (Malachi 4:1, NIV).

Those who don't believe in Christ at this time will be destined to a place where there is weeping and gnashing of teeth forevermore. But to those who believe and stand strong in their faith in the Messiah, it will be a great day.

"But you, brothers and sisters, are not in darkness so that this day should surprise you like a thief. You are all children of the light and children of the day. We do not belong to the night or the darkness" (1 Thessalonians 5:4–5, NIV).

Believers in Christ are children of the day; therefore, the Day of the Lord should be a day that the remaining believers, also known as the remnant, have endured to the end and shall be rewarded. These are the ones that will be prepared and ready for the final call...the final blast...which is the great trumpet. Believers should always be awake and watchful. Full of faith, confidence, patience, expectation, and in continual prayer. This is not only the final blast but also the final call to come to Him. Remember, God is the initiator of our spiritual communication, and we are to be the recipient. To complete the loop of communication, we should be the responder as well, meaning we take the seventh and final step in the process of communication by giving our response to Him.

"The day of the LORD is near for all nations. As you have done, it will be done to you; your deeds will return upon you own head. […] But on Mount Zion will be deliverance; it will be holy, and Jacob [Israel] will possess his inheritance" (Obadiah 1:15, 17 NIV).

The remnant should not fear this day but embrace this day, for this is a time when God will return and triumph. This will be a day when all nations and all kingdoms will behold God, and He will rule and reign with victory, and the Kingdom shall be His forever.

CHAPTER 23

THE SEVEN HORNS OF THE LAMB IN REVELATION

Horns are mentioned in Revelation 5:6 as it describes the Lamb who was slain, which is Jesus Christ. In this scripture, He has seven horns and seven eyes. For the sake of this reading, we will focus on the horns only.

As per our studies, horns mean power and authority; and the number seven is relevant to God's completion, perfection, finished work, fulfillment, and accomplishment. This signifies that the Lamb of God with the seven horns, who is Jesus Christ the Messiah, has complete power and all authority as the perfect sacrifice. The book of Revelation discusses how an angel of might with a loud voice asked who was worthy to break the seven seals and open the scrolls that were in the right hand of the one who sits on the throne. All the heavens, the earth, and under the earth had no one to be worthy enough…but one—the one who has triumphed. We see that Jesus Christ, as the Lamb of God, was the only one to do so. He had seven horns signifying all power and authority for all times in heaven and on earth, giving complete access to each of the seven seals that were to be opened:

> *Then I saw a Lamb, looking as if it had been slain,*
> *standing at the center of the throne, encircled by the*

four living creatures and elders. The Lamb had seven horns and seven eyes, which are the seven spirits of God sent out into all the earth. He went and took the scroll from the right hand of him who sits on the throne. And when he had taken it, the four living creatures, and the twenty-four elders fell down before the Lamb...

Revelation 5:6–8 (NIV)

The above scripture shows the complete authority and power of the Lamb in heaven. As the Lamb of God, He has the power and equal authority to rule with the one who sits on the throne. God, the Father, wrote the scrolls and sealed them, and only Jesus, the Lamb of God and the Son of God, had the authority to open and execute them. These seals contain the judgments of God reserved for the last days. This is the response from heaven to earth for those who choose not to give their hearts to Him and serve Him in the last days. The judgment of wrath will come from the sound of seven trumpets in heaven as a response to the sound of sin that has been released from the earthly horns of the wicked. As these seals are opened, the wrath of God's judgment will be released to the earth with the sound of a trumpet for those who choose to ignore the warnings and proceed to follow the ways of evil and wickedness. One would think that the wrath would come from God, the Father, and Jesus as the Lion of Judah. On the contrary, this wrath comes from God, the Father, and Jesus, as the Lamb who was slain. Throughout Revelation chapter 6, as Jesus opens the seals, it continually says, "When the Lamb opened the first seal... second seal, third seal," etc. In verses 15 to 16, we see that those in high places of rulership and authority on the earth feared and had to submit to the One who sits on the throne and the Lamb by wanting to be hidden from their wrath. Again, emphasizing Jesus, the Lamb of God, has *complete* power and authority over all, from the highest in status to the lowest in status... which is symbolized by the Lamb's seven horns.

> *Then the kings of the earth, the princes, the generals, the rich, the mighty, and everyone else, both slave and free, hid in caves and among the rocks of the mountains. They called to the mountains and the rocks, "Fall on us and hide us from the face of him who sits on the throne and from the wrath of the Lamb! For the great days of their wrath has come, and who can withstand it?"*
>
> **Revelation 6:15–17 (NIV)**

The above scripture shows us the complete power and authority of the Lamb on earth. There is one scripture that comes to mind that depicts His complete power over all living creatures and things in heaven, on earth, and under the earth, in one simple verse.

"That at the name of Jesus every knee should bow, in heaven and on earth and under the earth, and every tongue acknowledge that Jesus Christ is Lord, to the glory of God the Father" (Philippians 2:10–11, NIV).

I also believe the seven horns of the Lamb to be straight and not curved, which demonstrates Jesus' leadership and kingship as the Lamb of God. This also represents His governmental rule, leadership, His divine kingship, and royalty over the world. Jesus received *complete* power, *complete* authority, *complete* dominion, and *complete* authority after He finished (completed) the good work by walking the earth for thirty-three years, understanding our ways, teaching us the ways of God, and ultimately giving His life for the remission of our sins, which was His purpose here on this earth. He died and rose again, conquering death and gaining the victory, authority, and power over death. Jesus completed the promises of the covenants to man made by God that we discussed in the beginning of this book by fulfilling what needed to be fulfilled and making obsolete the ones that needed to be made more perfect by becoming the sacrificial Lamb.

1. *Edenic Covenant (Garden of Eden)—restored*—even though Adam brought death, Jesus brought life as the Lamb. The Garden of Eden was restored where the river of life flowed from the God's throne and of the Lamb. This was a city where God and the Lamb lived and where the tree of life stood, bringing healing to the nations (Revelation chapter 22).

2. *Adamic Covenant (The Promise to Adam and Eve)—fulfilled*—the enemy and woman were enemies (Revelation chapter 12). Jesus, as the Lamb of God, defeated the serpent/dragon, thus making the bride of the Lamb (the woman) victorious (Revelation 20:10).

3. *Noahic Covenant (The Promise to Noah)—fulfilled*—life on earth will not be destroyed by a flood again; but instead by death, famine, and sword through the judgment and wrath of God, the Father, and Jesus, the Lamb (Revelation 6:8).

4. *Abrahamic Covenant (The Promise to Abraham)—fulfilled*—the nations came forth as promised (twelve tribes of Israel), the land was given to the nations as promised (the new Jerusalem, the Holy City), and Jesus came as a Savior to the nations as promised through the shedding of His blood as the sacrificial Lamb of God. This is the new Jerusalem, where man and God live together (Revelation chapter 21).

5. *Mosaic Covenant/Sinai Covenant (The Promise to Moses)*, also known as the Law of Moses—*fulfilled*—the spiritual Israel has now become a holy nation and a royal priesthood, God's special possession because of the sacrifice of the Lamb of God (1 Peter 2:9, Revelation 1:6).

6. *Davidic Covenant (The Promise to David)—fulfilled*—David's name was made great because Jesus, the Lamb of God, came as the Root and Offspring of David (Revelation 22:16). He gave the spiritual Israel a home where they would no longer be oppressed by their enemies

(Revelation 21:3–4). The house of David indeed endured forever through His offspring, Jesus, the Lamb of God (Revelation 5:13).

7. *New Covenant (The Promise to us through Jesus)—fulfilled*—because of the blood of the Lamb, we have been given access to enter the Holy City and live with Him forevermore based on our deeds and the proclivity of our hearts (Revelation 22:12–16).

Jesus, as the Lamb of God, completed this by serving, remaining sinless, and through His sacrifice. He made this sacrifice once and for all, saving mankind and thus gaining power as the perfect Lamb of God. The term "once and for all" means that He is the perfect sacrifice and will continually be viewed in the heavens and in the sight of God as the Lamb who was slain. So that God can always look upon Him as the ultimate sacrifice, remember His sacrifice always, and respond by forgiving the sins of humanity always through His infinite mercy. The blood of the Lamb is always sufficient.

Adam, the first man, sinned and caused the curse for humanity. Man needed to be reconciled with God. The only way that could be done was through a man that was holy and free from sin to take on that mission for the sake of saving man. Jesus, the Son of God, was the only One worthy enough to do so. That is why the heavens sang a new song as the Lamb of God opened the scroll. Their song explained the power behind His sacrifice as the Lamb of God, which also demonstrated the horns speaking of His fullness of power and authority.

And they sang a new song, saying: "You are worthy to take the scroll and to open its seals, because you were slain, and with your blood you purchased for God persons from every tribe and language and people and nation. You have made them to be a kingdom and priests to serve our God, and they will reign on earth."

Revelation 5:9–10 (NIV)

The first Adam introduced sin and death due to His disobedience to God. So, it had to take a man to bring forgiveness and redemption from sin and life to set man free from the curse of death. That sacrifice had to be pure, free from defect, free from sin, innocent, and holy, which was Jesus Christ Himself. He came down to earth and gave His life as an innocent lamb to the slaughter. He walked here on earth and finished His task by shedding His blood on the cross. The cross is the altar, and Jesus is the Lamb. He paid the price with His blood, bringing redemption and, in turn, giving us salvation. That is why Jesus said, "It is finished." He finished and completed the work of His purpose on earth by giving salvation to mankind, making God accessible to us through His blood as the Lamb. He completed what was necessary to reconcile man back to God He finished and completed the requirements of God that save mankind from death due to sin by the shedding His blood as the Lamb, making mankind acceptable to God in heaven. Through His sacrifice as the Lamb of God, He completed what was necessary to gain complete authority and power with the Father over all things, which was not limited to earth and heaven but also under the earth and within the seas. We can see that all the angels, living creatures of the earth, under the earth, and seas, and elders worshiped the Lamb. They worshiped the Lamb of God, communicating to Him through voice, words, and postures.

> Then I [John] looked and heard the voice of many angels, numbering thousands upon thousands, and ten thousand times ten thousand. They encircled the throne and the living creatures and elders. In a loud voice they were saying: "Worthy is the Lamb, who was slain; to receive power and wealth and wisdom and strength and honor and glory and praise!" Then I heard every creature in heaven and on earth and under the earth and on the sea and all that is in them, saying: "To him who sits on the throne and to the

Lamb, be praise and honor and glory and power, forever and ever!" The four living creatures said, "Amen," and the elders fell down and worshiped.

Revelation 5:11–14 (NIV)

He has power and authority over all—"all," meaning completeness, which demonstrates that he rules in completion and perfection. Therefore, the Lamb with the seven horns is a descriptive picture of what the Horn of Salvation looks like. The Horn of Salvation is Jesus reigning in complete power as the Perfect Lamb of God. He completed the Law of Moses by becoming the ultimate sacrifice giving us atonement for our sins. The tabernacle is no longer a place built by man for God to dwell in; it is now within our hearts. Jesus, the Lamb of God, completed His purpose, completely restored mankind back to God through His sacrifice and by His name, and now rules with complete victory, glory, power, authority, and dominion as the Horn of Salvation, who is the Lamb of God!

Without the Lamb of God, we would be stuck in a life and world with no hope, destined to eternal death. To God be the glory that is not our story because we have been given access to God through the blood sacrifice of Jesus Christ, the Son of God. Humanity is not left alone and is not without hope, and we have been given the Comforter, who is the Holy Spirit, to help us in our walk with Christ so that we may live a life for Him, staying in communion with Him, and ultimately have everlasting life because we desire to serve Him and be One with Him where we will worship Him forever more. Through His complete and perfect sacrifice as the Lamb of God, we have been given the right to be one with the Father, one with the Son, and one with the Holy Spirit in completion and perfection. The sacrificial blood of the Lamb of God has given us full access to spiritually communicate with God through His blood—with no hindrances by the correct use of our earthly horn. His blood sacrifice as the Lamb of God has saved us from death, demonstrating His power and authority, making Jesus the Horn of our Salvation.

CHAPTER 24

THE SEVEN TRUMPETS IN REVELATION

The Lamb of God was the only one worthy to take the scroll in the right hand of God and open the seven seals. These seals unlocked the judgments that were to be released on earth. In the book of Revelation, there were seven trumpets blown after the seventh seal was opened in Revelation 8:6–13. This came into play after there was silence in heaven for half an hour. To cause silence in heaven means there was sound before in heaven signifying that heaven is a place of sound. However, for this moment, all sounds in heaven ceased to make way, make room in preparation and expectation for the final and great result that would come from the opening of the seventh seal. All of heaven stood at attention and revered this moment. After the silence, seven angels who stood in position before the throne of God were given a trumpet. Seven angels, seven trumpets, seven sounds of communication, seven results. As a reminder, trumpets are horns; horns communicate, horns release sounds that produce results. As we previously discussed, horns stand as the father of all instruments in heaven. This instrument is one that is placed in high regards in heaven. The angels could have received any other instrument after the silence and opening of the seventh seal, but God's instrument of choice for them was the trumpet. This leaves us to understand that the result that would come from the angels blowing these trumpets at this given time had to be of great significance. And so it was, these trumpets were the chosen instrument of heaven to release the woes into the earth.

The seven angels were fully prepared to sound their trumpet at the appointed time, which took place after the angel with the golden censer hurled the censer filled with fire from the altar into the earth. Each angel followed protocol by blowing their given trumpet one after the other. After the trumpet sounded, there was a result. This goes to show that there is always an effect of a trumpet that is blown—it is never blown in vain. We must understand that whenever a trumpet sounds, there is always a response, and there will always be a result. Heavenly trumpets are instruments of communication; when they are blown, we can always expect something to follow thereafter. God wants us to understand that this is true for both heavenly and earthly horns.

According to Revelation chapters 8 to 9, here are the assigned results for each trumpet sound from the seven angels in heaven:

Angel 1 blows his trumpet: Hail and fire mixed with blood were hurled down to earth, causing a third of the earth, trees, and all the green grass to be burned up.

Angel 2 blows his trumpet: A huge mountain ablaze fell into the sea, causing the sea to turn into blood. One-third of sea life died. One-third of ships were destroyed.

Angel 3 blows his trumpet: A great star that blazed fell from the sky, destroying and making bitter one-third of the river and springs of water. People died from these waters.

Angel 4 blows his trumpet: One-third of the sun was struck, one-third of the moon, and one-third of the stars—causing a third of them to get dark. A third of the day was without light, and so was a third of the night.

It got more intense after this...because the three woe judgments will follow.

Angel 5 blows his trumpet (Woe #1): A star fell from the sky to the earth, which received the key to the shaft of the Abyss. It refers to this star as "he," which shows that the stars are alive and spiritual beings. The fallen star is Satan, which can be found in Isaiah 14:12. Satan is the fallen angel originally known as Lucifer. The scripture goes on to say, "The star was given the key to the shaft of the Abyss. When he opened the Abyss..." (Revelation 9:1b–2, NIV) The Abyss is a place that houses evil spirits. This star was given a key, which means this star had the ability to receive it. This shows that there was something or someone that granted the authority to this star to have this key. This higher and authoritative power is God. God had to permit this to happen. Not only that, but it also says, "[...] he [the star] opened the Abyss" (Revelation 9:2, NIV), meaning that the star took action to do something about what he received and used that item to bring a result. A key gives access, and a key opens. Satan was given a key; he knew that he was supposed to open something. In his case, it was the key to the shaft of the Abyss. He understood this and utilized it. As a result of him using the key to open the shaft of the Abyss, smoke was released from it. This smoke darkened the sun and sky. Locusts came from the smoke to attack and torture the people of the earth who did not have the seal of God on their foreheads. The locusts came forth as an army of the Lord, likened to horses in battle. This woe lasted for five months. Five representing God's grace. He could have killed the people at this time but did not. It says that this angel was the angel of the Abyss, known as "Abaddon" in Hebrew and "Apollyon" in Greek, which means "destroyer." This was Satan.

Angel 6 blows his trumpet (Woe #2): a voice from the four

horns of the golden altar that stood before God. This voice instructed angel number six to release the four angels bound at the great river Euphrates. These angels were prepared and ready for this appointed time to release and kill a third of mankind through plagues of fire, smoke, and sulfur. Even though these woes were so drastic, the survivors did not repent and turn from their wicked ways.

After that, the Bible says a mighty angel descended from heaven that placed one foot on the sea and his other foot on the land. In his hand was a little scroll. This angel released a sound like a lion, and the voices of the seven thunders spoke, but these words were not recorded as commanded by the voice from heaven. The angel mentioned that there would be "no more delay" as he raised his right hand to heaven. This angel swore by God and went on to say that God's mysteries (even that which God revealed through the prophets) would come forth and accomplish what it was set out to accomplish. This voice commanded John to take the small scroll from the angel and eat it. John ate it; it was sweet to taste but sour in the stomach. He was then commanded to "prophesy again about many peoples, nations, languages and kings" (Revelation 10:11). John was given a reed to measure the temple of God and the altar with the worshipers and refrain from measuring the outer court, which was given to the Gentiles. The word goes on to say the holy city will be treaded upon for a total of forty-two months, but at this time, there will be two witnesses appointed to prophesy to the people, which was discussed in the previous chapter. This is the time when God's mercy is soon to run out because the seventh and final trumpet is about to blow.

Angel 7 blows his trumpet (Woe #3): There was a release of loud voices in heaven announcing that the kingdom of the world was becoming the kingdom of the Lord and His Messiah. The twenty-four elders that were seated upon their thrones fell down upon their faces worshiping God and Jesus, proclaiming what God has done, and giving Him thanks. This caused the temple of God in heaven to open, and the ark of His covenant was visible (Revelation 11:19).

The final trumpet will seal the fate of destruction to the unbelievers and the unrepentant and to seal the times. Satan will be judged and defeated. All will see and know that the God of the universe is the One and Only True God, and they will see that Jesus is the Son of God. This clearly depicts that every knee shall bow, and every tongue will confess that He is God.

God will triumph, and the Holy City will come down from heaven. The Bride and the Lamb will be together in the new Jerusalem. There will be a new heaven and a new earth. There will be no need for a temple and no need for light because The Lord God Almighty and the Lamb will be just that. Eden shall be restored, and the water of life will flow from the throne of God and the Lamb. God the Father, God the Son, and God the Holy Spirit, who is the Trinity, will be evident and demonstrating the power of unity. The Lord, thy God, is One.

God showed His power and might by bringing the great tribulation here on earth; this will be a great and terrible day. It is the Day of the Lord. He did this through the means of the sound of the seven trumpets. It was the release of destruction that came to the earth and to the opposers of God. Just as how God created the world and all that is in it within seven days, He permitted destruction to the earth through the sound of seven trumpets. The book of Revelation speaks so much about the number seven, and I believe the number seven is also related to God's creation as well when it comes to building up and tearing down. Keep in mind that God used His voice, which we learned to be the voice of the trumpet (shofar), to create the world in seven days. He said, "Let there be...," and it was. God used the sound of the seven trumpets given to the angels to also destroy. He gave the permission to destroy, and so it was. Seven days...seven trumpets—this is the story of creation.

Let's briefly compare when God created the heavens and earth with the sound of His voice (the great trumpet) versus when God destroyed it with judgment with the sound of the seven trumpets.

"God Said" (The voice of the great trumpet)	In the Beginning God Created the Heavens and the Earth (Genesis chapters 1 to 2)	God Judged (Angels sound their trumpet)	The End Times (Seven Years of Tribulation) and a New Heaven and New Earth Are Created (Revelation chapters 8, 9, and 11)
Day 1	God created light and darkness.	Trumpet 1	Hail, fire, and blood sent to the earth. (One-third of the earth, trees, and grass burn up.)
Day 2	God created the sky and seas.	Trumpet 2	Something like a mountain is thrown in the sea. (One-third of sea life dies, and one-third of ships are destroyed.)
Day 3	God created land and vegetation.	Trumpet 3	A great star falls into the rivers. (One-third of fresh water and rivers became bitter, causing death to those who drink from it.)
Day 4	God created the sun, moon, and stars.	Trumpet 4	One-third of the sun, moon, and stars are struck. (One-third of their light becomes dark. One-third of the day and night are kept from shining.)

Day 5	God created living creatures in the seas and birds in the sky.	Trumpet 5	Satan given the key to the abyss, (releasing locusts to the earth to torture those without the seal of God).
Day 6	God created animals and mankind.	Trumpet 6	Four angels released from the Euphrates river. (Killing one-third of mankind with three plagues: fire, smoke, and sulfur, but survivors still did not repent.)
Day 7	God completed the heavens and the earth, rested, and made this day holy.	Trumpet 7	It is finished. The kingdoms of the world become the kingdom of the Lord and the Messiah. Babylon falls, and Satan is defeated. Satan and the unrepentant are thrown into the lake of fire. A new heaven and a new earth are created where God, the Lamb, and the Bride live as one in the Holy City.

Additionally, all of this happened at the sound of the seventh trumpet, seven meaning completeness. God completed the good work and defeated Satan once and for all. All kings and kingdoms were rendered powerless and had to submit to the One and True God, the Holy One of Israel. For a brief period, the enemy reigns, but this was only for a time, which was permitted by God. In the end, God defeats the enemy completely. It was finished.

Let's take time to selah...

As we can see, something happens in response to the sound of the trumpet in heaven. Sounds will always emit a response. God could have had the angels use any other instrument or make any type of action as they were used to release the signs of the times, but God chose to give them trumpets. Why? The sound of the trumpet is extremely significant. It is the instrument of heaven. Remember, what is done on heaven shall also be done on earth. When we blow our trumpets, God will remember us and remember His promises. The trumpet is used as a powerful instrument of communication in the heavenlies, which causes a powerful result and response both on heaven and on earth. It is imperative that we know the power behind the sound of the horn. If the sound of the trumpet causes heaven to respond and results to take place on earth, that means the sound of our trumpet here on earth causes results to take place in heaven. It is a holy exchange, which is healthy spiritual communication. We just read about the seventh trumpet; we also see the response of God Almighty at the sound of this trumpet. Remember, the seventh concept of communication is the loop of communication; it is the response the recipient gives back to the sender.

As we previously studied in the earlier part of this book, the seventh step does not always happen. But if the communication is healthy, that means the seventh step has been reached. In this case, the seventh trumpet was blown, and there was a response. Again, trumpets are the instruments of spiritual communication. At the sound of the seventh trumpet, a response takes place by God when God defeats the enemy and redeems His followers, which ends in a grand finale of heaven and earth coming together.

God and man will be back together as it was originally ordained to be. No more sorrow, no more pain, no more oppression, and no more separation. Man will be able to worship God without hindrance, and God will be able to live among His people. It will be a continuous loop of communication; He will bless us with everlasting life and the access to remain in His presence; in return, we will worship Him forever; as we worship Him, He will reveal more and more of Himself to us, we, in turn, will stand in amazement and won't be able to help but give Him the glory through our praise and worship. This will allow the loop of communication to continue forevermore. It will never get boring because God will always have something more glorious to show us every time we worship Him. That is why the angels continuously say, "Holy, holy, holy," because they are amazed at each ray of glory God reveals to them. Our awe of God will be everlasting; that is just how big our God is.

CHAPTER 25

THE ARK OF HIS COVENANT—THE MOST HOLY PLACE OF SPIRITUAL COMMUNICATION

We just discussed the seven trumpets blown by the seven angels. For this chapter, I want us to focus on a specific revelation that we did not discuss before, which happened at the sound of the seventh trumpet. When the seventh trumpet sounds, worship takes place, and then God's temple opens. When God's temple opens, the mystery that is housed within the temple in heaven will be opened, giving all who worship Him the opportunity to see the ark of His covenant.

"Then God's temple in heaven was opened, and within his temple was seen the ark of his covenant. And there came flashes of lightning, rumblings, peals of thunder, an earthquake, and a severe hailstorm" (Revelation 11:19, NIV).

This signifies that the sound of the seventh trumpet makes way to access what was closed in heaven and to the unveiling of His mysteries. We can also see that in this passage, the Word of God differentiates the ark in heaven from the ark on earth as the ark of "*His*" covenant rather than ark of "the" covenant. The ark of *His* covenant is what the ark of the covenant on earth was built and constructed in the likeness of. The one on earth was only a replica of what is already in heaven. The ark of *His* covenant ("His" showing ownership of the covenant) is what belonged to God Himself, without the hands of man being involved and without the boundaries of earth being involved. We previously discussed that anything of the earth has limitations because it is bound to the limitations of what will soon perish. The only thing that is not bound to earth is the spirit because the spirit is eternal. God is spirit; He is eternal. He is and always will be alive forevermore. Anything that belongs to God reflects His characteristics and will also remain forevermore. That is why there is a clear distinction between the ark of the covenant versus the ark of *His* covenant. The one of the earth will not last, therefore, has boundaries, but the one in heaven belonging to God Himself is boundless.

We previously learned the protocol of the tabernacle after He gave specific instructions to Moses. The ark of the covenant was housed within the most holy place, separated by a veil, where His Shekinah Glory was enthroned between the cherubim. Within this ark contained His laws, the Ten Commandments representing the laws the people must obey, the staff showing His chosen one, and the bread (promising that He will always provide). I view the ark as a representation of something that preserves what was. God was showing the people that He is preserving the contents within the ark for them to remember who He is to them (the Israelites) and to remember what He expects of them and remember that He will stand by His promise if they stay faithful by worshiping Him only with their whole heart.

The tabernacle, the most holy place that contained the ark of the covenant, could only be accessed once a year by only one, the chosen one, who served as the high priest to intercede on behalf of the people. All others were closed off and restricted from entering that place, demonstrating they only had access to God in an indirect fashion, which meant limited access and limited communication with God. They had to communicate to God through someone, not directly, and could not even enter the tabernacle to behold the beauty of His presence for themselves. But here in Revelation, we see that God's temple was opened, and the ark of His covenant was revealed for all in heaven to see. Through Jesus, who is the chosen one, the High Priest forevermore, is not only interceding on behalf of us, but through His sacrifice, the veil has been torn; He has given us the access to communicate with God directly as it was originally ordained and designed to be. We will be able to see the ark of His covenant for ourselves.

The ark of His covenant is within the most holy place in heaven. This is the place where His glory, His presence, and His throne are forevermore. That is why the book of Revelation consistently refers to God, the Father, as the One who is seated on the throne because that is who He reveals Himself to be at this point. There will be no more separation between God and mankind. We will be able to enter in. That's why the Word says there will be no need for a temple because God and the Lamb will be the emple.

> *I did not see a temple in the city, because the Lord God Almighty and the Lamb are its temple. The city does not need the sun or the moon to shine on it, for the glory of God gives it light, and the Lamb is its lamp. The nations will walk by its light, and the kings of the earth will bring their splendor into it. On no day will its gates ever be shut, for there will be no night there. The glory and honor of the nations will be brought into it. Nothing impure will ever enter it, nor will anyone who does what is shameful or deceitful, but only those whose names are written in the Lamb's book of life.*

Revelation 21:22–27 (NIV)

We can also find in scripture that from this place, where the ark of His covenant is, came "flashes of lightning, rumblings, peals of thunder, and earthquake, and a severe storm" (Revelation 11:19). As we learned in the beginning part of this book, that where the God of Glory is, there you will find lightning and thunder…we also learned that the thunder of heaven is the voice of God. The voice of God is powerful and comes by way of the Heavenly Horn, Jesus Christ. If God's voice is present and being heard, that means communication is actively in motion, showing that a relationship is established. This shows us that the seventh step has been reached, causing the loop of communication to be at work, and there is a response. Remember, in communication, there must be a sender and a recipient, and if there is a response, there is a loop that has gone into effect. That shows there is a flip in roles; the recipient becomes the sender during their response. This loop signifies healthy communication and the presence of relationship.

We already know that God is the initiator of communication. He was the sender of the message first. What was His message? His message is His covenant that started from the beginning of time and throughout the Word of God. Anytime He makes a covenant, that means He is releasing His voice and communicating to the recipient. His voice is His horn. Yes, He made several covenants throughout the Word of God. However, on a whole, His main message is that He loves us with an everlasting love and desires our response to love and obey Him with all of our heart and soul. If we respond in that manner, He will be our God, and we will be His people. When He made His covenant, it was recorded in the heavens and preserved within the ark of His covenant to remain forevermore and remembered by Him forevermore. He will always stand by His promise. The ark of His covenant is a representation of spiritual communication and serves as the headquarters of communication between man and God. This is the place of preservation of relationship with His creation.

Now that we understand His part. How do we fit in? We know that we are the recipient of His message. To have healthy communication with Him, we must respond to complete the loop of communication, signifying relationship. Our response to His message is our worship. Meaning we are doing exactly what He asked us to do, which is to love Him and obey Him with all our heart. Our worship is our message. When we worship, we are now the sender of the message, and He becomes the recipient. Our heart must be connected to Him; our heart is the place of worship. Our heart is our earthly horn, and it is also where the ark of the covenant now resides because it is the place of communication between God and us. It is a place of power, authority, and where we receive a response. When we worship, our heart, which is the place of the ark of our covenant, makes sounds of power in the heavenlies. God makes powerful and loud sounds in the heavenlies from the ark of His covenant with rumblings, peals of thunder, and an earthquake. All of these are representations of sounds that are powerful and loud. Remember, we are made in His image. What He does, we replicate it. Our communication is also loud and powerful!

We can see this in action in Revelation 11:15–18; this is where the *loud* voices in heaven began to give worship by acknowledging the Messiah and God Almighty declaring the Kingdom belongs to them. These voices in heaven are the ones who have given their lives to serve Christ while on earth. Their voice is their voiceprint in heaven, the voice of their heart, and the voice of that which was translated in heaven from their earthly horn when they were on earth. Meaning, while they lived on the earth, they utilized their earthly horn; as they used it, the heavens captured the sound, translated the sound into their heavenly voiceprint, registered it, and then it became activated. Once they left earth, their voiceprint was already registered and therefore utilized in the heavens as their heavenly identification. Since we are made in the image of God and mini versions of God, our voiceprint in heaven can also be referred to as our heavenly horn.

As we go back to the scripture, we can see that these loud voices made a response after the seventh trumpet was blown. Don't forget...seven is completion. Seven is also the step of response in communication. We can also take note that the trumpet was blown, emphasizing how heaven uses horns to communicate and how a response takes place after. Here, we also see the worship in heaven going forth when the elders who were seated on their thrones fell and worshiped. All were worshiping God and the Lamb. We see that after they sent their message of worship, God responded with loud sounds of thunder and more. Worship is our means of communication with God while we are here on earth and when we go to heaven. Worship is the key to our relationship with God and the key to healthy and maintained communication with Him.

It is vitally important to sound our earthly horn, the voice of our heart, by accepting and responding to His voice, the place of His covenant. He will stand firm to maintain His promise with us; it is already preserved in heaven, waiting for us to receive if we simply obey, love, and worship Him with our whole heart and keep. The ark of His covenant is a reminder that the separation from a veil that blocks the access to His temple and most holy place will be no more. The doors to His temple will be opened, and His ark will be seen. His ark is the place where God is enthroned and where Jesus has been exalted as the Horn, the High Priest, and the Lamb of God for all humanity. The separation between God and man will be no more. The ark of His covenant will stand as a place of communication and oneness with mankind and where our heavenly horns will sound, worshiping Him for all eternity. God, in turn, will respond with thunder, and His heavenly horn will respond with the sound of the trumpet drawing us all together—the sound of victory with His Bride.

The Bride shall be alive and in communion with Christ! The

Bride, the Bridegroom, the Father, and the Holy Spirit will be One as planned.

CHAPTER 26

THE HEAVENLY HORN AND EARTHLY HORN CONCLUSION

As we come to a closing in this book, you may wonder, "What does this all mean? How does it all come together, and what does this have to do with me?"

Well, to answer that, let's go over how this book was birthed. This book came through a dream that God gave me about what the choir in heaven looked like, which I described in the beginning of this book. As a refresher, I will summarize the dream in a few words. The dream was about spiritual beings in heaven, dressed in white, singing unto the Lord and worshiping the Lord, with mouths made of a horn. The Holy Spirit shined a light on what these horns meant as I began to write in obedience by revealing that horns represent communication. As He revealed the horns being a symbol of communication in heaven, that means He was revealing that horns represent communication on earth as well. What is done in heaven, may it also be done in earth.

With all that we have learned within this reading, we can see that horns are more than an instrument of sound that can be audibly heard by the natural ear. Although natural horns, like trumpets and shofars that man can physically play, were discussed in this book, the real horn that was emphasized was that of the spirit. These spiritual horns are what can be referred to as horns of heaven and earth, and the sound that comes from them is the voice of the heart. Our voice is not limited to the sound of our natural voice because the sound that God interprets comes from the sound of our earthly horn, which is our heart. Horns of the Spirit, known as the heavenly horn and earthly horn, are spiritual wind instruments birthed from eternity, symbolizing power and authority and a gift that God has given mankind to stay connected with Him by maintaining healthy communication with the voice and sound of our heart. These horns are powered by the Holy Spirit because He is the breath and wind within them that produces the sound and brings life to the sound.

Healthy communication comes from speaking to God by way of the heart because He does not look on the outer. We talked about how communication has seven concepts. Healthy communication is complete and made perfect with God when the seventh step is reached, but the seventh step is not always reached. The seventh step is when the receiver of the message responds, which creates a loop of communication. This loop is when there is a sender of the message, the message is received, and then the receiver responds by sending a message back, and the communication continues in this matter. This demonstrates healthy communication and serves as evidence that a relationship exists between both parties, which, in our case, is between God and man.

Our heart is our earthly horn; it is our means of communication to God through worship, prayer, and intercession. It is a gateway to accessing heaven from earth by making that which is in heaven be brought to earth. Our earthly horn is the sound of our heart and voice of our heart.

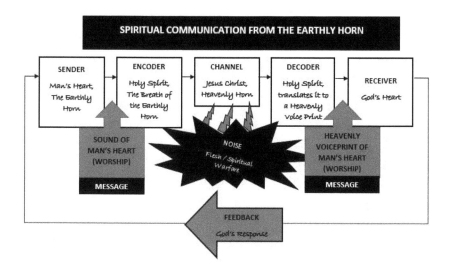

God's heart is the heavenly horn and His means of communication to us as humanity. This horn is also the gateway to mankind, making what is in heaven accessible to mankind on earth.
The heart of God is Jesus Christ, who reigns as the ultimate Horn
of all horns, who is the Horn of Salvation; through Him, we have
access to God, creating the ability for God to hear the sound from
the earthly horn of mankind and respond to mankind. We must
also remember that God is the initiator of communication; it is
God who first relayed a message to us from the beginning of time
to worship Him and be one with Him. He is the first to send the
message; we are the recipient.

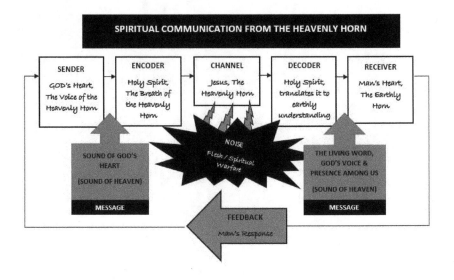

It is for us to respond to His desire for us to worship Him and stay in communion with Him by the help of the Holy Spirit. As we do this, we build a relationship through our earthly horn with God, where He communicates with us, and we communicate with Him. He guides us by the Spirit, and we respond by the Spirit; we communicate with Him by the Spirit, and He responds by the Spirit. There is power that comes from the heavenly horn and the earthly horn because there is a kingdom exchange that takes place from heaven to earth and from earth to heaven. That kingdom exchange makes communication complete, completing the steps and loop of healthy spiritual communication...that power comes from the response of the heart, which is translated in the heavenlies by the power part of the Trinity, who is the Holy Spirit.

God placed an emphasis on our heart, our earthly horn, by stressing the importance of the heart during the time of creation. This importance of the heart still stands to this very day when He created you, me, and all of mankind. Remember, the heart is the first organ that God creates from within the womb depicting by sound that there is life; it is a necessity for survival and, therefore, a priority for life. When you and I were being created within our mother's womb, the sign of life and what communicates that life is existent within the womb was our heart. The sound of our heart is continuous from the beginning of our life to the end of our life, symbolizing we have been given life here on earth, a gift from only God in heaven. But our life is more than just living for happen sake; it is for the purpose of worshiping God and being used for His glory.

We worship God by giving our hearts to Him; when we do that, everything else we do in life is only an expression and manifestation of the worship we have within our heart. Our earthly horn was created by God to not only stay in communication with Him but also for one more thing. We must understand that our earthly horn can be used not only for communication purposes but can be taken to a maximum potential that God has given it. That potential is for us to reign on earth with the power and authority that He has granted unto us.

There are many people that don't take the opportunity to utilize the potential to walk in authority and power as God has ordained because they don't know who they are in Him and are not connected or not completely connected. That power comes through the Holy Spirit, who serves as the maintainer of our spiritual communication between us and God and who can also perform through us with power and authority. If we know who we are in God, and stay connected through our earthly horn, making our voiceprint heard and known in the heavens, He can perform through us for the benefit of His Kingdom. He has given us the power to communicate with Him by releasing our sound to change situations. God has given us the power and authority to use our earthly horn to gain access to heaven and command that which is in heaven to be brought to earth through our communication with Him. The horns represented in this book symbolize the communication between God and man.

The entirety of this book covers a great deal of subject matters, but all these subjects tie in with one another for the purpose of revealing the mystery behind spiritual communication and how it relates to the horn. We talked about how the horn can be represented in different ways, such as sound, the voice, and wind instruments, such as the trumpet and/or shofar. We talked about how creation came into being through sound by the sound of God's voice. We came to understand that God's voice comes in different forms and different sounds, including thunder, whispers, symbols, impressions, through writing, through prophets, through His acts of power, and more. The sound of the horn is communication, and we see how communication between heaven and earth was symbolized through Jacob's ladder. It is by sound that God showed that He had a desire to have a relationship with someone like Him through communication of a heart of worship. We see how creation sinned, causing the communication of man to be disconnected with God, creating a barrier in the direct communication between God and mankind.

We see how the Trinity created a successful business plan to reconnect man back to God and how God communicated these solutions to His people through multiple covenants, which included God revealing Himself at Mount Sinai to Moses, the mountain of communication from God to earth, with a loud sound of the trumpet. At this mountain, God communicated with man by making a covenant and the laws of Israel. At the mountain of communication, He demonstrated what it was like to have a relationship with Him. When we commune with Him, we look like Him, Moses was one who was close to God, stayed in communication with God, and the face of Moses radiated with brilliance like that of many horns to the eyes of man by simply being in God's presence and relating with Him. God communicated the pattern of worship in heaven through making an issuance to build the tabernacle and the various sections of it to match the blueprint of worship in heaven. This blueprint was the means of communication from man to God through sacrificial worship. This caused a need for priests, those who were set apart for the service of God within the tabernacle, so that man could communicate with God by providing blood sacrifices and offerings to receive a response of forgiveness and atonement for their sins.

We see there was an order to the tabernacle that had to be followed for mankind to gain access and communicate with the Holy God who dwelled within the tabernacle. We see later that God fulfilled the requirements of the law and tabernacle through giving His Son as the ultimate sacrifice, tearing the veil from top to bottom in the temple, symbolizing there are no more barriers between the communication of God and man because of the blood of Jesus. So that the sins of man can be atoned, once and for all, canceling out the need for daily blood sacrifices at the tabernacle. Jesus fulfilled the law as the Lamb and the High Priest, causing the tabernacle to be rebuilt within our hearts and within our bodily temple, which now serves as the headquarters for communication and a dwelling place for God.

We see how the horns within the tabernacle stood as a symbol communicating the existence of Jesus as the Horn of Salvation and His power to save us. We see how the blood upon the horns within the tabernacle symbolizes His sacrifice as the Lamb of God and how it communicates to us that He has paid the price for our sins. The horns and blood upon the horns of the tabernacle show His redemptive power and authority that gave us access to God every step of the way so we could stay connected. We are now living tabernacles and have become present priests for the service of God, and it is for us to stay in healthy communion with God by following the spiritual blueprint in our walk with Him by blowing our earthly horn with the help of the Holy Spirit, the one who is the wind within our horn.

We are not only priests, but we have also been called to be watchmen upon the walls within the earth to foresee what God is saying, which comes through our relationship with Him. In doing so, we can be effective in the lives of others by blowing our horns, forewarning them about the dangers of sins, and sharing with them God's call to them to love Him, obey Him, and turn from their wicked ways so they, too, may receive His mercy, grace, and forgiveness. This will give them the opportunity to get connected with Him, be one with Him, and understand the meaning of their earthly horn and utilize it.

We also discussed God as the initiator of communication by being the voice of the heavenly horn, the Holy Spirit being the maintainer of communication by being the breath of the heavenly horn, and Jesus as the way of communication by being the actual Heavenly Horn, more specifically the Horn of Salvation. We talked about how the Trinity (Father, Son, Holy Spirit) communicated with one another throughout the history of time to continuously find solutions for man to stay in communication with God. We see how important it is for them to work in unity; one cannot move without the other. The Trinity is the actual foundation and patriarch of what true healthy spiritual communication is all about and how success comes from their union. We are living testaments of their success because we have access to God and have been granted the victory over the enemy.

We went over the various sounds of the earthly horn and how it communicates from the heart of man to God, making our voiceprint known in the heavens, causing a response from heaven to man. Everything that comes from our heart and earthly horn is simply an expression inwardly or outwardly by different sounds that can include our spirit, soul, and body, our five senses, and through verbal, nonverbal, written, or visual. Man may interpret these expressions in a minimized way or none at all, but God understands the communication of our earthly horn completely because He looks at the root of the expression, which is the heart.

Jesus Christ is the Heavenly Horn and the Horn of Salvation. His horn was exalted by God because He was lifted for all to see in the presence of His enemies. He made Himself low, not considering Himself equal with God for His own benefit, and because of this mindset, God exalted Him to be equal with Him, according to Philippians 2:5–11. He came as the perfect example for us here on earth, in the form of man, to make the way for us, and show us a better way. Jesus did this all by staying in communication with the Father in heaven through His earthly horn while walking upon the earth as man, which resulted in gaining authority as the Horn of Salvation for us all.

We, too, will experience our horn being exalted because He will lift us up from our state of lowliness of the limitations that come from being in this world to being brought high to be with Him. This happens if we stay connected and maintain our relationship with Christ through the continuous use of our earthly horn. We must emit heavenly sounds from earth to heaven, which activates and maintains our voiceprint in the heavens.

The heavenly horn is God's means and solution for staying in touch with us and wanting to relate with us. He longs for our heart…a heart that worships Him with the free will that He has given us. The heavenly horn is the sound of heaven. He is the sound of the trumpet of heaven connecting God to the earth and mankind to the heavens.

God wants us to listen for the sound of His horn, be prepared like the watchman He has called us to be, and be ready to meet with Him in His fullness. He already blew it once, which was the first trumpet, at Mount Sinai, inviting His bride to accept His proposal to come and be one with Him. We have two more to go. One day the last trumpet will sound to meet Him, the Horn of Salvation, and the Bride of Christ will be caught up in the air. Then the final blast from the great trumpet will sound, and the tribulation will come for those whose hearts were not ready and whose earthly horns were not in tune with Him. The judgment of God will then be released by the power and authority of the Lamb of God and the One who sits on the throne. This judgment will be communicated from seven horns (trumpets) within heaven.

But praise be to God for those who are left upon the earth whose hearts have found Him; they will become God's remnant, who have maintained the pure and holy sound of their earthly horn and have endured until the end. They will be saved because of the Heavenly Horn, who is the Horn of Salvation. They will live with God, who sits on the throne, the Lamb, and the river of life who is the Holy Spirit, forevermore. If we stay in communication with God, we will be prepared, which will allow us to ascend with Christ during the last trumpet call, which is the best time to be prepared to avoid being here on earth during the times of judgment.

Just as God has various calls from His trumpet and heavenly horn, we do too. Remember, your earthly horn has various calls, different meanings, which can be expressed in multiple ways. If we sound it purely, God will hear from heaven and respond.

Make sure your earthly horn is in tune! Stay in worship, stay in prayer, and keep watch. Your earthly horn can be out of tune with God, causing a displeasing sound to be released in the heavens, which also is followed by a negative response. It can be out of tune when our heart is disconnected with Him through sin without repentance. Let that not be said of you. Instead, keep your horn tuned up. A lot of times, we fall short of God's glory, causing our sound to be off at times. If, however, we get back in right standing with God by aligning our hearts, keeping our hearts clean by staying repentant, submitted, humble, and connected through prayer and worship, our earthly horn will have a sound, acceptable and pleasing, that communicates to God without inhibitions.

Is your horn out of tune or in tune? Whatever your answer may be, keep your horn tuned to the frequency of the Spirit of God. Just like an instrument needs to be tuned to the right note before we play it, we have to make sure our earthly horn is tuned correctly to God. For we are living instruments for God, and we have God-given power and authority to change atmospheres…we just have to utilize it. We were created to worship—this is our means of communication from our earthly vessels to our Heavenly Father. Worship is the sound of our heart. Worship has a sound and makes a melody. Our life is a song to God. Everything we do inwardly and outwardly makes different sounds from our earthly horn, the same way instruments have different keys, notes, and sounds. Our instrument is unique to us as the owner; when we sound our earthly horn, it creates a voiceprint in the heavenlies that was translated by the Holy Spirit identifying you as the owner. Your voiceprint is specifically assigned to you and no one else because it is your personal identification in the heavens. Use it so that God the Father, the Son, and all those within the heavens are familiar with you and know you through the sound of your horn and your voiceprint.

Worship God, be watchful, and stay in communion with Him, with all of your heart, all of your soul, all of your spirit. God desires that from you; He desires you to communicate with Him daily and for Him to be able to use you here on earth for His purpose. In Him and through His connection with Him, you are hooked to the source of all power and authority, exemplifying that you were made in His complete and perfect image. This fulfills His original desire, design, and plan of God, for mankind to be one with Him—for us to worship Him, love Him, communicate with Him, and have dominion with Him.

He wants to have healthy spiritual communication with you. There is power behind your horn, your trumpet, your voiceprint, your heart, and your sound! The heavens demonstrate it, and the earth testifies of it. Jesus sounded His horn, stayed watchful, stayed connected with God, and received all power to rule. He prepared the way for us. Sound your earthly horn, make changes on this earth by the power and authority granted unto you through Jesus' name. Make a difference with your horn by staying connected with God...like Abraham, Isaac, Jacob, Moses, Joshua, Gideon, Hannah, King David, Peter, James, John, the woman with the issue of blood, the woman with the alabaster jar, and so much more did...they used their earthly horn, they stayed connected with the source, they worshiped, they prayed, they used their earthly horn to change their situation, stayed watchful, and were used with power. The sound of their earthly horn communicated to God by making their voiceprint known and heard in the heavens because their heart was in tune with God. Their heart expressed their love and worship for Him. They avoided being like doubting Thomas because their faith and belief were intact, free from doubt, and God responded to them with power. This is the power behind the horn, and this is the kingdom exchange that takes place through spiritual communication from heaven to earth and from earth to heaven.

Go beyond just making a sound from your earthly horn. Use the authority and power that comes from your earthly horn by depending on the Holy Spirit, keeping watch, understanding who you are, and understanding this powerful tool and instrument that was gifted to you from the heavens above from the time of birth. Sound your earthly horn by staying in communication with Him; God will hear from heaven, remember you, remember His covenant, and respond!

It is time for you, it is time for me, and it is time for the Body of Christ to wake up and stay alert, to use our earthly horn, which is the instrument and weapon that God has given us to prepare for His return. We must rise from our slumber as a church and blow our trumpet with power and authority. We must stay in communion with Him with the gift of free will through our earthly horn, which is from the true worship of God within our hearts. That way, we can learn everything there is to know about Him during our allotted time here on earth through a healthy and consistent relationship with Him. As we are connected, we will hear His voice (His horn), preparing us for the trumpet call from His heavenly horn. As we worship, pray, and keep watch through our earthly horn, our voiceprint is being registered in the heavenlies, preparing way for our heavenly horn to be activated, ready, and established for that day when we are to be with Him forevermore. When He returns, we will become one with Him moving from the position of a bride to being His wife.

As this happens, the ark of His covenant, which is the headquarters of spiritual communication containing His everlasting and fulfilled promise, shall be revealed to us all. We will behold the ark of His covenant within the holy of holies in heaven, where we will worship God and the Lamb with heavenly songs and from our heavenly horns. We will join the angels, elders, and living creatures within heaven, and we will all blow our horns, making sounds of worship. These songs of worship will be maintained by the Spirit, who will always fill our horns of communication with His breath and life, translating our message of communication to God and the Lamb through what will then be our heavenly horn and where we will always receive an eternal response. There will be no noise or distractions from the flesh and enemy to hinder our communication because flesh will be no more, and the enemy will be no more. Only the Spirit will prevail. The sound we will hear is the sound of worship and the sound of the presence of God and the Lamb. The sound of worship will be the song of creation. The sound of the presence of God will include His voice containing flashes of lightning, rumblings, peals of thunder, and quaking. The sound of the Lamb will be like a trumpet blast of many waters, which is the resounding sound of the great trumpet (Revelation 1:10, NIV). This will be a place of rest where communication between God and His creation will be consistent and healthy. Worship will be sent from creation and received by God and the Lamb. His presence will be sent from God and the Lamb to creation and received by His creation. There will always be a response from both parties, which will be an eternal and everlasting response completing the loop of communication. This eternal response is the power of the response.

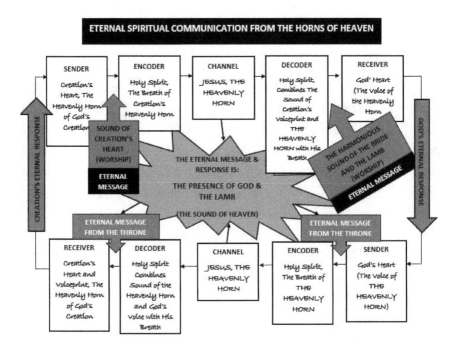

This brings us back to the vision God gave me about the choir of heaven that had mouths made of a horn. No noise and no distractions were present. There was only the sound of worship accompanied by God's presence.

Your earthly horn is the sound of your heart, your voiceprint, your trumpet, your shofar, and your ram's horn. There is power in the sound of your horn and power in the response. It is time to wake up; it is time to sound your horn, take authority, and use it for the time of His return is on the horizon!

"And do this, understanding the present time: The hour has already come for you to wake up from your slumber, because our salvation is nearer now than when we first believed" (Romans 13:11, NIV).

CHAPTER 27

ACTIVATION OF THE EARTHLY HORN PRAYER

With that being said, I pray that God has unfolded the hidden mysteries behind spiritual communication by way of the heavenly horn and earthly horn. May the breath of the Holy Spirit come as a mighty rushing wind to surround you. May the Ruach of the heavenly horn blow upon you to activate the sound of life and the sound of your earthly horn from within.

May you blow your earthly horn without hindrance, and may your sound be pure and holy. May it sound with clarity, be in tune with God, and be in the correct frequency of God creating and maintaining your voice print in the heavenly realm. May you be in communion with Him with the anointing of a royal priest as God has called you to be with power and authority. May your communication through worship and prayer with the Father of heaven be solid and sound like never before. May it reach the heavens and cause a response that will change that which is on earth to line up with that which is in heaven. I pray that God will instill within you a brand-new perspective of what it means to communicate with Him by the earthly horn and give you your own revelation so that He may have His purpose done through you at a maximum level for Him.

I pray God has imparted within you a revelation like never before and deep understanding about the horns of heaven and earth through the reading of this book. I pray that what He has given unto you, you will impart to others. I pray that your love for Him and communication with Him is refreshed and revived and that you will utilize your earthly horn with authority and power granted unto you by the authority of Jesus Christ. I pray that you will not only be connected like never before with God through the sound of your earthly horn but also be able to make changes and change atmospheres by the power of the Spirit that activates your horn.

May your earthly horn remain in tune with Christ, be maintained by the spirit, and be heard by God always. May you be effective and remembered here on earth and clearly known in the heavens by the sound of your voiceprint released from your earthly horn, which comes from the voice of your heart. May your heart release a sound from your earthly horn, demonstrating to God that you love Him with *all* your heart and *all* of your soul. May you stand, be in position, be awake, and keep watch with the anointing of a watchman on earth, making the call by sounding your horn to others within the world with the power and authority of Jesus to turn to God and make preparation for His return. May your heart be one with Christ, and your faith and belief in Him be strengthened as you prepare for the sound of His great trumpet as He calls His bride. May the loop of communication between your earthly horn and the Heavenly Horn, who is the Horn of Salvation, continue to sound forevermore. With this sound, may the spiritual communication with God, the Father, God, the Son, and God, the Spirit...the Holy Trinity stay activated and used with power and authority always. I pray that you will hear and take heed to the sound of the heavenly horn by always responding. May the sound of your earthly horn always be heard with holiness and purity, and may God in heaven always respond. Amen.

ABOUT THE AUTHOR

Sharlene Hylton is an author and journalist who lives in the Dallas/Fort Worth area of Texas. She is happily married and a proud mother of four children, three daughters and a son. Her parents are from the beautiful island of Jamaica, and her upbringing reflects her tenacity to pursue the unimaginable by embracing challenges, reaching for the highest goals, and staying in the mode of learning.

She received her spiritual training from True Worshipers Global Worship Center (TWGWC), located in Carrollton, Texas, under the teaching of Apostle Margelee Hylton, who is not only her pastor but mother as well. Sharlene serves at TWGWC as a dance minister, prophetess, youth teacher, and a minister of sound, music, and media.

She is the author of *Glory Revealed: An In-Depth Understanding of What the Glory Is All About* and blogger of Thoughtful River. She has a background in communication, customer service, and construction, which she also uses for the benefit of God's Kingdom. In 2014, she received her bachelor's in journalism and mass communication with a minor in psychology, summa cum laude, from Ashford University. She is a proud member of Golden Key International Honor Society, Alpha Sigma Lambda Honor Society, and the Society of Professional Journalists (SPJ). She is also a part of the first completely online chapter of SPJ, which is a historical moment for SPJ, known as the Society of Professional Journalists at Ashford University.

She is passionate about the things of Christ. Her mission is to encourage her readers to go higher in their walk with God and to bring them to a place of authority, accountability, and purpose for the glory of Jesus Christ. Her scriptural-based writings allow her readers to receive an in-depth understanding of the Word of God by breaking down scriptures with a simple explanation that can be tied in with everyday circumstances from a higher perspective. Her goal is to reach the world through her writings to share the Gospel of Christ and to understand that life really begins with Jesus. Her mission is to use her gift of writing to share the importance of worship, how to maintain communication with Him, how to live a life of honor and reverence to God, and to inform the world how it is necessary to have the Holy Spirit in their lives. Through her writings, she hopes to have her readers be saved and for those who are already saved to be brought closer to Jesus Christ.

BIBLIOGRAPHY

Bar-Ilan University (2013, September 1). *The Meaning of the Shofar—Prof. William Kolbrener* [Video File]. Retrieved from https://youtu.be/vEEtYAfaH_s

Bible Hub (2022). Mizbeach. *Biblehub.com.* Retrieved November 4, from https://biblehub.com/hebrew/4196.htm

Bible Hub (2022). Parts. *Biblehub.com.* Retrieved October 17, 2022, from https://biblehub.com/topical/p/parts.htm

Bible Hub (2022). Teruah. *Biblehub.com.* Retrieved November 4, 2022, from https://biblehub.com/bdb/8643.htm

Bible Hub (2022). Tsaphah. *Biblehub.com.* Retrieved October 17, 2022, from https://biblehub.com/hebrew/6822.htm

Bible Students Daily. (2017, January 2). "Study 8: The Tabernacle Coverings." *Biblestudentsdaily.com.* Retrieved from https:/biblestudentsdaily.com/tag/goat-hair/

Bible Study Tools (2022). Alexander. *Biblestudytools.com.* Retrieved October 18, 2022, from https://www.biblestudytools.com/dictionary/alexander/

Bible Study Tools (2022). Asham. Biblestudytools.com. Retrieved November 4, 2022, from https://www.biblestudytools.com/lexicons/hebrew/kjv/asham.html

Bible Study Tools (2022). Chata. *Biblestudytools.com.* Retrieved October 24, 2022, from https://www.biblestudytools.com/lexicons/hebrew/nas/chata.html

Brackman, Rabbi L. (2008, September 5). Why Jews are disproportionally successful. *Ynetnews.com. Jewish Scene Jewish World.* Retrieved from https://www.ynetnews.com/articles/0,7340,L-3592566,00.html#:~:text=Thirty%20percent%20of%20Nobel%20Prize%20winners%20in%20science,are%20disproportionally%20represented.%20Most%20 non-Jews%20also%20know%20this.

Cambridge University Press (2022). Anguish. *Cambridge Dictionary.* Retrieved October 18, 2022, from https://dictionary.cambridge.org/us/dictionary/english/anguish

Drew, C. (September 29, 2019). *Shannon Weaver Model of Communication—7 Key Concepts.* Helpful Professor. https://helpfulprofessor.com/shannon-weaver-model/

Free Dictionary (2022). Blueprint. *Freedictionary.com.* Retrieved October 18, 2022, from https://www.thefreedictionary.com/ blueprint

Healthline Media (2022). Hematidrosis (Sweating Blood): Causes and Treatment. *Healthline.com.* Retrieved October 18, 2022, from https://www.healthline.com/health/hematidrosis#causes

Lewin, Rabbi. (2019, September 23). *Shofar Sounds and Their Meaning| Rosh Hashanah* [Video File]. Retrieved from https:// www.youtube.com/watch?v=iybECuwzEAo

Linsley, Alice C., December 12, 2015. "The Gourd in Biblical Symbolism." *Biblicalanthropology.blogspot.com.* Retrieved from https://biblicalanthropology.blogspot.com/2015/12/ the-gourd-in-biblicalsymbolism.html#:~:text=The%20 Gourd%20in%20Biblical%20Symbolism.%20Gourds%20 were%20a,cedar%20decorated%20the%20inner%20sanctuary%20of%20the%20temple.

Lucia, R. (1994). "Effects of Playing a Musical Wind Instrument in Asthmatic Teenagers." *Pubmed.gov.* Retrieved from https:// pubmed.ncbi.nlm.nih.gov/7928933/. Accessed 14 October 2022.

Mahoney, K. (2018, December 29). "Understanding the Trinity." *Learnreligions.com.* Retrieved from https://www.learnreligions.com/how-can-god-be-three-things-712158

McLeod, S. (2021) Id, Ego, and Superego | Simply Psychology. *Simply Scholar Ltd.* Retrieved from https://www.simplypsychology.org/psyche.html

Merriam-Webster (2022). Ark. *In Merriam-Webster.com dictionary.* Retrieved October 18, 2022, from https://www.merriam-webster.com/dictionary/ark

Merriam-Webster (2022). Communication. In *Merriam-Webster.com dictionary.* Retrieved October 14, 2022, from https://www.merriam-webster.com/dictionary/communication

Sebastian, M. (2016, June 11). Why Are Jews So Successful? *Honor and Daring.com.* Retrieved from http://honoranddaring.com/why-are-jews-so-successful/

Sengar, C. "Science-Based Reasons Why Playing a Wind Instrument is God for Mind and Body." *Onlymyhealth.com.* November 6, 2019, https://www.onlymyhealth.com/playing-a-wind-instrument-is-good-for-mind-and-body-1573042902 Accessed 14 October 2022.

Shofar So Good (2021) "History of the Shofar." *Shofar.ca.* Retrieved from https://shofar.ca/history-of-the-shofar/

Stephenson, B. (2022). "The Sacrifices-Minchah." *Psalm11918.org.* Retrieved October 24, 2022, from https://www.psalm11918.org/Articles/What-Scripture-Says-About/The-Sacrifices/Minchah.html

Thompson, J. W. (2003). Horn. *Holman Illustrated Bible Dictionary* (pp. 782–783). Nashville, Tennessee: Holman Bible Publishers.

Razorplanet.com (n.d.). Brazen Altar [PDF File]. Retrieved from https://resources.razorplanet.com/516771-1557/1003701_THEBRAZENALTAR.pdf

ENDNOTES

1 Merriam-Webster (2022). Communication. In *Merriam-Webster.com* dictionary. Retrieved October 14, 2022, from https://www.merriam-webster.com/dictionary/communication

2 Drew, C. (September 29, 2019). Shannon Weaver Model of Communication—7 Key Concepts. Helpful Professor. https://helpfulprofessor.com/shannon-weaver-model/

3 Bible Study Tools (2022). Alexander. *Biblestudytools.com.* Retrieved October 18, 2022, from https://www.biblestudytools.com/dictionary/alexander/

4 Sengar, C. "Science-Based Reasons Why Playing a Wind Instrument Is Good for Mind and Body." *Onlymyhealth.com.* November 6, 2019, https://www.onlymyhealth.com/playing-a-wind-instrument-is-good-for-mind-and-body-1573042902. Accessed 14 October 2022

5 Lucia, R. (1994). "Effects of Playing a Musical Wind Instrument in Asthmatic Teenagers." *Pubmed.gov.* Retrieved from https://pubmed.ncbi.nlm.nih.gov/7928933/. Accessed 14 October 2022

6 McLeod, S. (2021) Id, Ego, and Superego | Simply Psychology. *Simply Scholar Ltd.* Retrieved from https://www.simplypsychology.org/psyche.html

7 Mahoney, K. (2018, December 29). "Understanding the Trinity". *Learnreligions.com.* Retrieved from https://www.learnreligions.com/how-can-god-be-three-things-712158

8 Sebastian, M. (2016, June 11). "Why Are Jews So Successful?" *Honor and Daring.com.* Retrieved from http://honoranddaring.com/why-are-jews-so-successful/

9 Brackman, Rabbi L. (2008, September 5). "Why Jews Are Disproportionally Successful?" *Ynetnews.com. Jewish Scene Jewish World.* Retrieved from https://www.ynetnews.com/

articles/0,7340,L-3592566,00.html#:~:text=Thirty%20per-cent%20of%20Nobel%20Prize%20winners%20in%20science,are%20disproportionally%20represented.%20Most%20non-Jews%20also%20know%20this

10 Free Dictionary (2022). Blueprint. *Freedictionary.com*. Retrieved October 18, 2022, from https://www.thefreedictionary.com/blueprint

11 Bible Hub (2022). Mizbeach. *Biblehub.com*. Retrieved November 4, 2022, from https://biblehub.com/hebrew/4196.htm

12 Bible Study Tools (2022). Chata. *Biblestudytools.com*. Retrieved October 24, 2022, from https://www.biblestudytools.com/lexicons/hebrew/nas/chata.html

13 Bible Study Tools (2022). Asham. Biblestudytools.com. Retrieved November 4, 2022, from https://www.biblestudytools.com/lexicons/hebrew/kjv/asham.html

14 Stephenson, B. (2022). "The Sacrifices-Minchah." *Psalm11918.org*. Retrieved October 24, 2022, from https://www.psalm11918.org/Articles/What-Scripture-Says-About/The-Sacrifices/Minchah.html

15 Bible Students Daily (2017, January 2). "Study 8: The Tabernacle Coverings." *Biblestudentsdaily.com*. Retrieved from https:/biblestudentsdaily.com/tag/goat-hair/

16 Thompson, J. W. (2003). Horn. *Holman Illustrated Bible Dictionary* (pp. 782–783). Nashville, Tennessee: Holman Bible Publishers

17 Razorplanet.com (n.d.). Brazen Altar [PDF File]. Retrieved from https://resources.razorplanet.com/516771-1557/1003701_THEBRAZENALTAR.pdf

18 Bible Hub (2022). Parts. *Biblehub.com*. Retrieved October 17, 2022, from https://biblehub.com/topical/p/parts.htm

19 Linsley, Alice C., December 12, 2015. "The Gourd in Biblical

Symbolism." *Biblicalanthropology.blogspot.com.* Retrieved from https://biblicalanthropology.blogspot.com/2015/12/the-gourd-in-biblicalsymbolism.html#:~:text=The%20Gourd%20in%20Biblical%20Symbolism.%20Gourds%20were%20a,cedar%20decorated%20the%20inner%20sanctuary%20of%20the%20temple.

20 Shofar So Good (2021). "History of the Shofar." *Shofar.ca.* Retrieved from https://shofar.ca/history-of-the-shofar/

21 Lewin, Rabbi (2019, September 23). *Shofar Sounds and Their Meaning| Rosh Hashanah* [Video File]. Retrieved from https://www.youtube.com/watch?v=iybECuwzEAo

22 Bible Hub (2022). Tsaphah. *Biblehub.com.* Retrieved October 17, 2022, from https://biblehub.com/hebrew/6822.htm

23 Bible Hub (2022). Teruah. *Biblehub.com.* Retrieved November 4, 2022, from https://biblehub.com/bdb/8643.htm

24 Bar-Ilan University (2013, September 1). *The Meaning of the Shofar—Prof. William Kolbrener* [Video File]. Retrieved from https://youtu.be/vEEtYAfaH_s

25 Merriam-Webster (2022). Ark. *In Merriam-Webster.com dictionary.* Retrieved October 18, 2022, from https://www.merriam-webster.com/dictionary/ark

26 Cambridge University Press (2022). Anguish. *Cambridge Dictionary.* Retrieved October 18, 2022, from https://dictionary.cambridge.org/us/dictionary/english/anguish

27 Healthline Media (2022). Hematidrosis (Sweating Blood): Causes and Treatment. *Healthline.com.* Retrieved October 18, 2022, from https://www.healthline.com/health/hematidrosis#-causes

CPSIA information can be obtained
at www.ICGtesting.com
Printed in the USA
BVHW050028110223
658309BV00010B/114